Living, Loving, & Lasting as a Coach's Wife

Insights From Football Coaches' Wives

Janet Hope
Liddy Hope
Sally Hope

COACHES CHOICE™

ISBN: 978-1-60679-250-6
Library of Congress Control Number: 2012955606
Cover design: Cheery Sugabo
Book layout: Roger W. Rybkowski
Front and back cover photos: Thinkstock
Author photos: Claire Haeg (Janet Hope), Bobbie Ruyle (Liddy Hope), Ryan Gibboney (Sally Hope)

Coaches Choice
P.O. Box 1828
Monterey, CA 93942
www.coacheschoice.com

Dedication

This book is dedicated to football coaches' wives—past, present, and future.

Acknowledgments

First and foremost, the three of us gratefully acknowledge all the wives who participated in this study, without whom it couldn't have taken place, and the American Football Coaches Wives Association (AFCWA) for allowing us to present our findings at their annual meetings. I'm grateful for the support I received from the College of St. Benedict/ St. John's University—financially and in the form of a sabbatical and research release time. In addition, I can't thank the late Suzanne Reinert enough for her work on the transcripts of the interviews and her other expert (and always cheerful) assistance on this project over the last five years. My colleagues Jeff Kamakahi and Sheila Nelson have also given me a great deal of support and help, as have Ryan Kutter, Heather Ley, and several of the student workers in my department. Finally, I thank my husband, Joe, for all his support, encouragement, and sacrifices—particularly his willingness to spend four weeks of his life in the car with me as we traveled more than 7,000 miles to do the interviews.

—Janet

This book is the culmination of the efforts and dedication of two women: Janet Hope and Sally Hope. I want to acknowledge their hard work, patience, and perseverance. Thank you for including me in this project. It has been an honor. I'd like to also thank Ali and my two lovely daughters, Emma and Maddy, for putting up with me during this project.

—Liddy

I would like to thank Dr. Bill Harper, former department chair of the Health and Kinesiology Department at Purdue University, who provided valuable suggestions and encouragement through the process of writing this book. In addition, I would like to thank fellow coach's wife Lorri Jackson for her feedback on our manuscript draft, Coach Shawn Clark for providing information on the typical day of a coach, Purdue Compliance Director Tom Mitchell for providing information on NCAA recruiting bylaws, and Purdue Assistant Director for Student Services Seth Schwartz for providing information on APR ratings. I must acknowledge and express my appreciation for the patience shown by my husband, Danny, when I was using the small amount of time we have to spend together to work on this book.

—Sally

Foreword

*"Every woman can be a great wife, but not
every woman could be a great coach's wife."*

I've made this statement in various interviews during my coaching career to make the point that the life of a football coach's wife is one that not every woman would choose and one that not every woman could handle successfully. *Living, Loving, & Lasting as a Coach's Wife: Insights From Football Coaches' Wives* paints a realistic picture of this life through the voices of experience: the coaches' wives themselves. While many articles and books about football coaches exist, this unique book presents a view of this increasingly challenging and life-consuming profession through the eyes of the women behind these men.

The coaches' wives speak openly and frankly about the common issues that coaching families encounter. As a football coach reading this book, I found some of the wives' insight to be predictable, some thought provoking, some brutally honest, some comforting, and some humorous (although those outside the circle of the coaching world may not pick up on the humor intended). Some information shared by the wives reminds us that, unfortunately, some aspects of our coaching careers add stress to the lives of our wives and children.

The book's inclusion of fact-based information about the day-to-day football-related duties of coaches (and their wives) is a positive step toward educating the general public about the demanding hours and the ever-increasing responsibilities that extend far beyond the team's game day performance.

Those who read *Living, Loving, & Lasting as a Coach's Wife: Insights From Football Coaches' Wives* will come away with a greater understanding and appreciation of the commitment made by all members of coaching families.

Danny Hope
Head Football Coach
Purdue University 2009–2012
Eastern Kentucky University 2003–2007

Contents

Dedication.. 3

Acknowledgments.. 4

Foreword.. 5

Preface... 8

Introduction: An Overview of the Coaches' Wives Study............ 9

Section I   Understanding Football Coaching Basics

Chapter 1   Responsibilities for Football Coaches and Their Wives 17

Chapter 2   Clock Management: Time in a Football Coach's World............ 33

Chapter 3   Instability in Coaching Football and the
            Importance of "Football Families" 41

Section II   Life With a Coach

Chapter 4   The National Anthem Gives Me Diarrhea:
            Life as A Coach's Child 61

Chapter 5   The Coach's Wife as a Career Woman............................ 85

Chapter 6   The Division of Family Labor..................................... 97

Chapter 7   On the Road Again: Moving for a New Job 114

Chapter 8   Life in a Fishbowl 126

Chapter 9   The Best Things About Life With a Coach........................ 138

Section III   Making Coaching Marriages Work

    Chapter 10 The Characteristics of a Coaching Marriage 149

    Chapter 11 When in Doubt—Punt! (and Other Coping Strategies) 168

Section IV   The Final Score

    Chapter 12 Parting Words From the Wives................................... 183

Conclusion 190

Epilogue.. 192

Appendix A: College Football Coaches' Wives Questionnaire.................... 194

Appendix B: Demographic Details of the College Football Coaches' Wives
                 Online Survey 202

References 208

About the Authors... 214

Preface

The purpose of this book is to provide insights from our study into the lives of women whose husbands are college football coaches. We want to explain through the voices of these women how they not only remain, but in most cases flourish, in marriages to men who often work on average 90-plus hours a week during football season, who travel extensively during recruiting, whose jobs are often terminated without notice after (or sometimes even during) a losing season, and whose earnings (depending on the husband's position and level) can be modest. We hope to dispel misinformation and incorrect assumptions about the lives of football coaches and their families. As we discuss themes that emerged from our study, readers will find that the information applies not only to the wives of college football coaches but to the wives of coaches at all levels of football. In addition, readers in other professions may recognize some of the positive and negative experiences and issues they share with the families of coaches while also becoming more informed about aspects of the coaching life that are unique to coaching families.

Introduction:
An Overview of the
Coaches' Wives Study

Several years ago, Janet attended a college football game where the Purdue Boilermakers beat the home team in the last few seconds of the game. This defeat so enraged the home team's fans that a number of them who were sitting close to her and in the same area as the Purdue coaches' wives screamed obscenities at the women and accused them in explicit and vulgar terms of sexual misconduct with the referees. This went on for as long as it took for the wives to exit the stands. Janet was horrified at the behavior of the home team fans but learned later that this kind of occurrence isn't unusual when a team loses a home game. She knew from observing the life of her daughter-in-law, Sally, and the lives of other coaches' wives she had met over the years that although their marriages were for the most part happy and successful, their husbands' careers created the need for them to make some personal sacrifices and cope with issues not found in non-coaching marriages. It seemed to Janet that the behavior she had just witnessed was one aspect of their lives that would be very hard to deal with and one which people unconnected with college football would know nothing about. At that point, she began to think seriously about conducting a formal study that would examine the lives of college football coaches' wives and provide information about the advantages and disadvantages of being married to men in this occupation. However, it wasn't until fall 2006 that she was able to even begin to work on it.

Janet knew it would be difficult to fit in this project with her other responsibilities as a professor of sociology and that she probably shouldn't undertake it alone. Luckily, her family includes a daughter and a daughter-in-law who have skills and education in disciplines that would allow them to approach this project from a broader perspective than would otherwise be the case. Both of them enthusiastically agreed to join Janet in this research. As a sociologist, Janet is primarily interested in the structure of families, the impact of forces outside the families on family members, and discovering what it is that makes families work. Daughter Liddy is a family social scientist, which means she looks at families from the perspective of several other disciplines as well as sociology. Liddy's interest and experience in research methods has been particularly valuable. Daughter-in-law Sally is married to Danny, the former head football coach at Purdue University. Sally's training is in education—particularly the pedagogical aspects—and physical education. Her contacts in the world of college football, her insights, and her knowledge of the sport have been invaluable. Some people might see the dynamics of this working arrangement as being fraught with peril, and it's true that our respective disciplines do mean we have different ways of thinking and writing. Nevertheless, the three of us worked very well together, and after almost four years spent on this project, we're still speaking to each other.

We believe that most of what the public knows about the wives of college football coaches is probably based on the images people see on Saturday afternoons during football season on TV or at the games. But are these images accurate? Are the wives really the poised and smiling women supporting their husbands from the stands through wins and losses, proudly decked out in the team colors (no matter how unflattering)? Or are they sitting in their seats sick with anxiety about the outcome of the game, knowing that another loss could mean their husbands' job will be gone and their families on the road again? Even if the latter is the case, an observer would never know it because the coaches' wives have learned to keep their public image intact. In her book *The Managed Heart: the Commercialization of Human Feeling*, sociologist Arlie Hochschild discussed what she calls "emotional labor." This, according to Hochschild, is "… the management of feeling to create a publicly observable facial and bodily display"—a skill that workers in several occupations, such as receptionists or flight attendants, use on a daily basis. It's also a skill that the women in our study and college football coaches' wives everywhere possess in abundance and which is an important part of their "job."

While few people who aren't connected in some way with college football would see being the wife of a coach as a job, that's precisely what it is. Former NFL head coach Steve Mariucci once said "the most difficult job on the team is that of the coach's wife" (Allen, 2007). While Coach Mariucci was talking about the wives of NFL coaches, his comment is every bit as true of college football coaches' wives. It's a job that the wives assume in addition to their own careers and the usual responsibilities that come with being wives and mothers. Not only do they undertake many team-related duties, but for the greater part of the year, they take on most—if not all—of the family responsibilities normally handled by husbands and fathers. One of our wives said of her husband: "He takes care of football, but my job is to make everything else work."

Through the voices of the wives, we acquaint readers with the reality of life "on the sidelines." We look at the aspects of their lives that bring them joy as well as those that create hardship and difficulty. We discuss the "coaching calendar" and how every aspect of the coaches' work and family life is affected by it, and we introduce the idea of time as a scarce resource. We identify the qualities of the coaches (according to their wives) and of the wives themselves that make it possible for their marriages to succeed. We examine parenting issues and what it's like to be a football coach's child. We explore the effects of the coaching profession on the wives' careers and the impact of the volatility of the profession on family and residential stability. In the last few chapters, we identify the ways in which the wives manage living under constant public scrutiny, the strategies they employ in coping with the vagaries of their lives, the special meaning of teamwork in their marriages and families, and what the wives want people to know about them.

We hope what we've discovered in our research will be of interest to the general public—even those who aren't particularly interested in football—because much of what we write about has value for husbands, wives, and families everywhere. We also see this book as a valuable resource for current coaches' wives by providing "normalization" as they seek reassurance that others share the life experiences unique to coaching families. It also contains important information for women who are planning to marry a coach and for men contemplating a career in college football coaching.

Methodology

Our data were obtained by using a mixed methods approach. We planned to obtain 100 or more responses from college football coaches' wives across the country to an online questionnaire and to conduct 20 in-person interviews. In fall 2007, we created a website that described the project and which contained a link to an 80-item questionnaire (see Appendix A). On the final page of the questionnaire, we asked coaches' wives living in the Midwest to contact Janet via e-mail if they were willing to be interviewed in person. Initially, the responses to the online questionnaire were slow arriving. We then put a notice on footballscoop.com, (a website that reports and tracks the movement of college football coaching jobs) with a link to our website. Sally attended the American Football Coaches Wives Association (AFCWA) conference in Anaheim in January 2008 to recruit more women. But even with that, we still had received only about 50 responses—not enough. Innovation was called for. Luckily, Janet had been granted a sabbatical for the spring 2008 semester to work on this project and had time to send individual e-mails to the head coaches of every NCAA football program in the country—around 500 altogether—asking that they forward or have someone forward the link to the website to their wives and to the wives of the other coaches in their program. Many coaches were enthusiastic about the project, while others ignored us. We quickly learned that when a program had a "football secretary," that person was the one to contact. Some of the coaches' responses were fascinating. This is one of our favorites:

> Honest answers from coaches' wives? Dear God, madam, what are you trying to do to us? If young women all over the country truly understand what it's like to be married to a football coach … we will indeed become an endangered species. Actually, I'm sure my wife would be glad to participate.

The number of usable responses when we finally closed the website at the end of March 2008 was 285. This is almost three times what we would have settled for and is a large enough sample to allow for some interesting statistical analysis. In addition, we had 25 women willing to be interviewed in person. That summer, Janet, along with Joe, her long-suffering husband, traveled to 15 different states. They went as far south as Florida and as far west as Oklahoma for the first trip, and for the second trip, they went to Michigan and Illinois. Altogether, Janet interviewed 16 wives by using a structured interview format but one that was flexible enough to allow her to explore unanticipated topics as they came up. (The names of these wives have been changed to protect their identities.) They put more than 7,000 miles on the car but had to stop at 16 interviews as gas was well over $4 a gallon at that time and grant funds were running low. This was unfortunate because we could have done four more interviews in the Carolinas, which would have given us the 20 we originally sought.

Demographics for the Online Respondents

Detailed demographic information is contained in Appendix B. Following is a brief overview:

- *Age:* The mean age of the wives is 39.2 years, with a range of 24 to 73. Their husbands' mean age is 41.5, with a range of 24 to 81. A two-year age difference separates wives and husbands, which is typical of husbands and wives generally.
- *Race:* The majority of wives and husbands are Caucasian (86.4 percent), with slightly more African American husbands (12.1 percent) than wives (7.1 percent).
- *Education:* The vast majority of respondents (87.5 percent) are well educated, with a bachelor's degree or higher levels of education, and 99.3 percent of their husbands have a bachelor's degree or better.
- *Marriage:* 99.5 percent of the sample is married, for a mean duration of 13.5 years. The range in number of years married is newly married to 52 years, and 8.2 percent of both husbands and wives had previous marriages.
  - ✓ 36.1 percent of the respondents are married to head coaches.
  - ✓ 8.8 percent are married to assistant head coaches.
  - ✓ 24.8 percent are married to coordinators.
  - ✓ 26.3 percent are married to position coaches.
- *Children:* 84.1 percent of the sample has children, and 1.1 percent of the wives were expecting at the time of the survey.
  - ✓ 36.7 percent have two children.
  - ✓ 27.4 percent have one child.
  - ✓ 20 percent have three or more children.
- *Employment:* 71.8 percent of the wives are employed outside the home, and 73.2 percent of those work full time.
- *Income:* Almost 60 percent of the sample reported a combined family income between $50K and $150K.
- *Coaching level:* The wives' husbands ran the full gamut of college levels:
  - ✓ 36.2 percent are from Division I BCS schools.
  - ✓ 19 percent are from Division I FCS schools.
  - ✓ 17.5 percent are from Division II schools.
  - ✓ 25.7 percent are from Division III schools.

Demographics for the Interviewees

Demographic details for the 16 wives who were interviewed reveal statistics similar to those of the online respondents:

- *Age:* These women are slightly older than the online respondents, with a mean age of 40.8 years. Their husbands' mean age is 45.3 years.
- *Race:* All the wives are white, and one of the husbands is African American.
- *Education:* Only one wife has less than a college degree, and all the husbands have bachelor's degrees or better.
- *Marriage:* The length of marriage for these couples ranges from 4 to 42 years, with a mean of 17.4 years.
  - ✓ Half of the husbands were head coaches at the time of the interviews.
  - ✓ Five were coordinators.
  - ✓ Three were position coaches.
- *Children:* Online respondents have a mix of children dynamics:
  - ✓ Only one of the interviewed wives has no children.
  - ✓ One wife has one child.
  - ✓ Eight wives have two children.
  - ✓ Four wives have three children.
  - ✓ Two wives have four children.
- *Employment:* The employment statistics are different from those of the online respondents:
  - ✓ 43.5 percent of this sample was employed full time.
  - ✓ 12.5 percent worked part time.
  - ✓ 37.5 percent weren't employed at the time they were interviewed.
- *Coaching level:* The wives' husbands ran a similar range of college levels as those who responded to the online survey:
  - ✓ Nine were affiliated with Division I BCS schools
  - ✓ Three were from Division I FCS schools
  - ✓ Three were from Division II schools.
  - ✓ One was from a Division III school.

Other Factors

While many aspects of their lives as college football coaches' wives were shared by our respondents, it was obvious from what they wrote online and said in the interviews that how they actually experience their lives depends on a number of factors. In reading the rest of the book, think about the following influences, which will be discussed in detail in later chapters:

- *Age:* Experiences in marriage are affected by the spouses' age and generation.
- *Life stage:* Marriage and family experiences are governed not only by chronological age but also by the spouses' life stage. These stages include young adulthood, the middle years, and the older years.
- *Presence and age of children:* The number and age of children in families affect many aspects of husband-wife relationships.
- *Husband's rank and level:* The level at which the coach's team plays and his coaching position make a difference in the wives' experiences.
- *Husbands' and wives' personal qualities:* Personal characteristics of both spouses have an impact on communication, decision making, conflict resolution, and many other aspects of the marriage.
- *Whether the wives knew what they were getting into:* Most situations people face in life are easier to deal with if they have some idea of what they'll encounter.

Summary

Even as the wife, stepmother, and sister of a coach, we learned things about the lives of football coaches' wives that we didn't know prior to beginning this study. It's our hope that through this book readers will develop an even greater understanding of the world of football coaches and their wives and families.

SECTION I

UNDERSTANDING FOOTBALL COACHING BASICS

Despite the deep interest in football in the United States, many misconceptions and much misinformation abound regarding the lives of football coaches. In Chapter 1, we provide basic information about the responsibilities of football coaches and their spouses' football-related expectations. In Chapter 2, we discuss coaches' demanding work hours and how these long hours affect the coaches, their spouses, and their families. Chapter 3 describes the harsh realities of job security (or insecurity) for football coaches and their wives and children and demonstrates the importance of the football "families" that are forged in this volatile profession.

1

Responsibilities for Football Coaches and Their Wives

Most of the information contained in this chapter doesn't come from our data but from a variety of other sources, including informal interviews with coaches. We believe this chapter will enable readers to better understand our findings presented in later chapters. To comprehend the lives of the college football coaches' wives we interviewed, we have to first be familiar with the responsibilities of the coaches themselves and how these vary according to the season, the coach's rank, and the team's division. Generally, the coaching staff consists of the head coach, an associate (or an assistant) head coach, offensive and defensive coordinators, position coaches, and graduate assistants. Teams are organized into divisions and conferences as follows:

- *Division I BCS:* These schools have a limited number of full scholarships (tuition, books, and room and board) that can be awarded. Usually, they have fewer walk-on players (players without scholarship). Some conferences in this division are: ACC, Big 12, Big East, Big Ten, Conference USA, MAC, PAC-12, and SEC.
- *Division I FCS:* These schools are similar to BCS schools. The main differences are the overall talent levels of the players and the number of scholarships available. This division has the ability to "split" scholarships to include more players. Players may receive partial scholarships. Generally, FCS schools have more walk-on players than BCS schools. Some conferences in this division are: Big Sky, Big South, Ivy League, Ohio Valley, Patriot League, and Pioneer.
- *Division II:* These schools are smaller schools with competitive programs. Fewer scholarships are offered—if any at all (depending on school). The GPA requirements for eligibility are lower at this level. Some conferences in this division are: Central, Great Lakes, Great Northwest, Gulf South, Lone Star, Rocky Mountain, and South Atlantic.

- *Division III:* Schools in this division are the smallest of all NCAA schools. Scholarships aren't offered, but financial aid is available depending on the school. Many schools at this level are private and/or have very rigorous academic requirements. Some conferences in this division are: American Southwest, Centennial, Empire 8, Freedom, Heartland, and Southern Collegiate.

The Football Calendar

Unless members of the public are related to or are close friends with football coaches and their families, they probably have little idea of how coaches and their families live and how every aspect of their lives is influenced in one way or another by the football calendar. The type and extent of a coach's responsibilities depend on the time of the year, and although some differences may occur at the various levels (particularly during recruiting season), the typical football calendar is broken down into four basic seasons: football season, recruiting, spring ball, and summer. The football calendar determines the number of hours during each season that coaches have to work, the number of days they might be out of town, and the nature and extent of their other responsibilities.

Through the years, additional responsibilities that aren't directly related to the team's on-the-field performance have continued to increase, making a football coach's job more and more demanding. Some coaching responsibilities, such as monitoring student-athletes, making public appearances, and being interviewed by the media, are often ongoing and occur in more than one of the four seasons. It should also be noted that over the past few years, the time frame of recruiting has extended excessively into the football season, particularly at the Division I BCS level. The following sections outline the demands and overall "lives" of football coaches by season.

Football Season

Players return for pre-season camp during August, prior to the beginning of the fall semester. The regular season usually contains 10 to 12 games and generally ends in November. However, if a team is involved in post-season play, playoffs and bowl games usually take place from mid-December through the early part of January. Teams that participate in post-season play use the time between the end of the regular season and their post-season game(s) to prepare for their opponents.

During this period, a coach's time is spent preparing for practices, conducting actual on-the-field practice situations, preparing for meetings with players, meetings with players, breaking down the game films of opponents for tendencies, reviewing his own team's games film, and recruiting players. As noted later in this chapter, coaches have other duties that aren't directly related to the team's on-the-field performance that also peak during this season. Wives who responded to the online survey estimated how many hours their husbands worked per week during the football season, as shown in Figure 1-1.

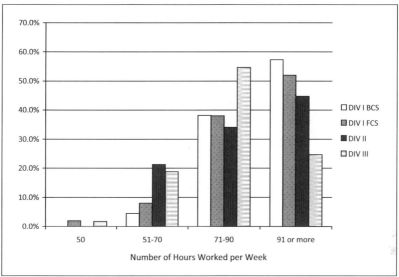

Figure 1-1. Wives' estimates of husbands' work hours during the football season (in percentages)

This chart clearly shows that with the exception of Division III, the majority of wives estimated that their husbands work 91 hours a week or more during the football season. In Division I BCS, more than half (57.3 percent) of the wives estimated that this is true of their husbands, while in Division I FCS, the percentage is almost as high (52 percent). In Division II, almost 45 percent of the coaches work in excess of 91 hours each week. According to football coaches' wives, the largest percentage of Division III coaches (54.7 percent) work between 71 and 90 hours per week during this season. A typical coaching week during the season may resemble the schedule shown in Figure 1-2.*

Recruiting

To explain the recruiting season by saying it lasts from one designated month to another would be misleading. Those in the coaching profession generally refer to the recruiting periods as mid-April through May and November through the end of January because those are the months in which coaches—in compliance with NCAA rules—are allowed to actually travel to see recruits. Signing Day for recruits is the first Wednesday in February, so that's usually considered the end of the recruiting period, although some student-athletes will sign letters of intent after that date. However, many hours are spent recruiting student-athletes beyond these designated travel times.

*The typical coaching workweeks shown in Figures 1-2, 1-5, and 1-8 are based on an interview with a Division I BCS offensive assistant coach and are a compilation of his experience as an assistant coach at the Division I FCS and Division I BCS levels. Typical coaching workweeks may vary from level to level and from staff to staff within the same level.

Typical Work Week During Football Season

HFC = Head football coach   ST = Special teams

Sunday

7:00	Grade video from previous day's game
9:00	Meet with recruits visiting campus (HFC: exit interviews with recruits/families)
12:00	Lunch
1:00	Offensive/defensive/ST staff meetings (discuss previous day's performance)
2:00	Staff meeting (discuss previous day's team performance; discuss injuries)
3:00	Team meeting (discuss previous day's team performance)
4:00	Meet with position players (discuss previous day's position performance)
5:00	Practice (media interviews pre- and post-practice)
6:00	Dinner
7:00–11:00	Offensive/defensive staffs meet to begin planning for next week's game

Monday

7:00	Write recruiting letters
7:30	Offensive/defensive staff meeting (preparing game plan for next week's game)
9:30	Academic meeting (discuss academic progress of all football players)
10:30	Offensive staff meeting (continue preparation of next week's game plan)
12:00	Lunch (HFC: weekly luncheon)
1:00	Offensive/defensive staff meetings
3:00	Staff recruiting meeting
4:00	Offensive/defensive staff meetings (HFC: film TV show)
6:00	Dinner (HFC: radio show)
7:00	Offensive staff meeting (HFC: defensive staff meeting)
9:00	Defensive staff meeting (HFC: offensive staff meeting)
11:00	Go home

Tuesday and Wednesday

7:00	Write recruiting letters
7:30	Staff meeting
8:00	Offensive staff meeting (first-down plays, etc.)
9:00	Prepare for practice (scripting)
12:00	Lunch (HFC: weekly press conference)
1:30	Prepare for position meeting
2:30	Meet with position players
4:00	Practice (media pre- and post-practice)
7:00	Dinner
8:00–11:00	Offensive/defensive staff meeting (work on game plan); call recruits

Figure 1-2. Typical workweek during football season

Thursday	
7:00	Write recruiting letters
7:30	Staff meeting
8:00	Offensive staff meeting (choose plays)
12:00	Lunch
1:30	Prepare for position meeting
2:30	Meet with position players
4:00	Practice
7:00	Family time!

Friday	
Home game: Recruits arrive on home game Fridays	
7:00	Work on individual player notes and handouts
7:30	Staff meeting (recruiting; meet with athletic trainer) Continued preparation for today's practice and tomorrow's game
2:30	Practice
5:30	Dinner
7:00	Walk through plays and formations with team
9:00	Team meeting

Away game:	
TBA	Team meeting
TBA	Position meeting
TBA	Practice
TBA	Travel
5:30	Dinner
7:00	Walk through plays
9:00	Team meeting

Saturday (Game Day)	
Home game:	
7:00	Breakfast with team; breakfast with recruits
8:00	Walk through plays
8:25	Depart for stadium
10:30	Meet with recruits visiting campus
11:00	Pre-game warm up
12:00	Game (post-game team meeting) (HFC: post-game media interviews)
6:00–9:00	Recruiting dinner

Figure 1-2. Typical workweek during football season (cont.)

The recruiting process is a long one. First, the coaches must evaluate prospective student-athletes to determine who would be the best "fit" for their school's division, league, and academics standards. This evaluation is done primarily through the viewing of game footage of the athlete and visiting the student-athlete's school during NCAA evaluation periods. According to the NCAA, the months of September, October, and November (the exact dates vary from year to year) are considered an evaluation period, during which 42 days could be designated as evaluation days—that is, a day on which a coach is engaged in the evaluation of any prospect. The Sunday following the last Saturday in November through the Saturday prior to the National Letter of Intent signing period is a contact period, with April 15 through May 31 also considered an evaluation period.

Traditionally, recruiting protocols relied heavily on high school football coaches to provide game film to the colleges, but today, advances in technology have led to the prospective student-athlete and/or his parents, guardians, or mentors taking a more assertive role in his promotion, which consumes many more hours of the coaches' time. In addition, numerous recruiting services promoting prospective student-athletes have surfaced. As a result of these changes, the amount of game footage a football coach must view to begin the selection process has greatly increased in recent years.

Coaches hope that the prospective student-athletes they've identified as good fits will be interested in playing football at their universities, so they begin to establish relationships with them. This means countless hours on the phone as well as countless hours on the road visiting the prospective student-athletes during contact periods. The *NCAA Division I Football Coaches Off-Campus Recruiting Guide* states that junior recruits may receive one phone call between April 15 and May 31 and that senior recruits may receive one call per week after September 1 and unlimited calls during the contact period. Two-year and four-year college prospects may receive one phone call per week. According to the NCAA, the Sunday following the last Saturday in November through the Saturday prior to the National Letter of Intent signing period is considered a contact period, during which six in-person, off-campus contacts per student-athlete are permitted. However, these student-athletes may opt to visit the college on their own to look around and to meet the members of the football staff during what would be considered an unofficial visit. Official visits (meaning the university pays the costs of transportation and meals for the recruit's visit to the campus) can be made after a high school senior's first day of classes. A prospective student-athlete may make five official visits, as allowed by NCAA rules. During these visits, coaches must be available to speak with recruits and host recruiting events. At this point, recruits may make a verbal commitment to a school, which is an oral promise to come to the school to play football. On Signing Day, the recruits sign a letter of intent and an athletic tender/ scholarship that makes the commitment more binding.

To get a feel for the current trends in football recruiting, one only needs to tune in to ESPN on Signing Day. There, highly touted recruits sit at a table with hats from a variety of schools before them. The media are poised to see which hat the recruit will select, and it may not be the school to which he had verbally committed. Numerous recruits have been known to change their minds at the last minute. Coaches can be heard lamenting that "the days of honoring one's word are gone," while others adopt the philosophy of "all is fair in recruiting—until the ink dries on the letter of intent."

Much like football season, recruiting season requires untold hours of work on the coaches' part, but during recruiting, the hours spent working often involve many nights away from home. During a typical recruiting day, the coach arrives at the first high school by 7:00 a.m. and will try to visit four to five high schools that day. Usually, he has little to no time for lunch. Home visits usually begin somewhere around 6:00 p.m., and the coach will try to get in two home visits per night. According to our online responses, the number of hours coaches' wives estimate that coaches spend at work during recruiting season by division is shown in Figure 1-3.

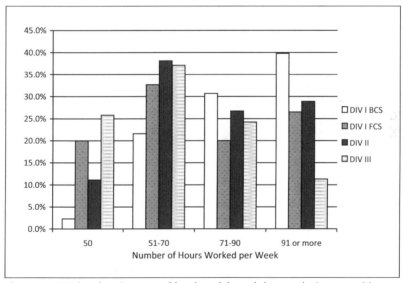

Figure 1-3. Wives' estimates of husbands' work hours during recruiting (in percentages)

Spring Ball

Spring ball usually begins in the first weeks of March and culminates in a team spring game during mid- to late April. This is the first practice opportunity of the calendar year for the team and gives insight into the potential position assignments for the fall season. The coaches' time is spent in preparing for practice sessions, conducting actual practice sessions, preparing for meetings with players, meeting with players, and breaking down practice film. Of the four football seasons, spring ball elicited the fewest comments from the respondents—almost certainly because the hours the coaches work are considerably fewer in contrast to their hours in the two preceding seasons. The chart in Figure 1-4 gives the hours worked by division during spring ball.

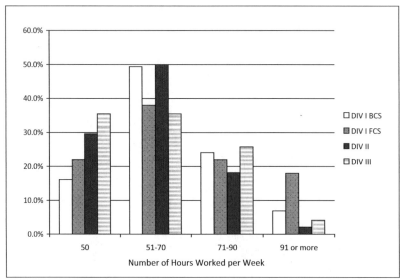

Figure 1-4. Wives' estimates of husbands' work hours during spring ball (in percentages)

In every division, the highest percentages of coaches work 51 to 70 hours a week during spring ball, according to their wives. No discernible themes emerged from our data for this season. A typical coaching week during spring ball may resemble the schedule in Figure 1-5.

Typical Work Week During Spring Ball

Monday

7:30	Staff meeting
10:00	Staff academic meeting (discuss academic progress of all football players)
11:00	Offensive/defensive staff meetings (work on practice plan)
12:00	Lunch
1:00	Offensive/defensive staff meetings (work on practice plan)
2:30	Meet with position players
4:00	Practice
6:00	Dinner
7:00–?	Offensive staff meeting (view practice video tape)

Tuesday/Thursday

7:30	Staff meeting
9:30	Offensive/defensive staff meetings (work on tomorrow's practice plan)
12:00	Lunch
1:00–?	Recruiting (call, email, Facebook recruits)

Wednesday/Friday

7:30	Staff meeting
10:00	Staff academic meeting (discuss academic progress of all football players)
11:00	Offensive/defensive staff meetings (work on practice plan)
12:00	Lunch
1:00	Offensive/defensive staff meetings (work on practice plan)
2:30	Meet with position players
4:00	Practice
6:00	Dinner
7:00–?	Offensive/defensive staff meetings (view practice video tape)

Saturday

7:30	Staff meeting
9:00	Practice
12:30	Offensive/defensive staff meetings (watch practice video)
3:00	Done

Sunday

Off	

Figure 1-5. Typical workweek during spring ball

Summer

Of all the seasons, summer corresponds most closely to the academic calendar of the school. The summer season begins at the close of the spring semester and ends in August when players return to campus for pre-season training. While June and July are typically the months when coaches schedule vacations and downtime with their families, many of them are also involved in summer camps for high school and younger players during those months. These camps are a way for coaches to add to their earnings, and they also produce revenue for the colleges and universities that employ them. However, the camps do encroach on the coaching family's time together and do place limitations on when family vacations can take place.

The wife of a Division I BCS defensive coordinator told us: "Our family time is typically in July, when we recharge our batteries and spend a lot of time together as a family." This appears to be the most common month for the coaches to take time off, and as Figure 1-6 reveals, the hours they work are considerably fewer than for any of the other seasons.

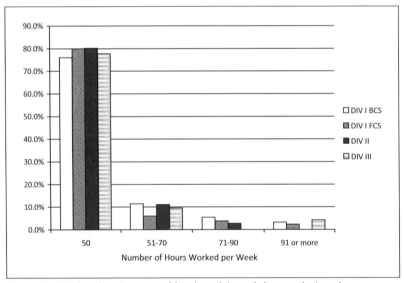

Figure 1-6. Wives' estimates of husbands' work hours during the summer (in percentages)

It's interesting to note the differences that arise when we break down the 50 hours or less classification into 10-hour increments, as shown in Figure 1-7. Even though the summer is the time of year when coaches work the fewest number of hours, according to Figure 1-7, the majority of them are still working at least as much as or more than a "normal" 40-hour workweek. A typical coaching week during the summer may resemble the schedule shown in Figure 1-8.

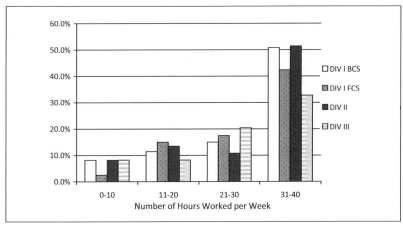

Figure 1-7. Wives' estimates of husbands working 50 hours or less in summer (in percentages)

Typical Work Week for Summer	
Monday–Friday (no camps)	
7:30	Staff meeting
8:30	Work on playbooks for upcoming season/recruiting
12:00	Lunch
1:00–5:00	Work on playbooks for upcoming season/recruiting
Camp Days	
7:30	Staff meeting
10:00–1:00	Camps
1:00–5:00	Work on playbooks

Figure 1-8. Typical workweek for summer

Other Duties and Responsibilities

While living with and adjusting to the football calendar has a huge impact on a coach and his family, other areas of a football coaching career also make demands on the coach's time. Again, variations occur according to rank and division.

Monitoring Student-Athletes

Football coaches spend many, many hours with student-athletes once they're on campus. As a result, close relationships are formed between the players and their coaches. Coaches are often the people these young men come to when they're experiencing personal, academic, or football-related issues. Fair or not, the coaches are held accountable for players' off-the-field behaviors.

Monitoring Academic Progress by Student-Athletes

In recent years, football coaches have become more accountable for the academic performance of their student-athletes. A key factor in this trend was the introduction of the NCAA's Academic Progress Rate (APR), as explained in Figure 1-9.

Academic Progress Rate

The Academic Progress Rate (APR) was established by the NCAA as a "real-time snapshot of every team's academic performance at a given time" (Brown, 2005). The first year of data for this program was collected in the 2003–2004 academic year. Current scores are based on the most recent four years of data that have been collected for each team. APR scores are calculated as follows:

> The APR is calculated by allocating points for eligibility and retention—the two factors that research identifies as the best indicators of graduation. Each [scholarship] player on a given roster earns a maximum of two points per term, one for being academically eligible and one for staying with the institution. A team's APR is the total points of a team's roster at a given time divided by the total points possible. Since this results in a decimal number, the CAP decided to multiply it by 1,000 for ease of reference. Thus, a raw APR score of .925 translates into the 925 that will become the standard terminology. (Brown, 2005)

Teams with APR scores below 930—considered equivalent to a 50 percent graduation rate—won't be eligible for post-season competition. A perfect score is 1,000.

Figure 1-9. The NCAA's Academic Progress Rate

Most universities have academic support staff—at least at the Division I level—whose job descriptions include monitoring student-athletes' academic progress. However, with stricter standards being implemented and harsher consequences being levied for poor academic performance, football coaching staffs have been thrust into additional academic duties at many universities.

Public Appearances/Fundraising

Football is a revenue sport that accounts for a large percentage of the athletic department's budget. The more tickets sold to football games, the more money that's brought in. Therefore, fan support and ticket sales are crucial. To generate interest in the football program, the head coach is often asked to make public appearances at various alumni, booster, and community functions. These obligations are year-round but tend to peak just prior to the football season and during the season itself.

Media Obligations

The ever-increasing media coverage of sports requires coaches to be available to talk to the media. Post-game press conferences, weekly press conferences, radio shows, TV shows, league conference calls, and day-to-day media interviews take up many hours in a head coach's day. Assistant coaches also participate in these interviews; in fact, media demands have become so overwhelming that many programs have adopted strict guidelines for when and where members of the media may interact with coaches. Many programs have closed practices so outsiders, including the media, can't attend.

Managing the Football and Support Staff

Coaching staff meetings are mentioned in the sample daily schedules shown earlier in this chapter. However, coaches also spend time meeting with support staff members, such as the team physician, team trainer, strength and conditioning coaches, academic counselors, and the recruiting coordinator. Football coaches are also expected to attend athletic department meetings. As we discuss in depth in Chapter 4, coaching staff turnover is a reality in football. Coaches may choose to leave for a variety of reasons or they may be dismissed by the head coach. Most coaching changes occur from November through February. The process of interviewing new coaches takes many hours of the head coach's time.

Expectations for Football Coaches' Wives

While the coaches perform many duties to ensure the success of their football teams, coaches' wives also play an integral role in the teams' success. Although not employed by a school to do so, these wives are often expected to serve as ambassadors for the football team. This is especially true of the head coach's wife, who's frequently referred to as the "first lady" of her husband's team.

The nature of these responsibilities and the extent of the head coach's wife's involvement with the team may include appearances at formal functions, hosting get-togethers for the assistant coaches' wives, and making speeches on behalf of their husbands. It should also be noted that wives associated with teams at certain levels may undertake some very unique responsibilities due in part to the lack of support personnel. Coaches' wives may opt to perform duties that would otherwise fall on the shoulders of the head coaches, assistant coaches, and support staff, such as washing team uniforms, helping with practice field and facilities maintenance, and taking care of office work.

Just as it does for their husbands, each season brings with it its own set of circumstances, issues, and responsibilities for the wives. In addition to their family obligations, wives also have certain team-related and program-related responsibilities that correspond with the seasons of the football calendar, for which they must make room in their schedules.

Football Season

Even before the actual football season begins, wives are involved in some pre-season activities. When the players return to campus and two-a-day practices begin in mid-August, many wives make it a point to be visible and supportive to the team. Several wives mentioned that they often see themselves as surrogate mothers for the players and especially try to be available to the freshmen when they first arrive on campus, as many of these players are away from home for the first time. Megan Mullen, the wife of Mississippi State head football coach Dan Mullen, has said of the pre-season "craziness":

> You can absolutely tell it's time. Not only are you dealing with all of your family and them wanting to come to games, but you are getting the wives on board because we've got three wives moving here this year. Tuesday night is the wives' appreciation dinner and it's basically the last supper with your husband before it starts. (Smith, 2010)

In addition, Megan spent pre-season time speaking at engagements, planning tailgates, and working on coaches' family nights (Smith, 2010). Just as the number of hours worked by football coaches reaches its highest point during the football season, the wives' team-related and program-related responsibilities also peak during this period. Game weekends can bring a variety of social functions that wives may be asked to attend. College presidents and athletic directors often host dinners for influential alumni and/or donors on the evening prior to home games, at which the coaches' wives are expected to be present. Game day itself is filled with numerous tailgating sites that request a visit from the coaches' wives. Some coaching staffs have a pre-game reception for the wives of the visiting team that's hosted by their own wives. In-season rituals, such as Friday night peanut butter sandwiches, Thursday night meeting cookies, and end of two-a-days ice cream bars, are established.

The season also brings with it an influx of out-of-town relatives and friends who come for the games. Kate, a young head coach's wife, mentioned in her interview that she sometimes feels as if she's running a bed and breakfast during the season, although she did say that most of their guests are close family members. Claire, also a head coach's wife, mentioned that on game weekends, their three guest bedrooms are generally filled with people—whether it's "former friends of her husband or other people that they know from everywhere." Not only are the wives often responsible for having people stay overnight, but they also find themselves preparing meals for large numbers of people, making hotel reservations, and accommodating requests for tickets to the games. Sally, one of the authors, keeps a "reservations book" so she knows how many will be staying in her home, who will be eating with them, who needs hotel reservations, and who needs tickets.

Recruiting

Recruiting can be divided into two parts: recruiting activities that take place on campus and in the local area and those to which the coach must travel—often for days at a time. Many wives are active participants in recruiting activities on campus and are instrumental in creating a sense of "family," which is one of the oft-cited keys to successful teams. A change in the recruiting calendar, particularly at the Division I BCS level, has seen recruiting—which once was given more emphasis in November, December, and January—move into the football season itself. This shift now presents additional in-season responsibilities for a coach's wife, such as pre-game recruiting receptions and post-game recruiting dinners, which she's expected to attend. Whereas 10 years ago a Division I BCS coach may have gathered with friends and family after a home game to celebrate a victory or bemoan a loss, current coaches at this level will probably rush home to shower, change clothes, get in the same car as his wife, and head straight to a recruiting function. Post-season recruiting functions are often held on Friday and Saturday evenings.

Spring Ball

Spring ball may be the period of the coaches' calendar that holds the most semblance of a "normal" working family routine, as it has a decrease in the rigorous schedule time seen during in-season and recruiting periods. Many of the coaches' responsibilities during spring ball focus on the actual practice time, so the number of team- and program-related responsibilities for the wives seem to be fewer in this period. However, because spring ball usually culminates in an annual spring game, some responsibilities may mirror an in-season game day and the responsibilities associated with it.

Summer

Summer is the "season" of a football coach's life when time is spent with the family. However, this family time is usually carefully planned around other football responsibilities and often lasts only a week or two. During the summer months, the head football coach (and sometimes various assistant coaches) is often asked to make public appearances in an attempt to create excitement and generate ticket sales in anticipation of the upcoming season. Statewide booster gatherings, golf outings, and rallies are common functions that the head coach's wife is expected to attend with her husband. Football camps for younger athletes are held during the summer months, and coaches' wives at certain levels may find themselves assisting in the operation of the camps in various capacities, such as helping at registration, managing meals/snacks, and other tasks.

Summary

A football coach's dedication to his profession and the constant hard work involved in being a head coach is evident from this chapter. The demands, duties, expectations, and obligations are relentless and not limited to just the football season. In addition to the coaching duties that one might imagine to be typical, coaches must oversee academics, adhere to guidelines, make media appearances, raise money, do charity work, and spend large amounts of time with the players—on and off the field. Expectations for coaches' wives include public appearances, hostess duties, coordinating events and activities to help create a sense of family among the team members and staff, and, at some levels, performing duties that are generally considered to be coaches' responsibilities.

In this chapter, we examined football coaches' lives by discussing the ever-increasing job responsibilities and expectations, the erratic schedules, and excessive hours necessary to fulfill these obligations. We also discussed football coaches' wives' contributions, as they often play integral roles in the achievements and perceptions of the football programs at their institutions. In Chapter 2, we explore the impact that consecutive months of 15-plus-hour days have on coaches and their families.

2

Clock Management:
Time in a Football Coach's World

Football coaching is an extremely competitive and unstable occupation. Whether coaches continue to be employed from year to year depends on a variety of factors—many of which are beyond their control. The long hours, the pressure to win, and the volatility of the profession make managing the job and the coaches' obligations to their families, friends, and life in general extremely difficult. The coaches' responsibilities discussed in Chapter 1 create extraordinary time constraints and immense pressure and stress, which in turn affect their families. Overwhelmingly, issues of time emerged as the dominant concern by respondents in our study. In this chapter, we examine the wives' perceptions of the impact of occupational demands on their husbands' time and the subsequent effects on the coaches, their wives, and their children. We conclude with a discussion of how the characteristics of time in the coaching world are different from those encountered in other demanding professions.

Time Demands

The demands and constraints placed on coaches depend on many variables beyond the "basic" job expectations and obligations. The amount of time coaches spend on the job and how it's spent are decisions often in others' hands, and they also depend on the season, the specific coaching rank, and the team's division. Talking about the work hours, one wife said, "It's different at different levels of coaching, but it's just their job, and their time is really not their own." In Chapter 1, our data clearly show that when compared with what most people would regard as a normal 40-hour workweek, the work hours of our respondents' husbands are excessive. No doubt about it—the long and erratic hours that football coaches work determine how much time the coaches have available to spend with their families and to engage in other activities unrelated to their jobs. As one wife put it: "Everything revolves around him and football. Football determines all decisions. His job always takes priority." Another wife talks about the

"… 'all or nothing' ebb and flow of the year—i.e., he is not truly present in our lives from the end of July to mid-November, then he is back and then he is gone during recruiting season, then back, then gone for spring football season."

Although most of the wives stopped short of identifying their husbands as workaholics, some did. One wife said, "In the off-season, I would like him to devote more time to family and his home, but he does not because there is no *off* season with him. He's a *workaholic.*" In the past, research has had difficulty in defining the term workaholism, but in a 2001 article, Robinson, Carroll, and Flowers suggest it's "… characterized by self-imposed demands, compulsive overworking, inability to regulate work habits and overindulgence in work to the exclusion and detriment of intimate relationships and major life activities." Although the wives' descriptions of their husbands' work lives resemble these characteristics of workaholism in several respects, this definition fails to capture the reality of coaches' lives for whom their work demands are *not* self-imposed nor are the coaches ultimately in charge of whether they overwork or regulate their work habits. Although the net result is probably the same, in most cases, the hours coaches work are almost certainly not of their own choosing.

Many of the wives in our study say they understand perfectly well that to be successful, their husbands must devote long hours to the job and make great personal sacrifices. They don't like it, but they realize that's just the way it is. The bottom line, according to most of our respondents, is expressed in this remark from one of the younger wives, who said "… it's just a cycle and you just have to do it." A few of our online responses reflected a different view of the coaches' excessive working hours:

> I did not want to be a coach's wife but tried to support his dream. I think that it is entirely too demanding of their time. If they were finding the cure for some disease, I could understand the hard work, but it is just a game.

> I married my husband before going through an entire season. If I had known all the hours involved with this occupation, I may not have married him. If it were not for the fact that I know coaching and football are passions, I would not be able to understand why anyone would want to give up so much of their life pursuing this career.

Even though the wives understand the amount of time their husbands spend on the job, they point out that the stress, strains, and constraints imposed on coaches by these time demands inevitably result in conflict between their jobs and their families. The concept of work-family conflict was identified by Greenhaus and Beautell (1985) to describe what occurs when the demands associated with work are incompatible with the demands of the family. Additional work-family conflict arises for the coaches because their nonstandard work hours are incompatible with the rigidity of their children's school schedules and the ways in which other families with fathers who work standard hours are organized.

In addition to season, rank, and level, the time the coaching staff spends on the job is also determined by the head coach's philosophy and attitude toward work and family. Some head coaches are serious about making sure their assistants have some opportunities even during the season to spend time with their wives and children. The priority some head coaches place on family is evident in their use of various strategies to make family time available for themselves as well as for their coaching staff. These strategies may include taking the families to away games and encouraging them to attend practices during the week, among others. Such family-friendly policies go a long way toward helping the assistants manage at least some of the work-family conflict they experience. A *Sports Illustrated* article describing Bob Stoops' program at Oklahoma said: "He holds Wednesday-night 'family meetings,' during which the coaches' spouses and their 30 kids turn the football offices into Gymboree. He doesn't start his day until 8:45 in the morning, so his coaches can see their broods off" (Reilly, 2006). On the other hand are head coaches who are notorious for keeping their assistants at the office for long hours. One wife mentioned a legendary older coach who routinely leaves the facility at midnight or even later, expecting that none of his assistants will leave before he does.

The Specific Effects of Time Constraints and Demands

The direct and specific effects of the constraints and demands on coaches' time are abundant, but the greatest costs, as expressed by the wives, is the small amount of time the men are able to spend with their wives and children, their inability to take care of their own personal health, and their missing out on many other personal aspects of their lives that most husbands and fathers take for granted. These personal aspects include time with friends and extended family, religious activities, and the chance to pursue personal hobbies and interests.

Coaches' Physical Well-Being

Many of our respondents expressed concern about their husbands' physical health. The wives reported that these health concerns are present for some coaches year-round, but they're more evident during the football season and recruiting because of the coaches' lack of time to devote to their own personal welfare. One of the most common concerns among the wives is their husbands' inability to sleep well, which results in exhaustion. A number of wives mentioned that their husbands were often up before 5 a.m. and rarely in bed before midnight during the season. Another health concern is the coaches' diet. While eating an unhealthy diet is a common (and almost expected) feature of recruiting season, it also occurs during football season, as coaches often don't take the time to eat well. Lack of exercise is also an issue. Many respondents echoed the concern of one wife: "He is so concerned about winning and he puts in so much time and energy into the job that he doesn't have time to work out." Other health issues mentioned were high blood pressure during the season and the lack of life satisfaction because of insufficient leisure time. Another wife said, "There is very little outside joy because of the lack of downtime—not a good quality of life." And yet another told us, "He can be too consumed with his job and he forgets to have fun and relax."

Lack of Time for Religious Activities

One issue that arose many times is the lack of time the coaches have for religious activities. Even though their wives may describe them as religious or spiritual and tell us that regular worship is important to many coaches, they're often unable to attend religious services, especially during the season and recruiting. Game days are almost always on Saturday, which means the coaches are usually at work on Sunday to review film from the game or are in meetings and working with the players. One wife mentioned that when her husband did attend church on Sundays, he was often confronted by fans who would ask him why he wasn't at work looking at film from the day before. For some coaches, the inability to attend church services is partially compensated for by the presence of a team chaplain, who holds services for the coaches and teams during the season.

Lack of Time for Personal Interests/Hobbies

Another area of concern the wives mentioned often is that their husbands had no time during the season (or at any other time, some said) for hobbies or personal interests. One wife said her husband's career drains him to such an extent that when he does have free time, he doesn't want to do much of anything except sleep. She wasn't alone. In addition, several of the wives said their husbands would like to pursue advanced degrees but have difficulty doing so. Despite fringe benefits that often include tuition remission, unless appropriate classes are offered during the summer, coaches find it difficult to take advantage of this benefit because of their long hours and erratic schedules.

Contact and Time With Extended Family

Living long distances from their parents and other relatives is a concern for the coaches themselves, who often find it difficult to maintain relationships with their extended family. Unless their parents, siblings, and other relatives are able to come to games or otherwise do the traveling, times together may be few and far between. One wife said: "He misses his family—all of whom live out of state. His schedule prevents him from going 'home' as much as he'd like."

However, some coaches are luckier and live and work in the same state as their extended families and are therefore able to work family visits into their schedules. Assistant coach's wife Justice told us that her husband is very close to his family and talks to his mom probably every day. She said his family always gets together for Easter and the Fourth of July as well as for other family celebrations.

Lack of Time for Personal Friendships

A coach's social life is also affected, and as far as personal relationships are concerned, football coaches have few if any friends outside of football, according to their wives. They've limited time available, which makes it difficult to keep in touch with old friends and difficult to make friends in a new community. Overall, the often nomadic nature of a coaching career can make it almost impossible to establish ties in any one physical location.

Other Family Needs

Comments by many wives emphasized how truly difficult accommodating family needs to the demands of the football year can be. Seldom do family events coincide even partially with the coaching calendar. For example, the wife of a Division II head coach said of her family:

> Our oldest was born in the summer right before football starts, so he's always been around for his birthday. My daughter, unfortunately, was born right smack in the middle of recruiting season, so very seldom was he home for hers. And sometimes, we would just have to delay her birthday. And my youngest is right during spring practice, so he's … it's a little bit missed sometimes. You know, you just have to just do it when you can.

One wife said, "I've had two children induced because they had to fit in with his schedule." She wasn't the only one to mention this. The wife of a Division I BCS head coach told us, "I had to plan every birth of a child and all major surgeries according to his schedule, not limited to but including two C-sections and a hysterectomy." In discussing the impending death of her terminally ill father-in-law, one head coach's wife said, "I remember my husband saying that it would really work well if he (his father) could die this week—the week we have an open week—this would really be the ideal time. …"

Characteristics of Time in the Coaching World

The specific effects of the time demands, expectations, and constraints of football coaching are evident, but what's less evident and perhaps more interesting are the characteristics of time in the coaching world—or what we refer to as the "coaching clock." What time means, how it's used, and even how it feels are all markedly different for coaches and their families than for non-coaching families. While many other people have demanding careers, we assert that the specific characteristics of time-related demands are different in the coaching world. In our study, these differences revolve around four areas, each of which is outlined in the following sections.

Ambiguity

A career in coaching is riddled with ambiguity; the coaches' lives are full of unknowns. (Here, we define *ambiguity* to mean a lack of definition and certainty.) The coaching clock is marked by demands beyond the coaches' control, is constantly shifting, and often consists of delays, unanticipated circumstances, and disappointment. Each situation and configuration of situations with which the coaches are confronted on a daily basis may have multiple parameters, multiple meanings, and multiple consequences. Will the team win or lose? Will the player sign? How will the fans react? What will the season bring? This uncertainty translates directly into how time is spent and perceived. This ambiguity is evident at every level of coaching and at every point in the coaching calendar, although its effects are most evident in the recruiting season.

Although other seasons, especially the actual football season itself, are demanding as far as time at work is concerned, they do offer a routine or sense of regularity that's missing from the recruiting season, which is built on ambiguity. Will the player commit? How long will it take? When will the coach be gone and for how long? Where? Such lack of certainty makes it hard for the coach and his family to plan anything, and the normal routines or even the creative strategies that work at other times don't work during this season. As far as off-campus recruiting is concerned, many wives said that long recruiting trips are the most difficult part of being married to a football coach. One wife said that she can take any demands during the season because at least he's home with them at night (even if not until late), but she really doesn't like it when he's on the road day after day. Many other wives talked about how hard recruiting season is for their children, especially when their father is away for a week or more at a time. This wife's comments are telling:

> I've learned that there isn't any point in arguing about having to do everything at the house even though I work a full-time job, and there isn't any point in arguing about never spending any time together as a couple or a family because he says there isn't much he can do about it. Sometimes, I have just had enough and explode, but then we have it out and the conclusion is there is nothing we can do about it.

Relentless Pressure

Many wives mentioned how their husbands' intense and consuming preoccupations with their jobs left the men with little capacity to think about anything else. Even when coaches are at home, many wives said that their husbands are never really off duty. One wife stated: "Even when Dad is home, he often has to be doing recruiting work. He doesn't have the energy to go out and play with the kids."

Advances in technology serve as a double-edged sword for the coaches and their families. While many of the advances, such as cell phones, the Internet, and portable computers, allow for more flexibility and availability for the coach and greater access to his family, they also create more opportunities for work in any number of places.

Coaches are always accessible to other coaches, players, and other work-related people. Several of the older wives mentioned how much worse the problem has become with the constant phone calls and text messages when the coaches are at home.

Some of our respondents told us that the only way they can get their husbands away from their cell phones is to go to remote areas where "... with any luck, cell phones won't work." One veteran wife told us about her family's vacations:

> It is the month of July usually or late June—[the] first three weeks of July. We used to go to a cabin in a real remote part of Washington State when the children were little. Even when the kids were older, we still escaped as a family [to a place] where cell phones don't work. ... If there is an emergency, it can wait a day or two.

Another young wife, married to a Division I head coach, said:

> When he can get away, these three to three-and-a-half weeks in the summer time, he needs to leave home. And then we just hang out at the beach. We do whatever but preferably in an area where cell phones don't work because otherwise he will not disconnect.

Double Duty

A creative strategy employed by many wives and coaching families is what we're calling "double duty." Double duty is the merging of two (or sometimes more) separate tasks into the same time slot. For example, taking the kids to practice as a way to spend time with family (task one) while the coach works (task two). Although this is an effective and creative strategy and solves one problem, it nevertheless adds to the relentless nature of the coaching clock by cramming every minute with as many tasks as possible. Coaching families have few options if they want to spend time together. However, the impact of this double duty shouldn't be minimized. In addition to allowing for little to no downtime, the coaching clock is stretched to the maximum.

Jamie, the young wife of an assistant coach, doesn't like her husband being absent from home during recruiting either, but she does enjoy participating in recruiting activities on campus whenever she can. She sees these activities as being the only opportunity for "dates" during this season. She said: "We get babysitters, and I'll go to a hockey game with them [the coach and recruits] and afterwards, they'll go out to supper, so I will usually go to that too. Otherwise, I wouldn't see my husband."

Other examples of double duty are taking lunch to the coach's office so his wife and children can spend time with him while making sure he takes time out for lunch, inviting players to their home so the coach can be with his children and his family at the same time, and, at some programs, having the wife help out at the football office and therefore have some additional time with her husband.

Preoccupation

Many wives mentioned that their husbands' "focus" on football peaks during the season. As one wife said, "… [E]ven if he is physically home, he is not mentally present." Another stated, "His focus is on football and only football during the season." A veteran head coach's wife agreed: "The coaches don't notice anything once the season starts." Others mentioned the constant "talking about football when we are together." In discussing her husband's total preoccupation with his job during the season and the fact that coaches don't notice anything once the season starts, Tina told the story about her new end tables. She said she bought the tables at the beginning of the season and that it took her husband until Christmas to notice them. Preoccupation to this extent results in a husband and/or father who might be physically present but is often emotionally and intellectually unavailable.

Summary

Excessive time demands are a reality in the coaching profession. The long working hours can affect the physical well-being of a coach as well as relationships within the coaching families and with extended family members and friends. Coaching families learn to efficiently organize events around coaching time responsibilities (although recent advances in technology have diminished the "leftover" time in a coach's day) and to plan family events accordingly. Although most of the "seasons" of a football coaches' lives consist of 70- to 90-plus-hour workweeks, the recruiting season seems to add additional time-related issues because the coach is physically gone from home for many days.

3

Instability in Coaching Football and the Importance of "Football Families"

*"There are only two kinds of coaches—those
who have been fired and those who will be fired."*
—Ken Loeffler

This is a commonly known saying in athletics. Although people in other occupations may also be at risk for job loss, the nature and severity of occupational volatility with which football coaches especially must contend is unique to their profession. What many people don't understand is that coaches don't just get fired when they mess up, but assistant coaches can also lose their jobs if the head coach of a program is fired, retires, or resigns. As several wives noted, when the head coach loses his job, that generally means a total of 10 other coaches will also probably lose theirs—no matter how well the assistant coaches may have performed individually.

Traditionally, head coaches had multiyear contracts that included a buyout clause and assistant coaches had one-year contracts. However, this seems to be changing, particularly at the Division I BCS level. Research cited in a 2009 *USA Today* article found six assistant coaches at major football-playing colleges with five-year contracts (three of these six coaches were at Oklahoma State), 12 with contracts of four years or more, 56 with contracts of three years or more, and 206 with contracts of two years or more (Wieberg, Upton, Perez, and Berkowitz, 2009). A 2011 *St. Louis Post-Dispatch* article quotes St. Louis attorney and agent Bob Lattinville as saying that about 25 percent of coordinators have retention bonuses similar to those that are being included in head coaches' contracts (Durando, 2011).

Traditional wisdom in football asserted that a head coach should be given at least four years at a program so that by year four, the team he's coaching consists of his own recruits. This line of thinking seems to be changing too. An article in *Sporting News* suggested that as head coaches' pay has increased, the expectations for success have too. The author believes that highly paid head coaches today operate (not by choice) on a three-year plan: "… [O]ne year to clear out malcontents and to get players to embrace your philosophy, one year to turn the corner and one year to show significant improvement" (Hayes, 2004). Some programs, though, don't offer coaches enough time to turn a program around or return it to former glory. In fact, in 2010, Rich Rodriguez was terminated at the University of Michigan after his third year, while in 2011, Turner Gill was dismissed at Kansas after only two seasons.

Although we've already alluded to high salaries for football coaches, we don't want to leave readers with the assumption that all coaches are paid equally and all are paid high salaries. A quick glance at the 2012 base salaries in the Division I BCS shows head coaches' pay ranged from $225,000 to $4,683,333 (USA Today College Football Coach Salary Database, 2006–2011). Generally, salaries for head coaches in other divisions are considerably lower than those of Division I BCS head coaches. Assistant coaches and coordinators are mostly very well compensated in Division I BCS programs, and numerous assistant coaches for Division I BCS teams make more money than head coaches in the lower divisions. Nevertheless, some of our participants pointed out that a disjuncture often exists between the amount of time and effort their husbands put in and the amount of money they're paid. One wife said, "My husband is not compensated for his effort and hard work." Another noted:

> A distressing aspect of being a coach's wife is the hours my husband puts into his work and not getting a lot of money for it. I see family members who put in the same amount of time as my husband and they get two times the salary as my husband. It is frustrating.

Several other wives point out that although their husbands may have a sizable salary one year, they may very well be out of a job the next year. While coaching vacancies are often the result of firings or retirements, the subsequent switching of jobs (frequently referred to by the media as the "coaching carousel") to fill these openings means that some coaching changes are the result of coaches leaving their current position for what's perceived to be a better job. An excerpt from a January 2012 article discusses the increasing occurrences of coaches not finishing their contracts:

> Of 120 coaches at [BCS] programs, 78 have completed three seasons or fewer, meaning a majority of football coaches have yet to see their first crop of freshmen graduate as seniors.
>
> [Todd] Graham left Pittsburgh for Arizona State with four years left on his contract; he took the Pittsburgh job two years after agreeing to a 10-year contract at Tulsa.
>
> Graham isn't the first coach to leave with years left on his contract. He won't be the last. He's not even alone in ugly exits. Arkansas coach Bobby Petrino left Louisville for the Atlanta Falcons less than six months after agreeing to a 10-year contract with the Cardinals. The stories go on and on.

And it's not just coaches leaving one job for another with a contract on the table. Athletic directors are just as finicky: Former Texas A&M coach Mike Sherman received a one-year contract extension on his five-year deal and a raise in July. He was fired Dec. 1. (Fox, 2012)

A January 2012 ABCNews.com article states:

> Coaches who come to define not just a team but a school, Hall of Famers such as Bear Bryant, Tom Osborne, Bo Schembechler, Bobby Bowden and Joe Paterno, seem to be going the way of the wishbone and tear-away jerseys in college football.
>
> "Look what's happening," Bowden told The Associated Press on Sunday, hours after Joe Paterno died at the age of 85. "Coaches getting fired in two years. Coaches making a million dollars here and they get $2 million and they leave. They break a five-year contract. You've got unloyalty at both ends." (Russo, 2012)

We noted earlier that when a head coach is dismissed, the entire staff is often also let go. However, when a head coach leaves to take a "more desirable" job, he may not always have the liberty or ability to bring his entire staff with him. Staff shakeups also occur when coordinators are named head coaches at other schools, causing the assistant coaches to have to decide whether to work for the current head coach or go to work for the previous coordinator. Coordinators are sometimes let go as the step preceding/preventing the firing of a head coach. The coaching carousel was in high gear following the 2011 season, as illustrated in a CollegeFootballPoll.com article dated January 31, 2012, that showed 27 Division I BCS head coaching changes had taken place for the 2012 season. This followed 24 Division I BCS head coaching changes in 2011 and 23 in 2010 (CollegeFootballPoll.com staff, 2010, 2011, 2012).

To further illustrate the precariousness of the coaching life, following the 2008 season, seven of the husbands of the 16 wives interviewed in the summer of 2008 had changed jobs. Five of the husbands were fired and two voluntarily changed jobs. Three of those fired were head coaches, one was an assistant coach who lost his job because his head coach was fired, and the fifth was a veteran coordinator. One of the two coaches who left his job voluntarily took a head coaching position in another state, and the other made a lateral move to a similar program—also in a different state. In addition, another veteran coordinator lost his job following the 2009 season when his head coach was fired. All the wives and children of these men have had to relocate as a result of their husbands' job changes. By the time the 2011 season ended, the careers of the husbands of our 16 interviewed wives looked like this:

- Seven were still at the same job.
  - ✓ Three from Division I BCS: five, six, and 12 years at the same school
  - ✓ One from Division I FCS: nine years at the same school

✓ Two from Division II: both at the same school for 10 years

✓ One from Division III: four years at the same school

- Six had been fired at least once
- One had retired
- Four had moved to better jobs at least once
- One sat out of coaching for a season
- One left the profession

To comprehend the frenzy surrounding job movement that occurs in the football coaching profession, one should experience the American Football Coaches Association convention. The AFCA is "… the only national organization solely dedicated to improving football coaches through ongoing education, interaction, and networking. Its primary goal is to provide resources for personal and professional development amongst the football coaching profession. The AFCA membership includes over 11,000 members and represents coaches and several stakeholders within the game of football. Any high school, junior college, international, semi-professional or professional football coach is eligible to become a member of the AFCA" (AFCA).

The annual convention is held each year in January—the peak of the coaching carousel. Picture thousands of football coaches gathered in a convention venue—many looking to improve their job situation by networking as many individuals as possible in a three-day span. One head coach commented to his wife that in years when he has openings on his staff it takes him as long as two hours to cross the lobby.

Football Scoop is a website (www.footballscoop.com) that keeps up with the latest "scoop" on coaching openings and is followed by many coaches and their spouses. The two-day excerpt (January 8 and 9, 2012) contained in Figure 3-1 gives an indication of the amount of movement taking place at that time. An interesting side note: One of the main sponsors of the website is a family relocation specialist that has the endorsement of the American Football Coaches Wives Association (AFCWA).

Our respondents frequently mentioned the instability and uncertainty generated by their husbands' career as being a constant source of anxiety to the whole family. People whose identity is defined mostly by their occupation (and football coaches certainly fit into this category) have great difficulty handling job insecurity because job loss means not only loss of income but loss of identity (Kuhnert and Palmer, 1991). All this creates considerable amounts of stress.

Snookie, a head coach's wife, points out that individuals outside of the coaching profession just "don't get" the fine line between keeping a job and being fired. She recalls having several childhood friends as guests at a pivotal game, which thankfully ended with her husband's team being victorious:

> The game included a blocked field goal that sent it into overtime and the quarterback's ability to stretch the ball over the goal line for the

game-winning touchdown. As we left the stadium, one friend said, "OK, let me get this straight. … Since that field goal got blocked and your quarterback was able to reach into the end zone, your husband still has a job. But if either one of those hadn't happened, you would all be getting fired?" I told her that she had summed it up beautifully. For the rest of the evening, they all took turns shaking their heads and saying things like, "I just cannot believe that," "How can you live like that," "Why would anyone go into coaching," etc.

A contributor to the wives' message board on Football Scoop wrote about coaching insecurity: "Everyone knows the stress involved in moving, but you don't realize the stress that comes before what I call the waiting game. This is the time when your life is in limbo and you don't know if you are staying or going." A number of our respondents said the same thing because at the end of each football season, they're facing uncertainty. Will the coach be fired? Will he be kept on for another year? Will the head coach lose his job and the assistants lose theirs too? Will the head coach take a new position and move his staff with him? For many, the anxiety of wondering if their husbands will have to take a different job only makes their lives all the more difficult. One young wife said:

> I get scared about the insecurity of his job. We are starting to think about having a family, and it really scares me that he will be fired. If he gets another position and we have to move, it is a different story. But it is scary being married to a football coach. You can never feel stable or too comfortable where you are.

And it's not only the zero job security in many cases that's the problem nor the fact these wives often realize that a move is unavoidable. It's also not knowing where they'll be moving to next. Although Jamie had no reason to believe her husband's job was in jeopardy at the time of her interview, she suffers from the same anxiety nevertheless. She said: "But every December, you always get nervous because there are so many coaching changes and you always wonder are you going to be here or are you going to be there, so that part is kind of scary."

Divisional differences also affect job security. For the most part, coaches in Division II and Division III move less often than their counterparts in Division I, but one DII wife told us: "It [job security] could change tomorrow. One thing you learn about football is that life is only what it is at the moment." Rachel, the wife of a head coach, told us she also feels safer at the Division II level. She said:

> I don't want that life for our family in Division I because I feel like Division II is a safer level. You just don't get fired at the drop of a hat. There seems to be a lot more stability and security at this level than at Division I. We talked about that quite a bit earlier this year, moving to [Division I BCS] or even [Division I FCS]. I was just very skeptical of that.

- *Penn State:* We have learned that Ted Roof will join the defensive staff.
- *Vanderbilt:* Word at the convention is that Tulsa's Van Malone will join the staff at Vandy to coach the corners.
- *Baylor:* We have confirmed Phil Bennett was offered the Tennessee defensive coordinator job and declined. He's staying in Waco.
- *Auburn:* Multiple sources telling us that Auburn has hired Falcons defensive coordinator Brian VanGorder as defensive coordinator.
- *Yale:* We hear that UConn defensive coordinator Don Brown has accepted the head coaching position at Yale. Have not confirmed. Will update.
- *Texas A&M:* We have confirmed Mark Snyder will become defensive coordinator at Texas A&M. Snyder is currently defensive coordinator at South Florida and prior to that was head coach at Marshall and defensive coordinator at Ohio State prior to that.
- *Arizona State:* We hear Pitt head strength coach Shawn Griswold left to take the same position at ASU.
- *Maryland:* Locksley's agreement is $500,000 for 4 years all guaranteed. Max bonus of $150k.
- *Oklahoma:* Mike Stoops will reportedly join the staff as co-defensive coordinator. Will update further later.
- *FAU:* Jared Allen will be retained. We hear he will coach the receivers.
- *Penn State:* We hear Buffalo Bills receivers coach Stan Hixon will be named assistant head coach / receivers coach at Penn State.
- *UCLA:* Sources close to the program tell us that Angus McClure will wind up coaching the defensive line. Unfortunately we hear that Inoke Breckterfield will be leaving the program.
- *Vanderbilt:* We hear James Franklin will likely hire Josh Gattis from Western Michigan as his receivers coach. Not a done deal yet though we hear.
- *Penn State:* Ball State offensive line coach John Strollo will move to Penn State in the same capacity.
- *Humboldt State:* We hear that Fred Kelley will be named offensive line coach. Kelley was at Sacramento State this past season.
- *FAU:* Sources tell us that Luke Meadows is leaving South Dakota State to serve as offensive line coach at FAU.
- *New Mexico:* We hear former Louisville defensive coordinator Kevin Fouquier has been offered the defensive line job at New Mexico.

Figure 3-1. Two-day excerpt (January 8 and 9, 2012) of coaching changes from Football Scoop

> I could be wrong, but what I see is a heck of lot more family movement and a heck of a lot less time at home. It is bad now, so I can't imagine it being any worse.

Even wives whose husbands are part of a program headed by a long-term coach aren't immune from anxiety. Marissa told us:

> You would think there is a little more stability when you have a head coach that has been here 20-plus years, but at the same time, there is

- *Redlands:* We hear that Kiyoshi Harris has been hired to coach the inside receivers. Harris was assistant head coach / offensive coordinator at Chaffey Junior College.
- *Memphis:* We have learned that Brad Cornelson has been hired to coach the receivers. Cornelson was the offensive coordinator at Northeast Oklahoma. We also hear that Justin Fuente has targeted Todd Dodge for quarterbacks coach. Dodge isn't a done deal yet.
- *Penn State:* Ron Vanderlinden has been retained.
- *Colorado State:* Sources tell us that Alabama offensive quality control Billy Napier will go with Jim McElwain to CSU as quarterbacks coach.
- *VMI:* We hear that defensive coordinator A.J. Christoff is retiring after 37 years in the profession. Some of the programs Christoff has coached at include Notre Dame, Alabama, UCLA, Colorado, Cincinnati, Idaho, Stanford and with the 49ers.
- *Illinois:* We hear that Toledo corners coach / special teams coordinator Steven Clinkscale will be joining Tim Beckman's staff at Illinois.
- *Syracuse:* Sources telling us that Doug Marrone is interviewing a number of guys this week for some defensive slots.
- *New Mexico State:* We hear that former Washington State offensive coordinator Todd Sturdy and Hawaii offensive coordinator Nick Rolovich are interviewing for the offensive coordinator job as well.
- *Washington State:* We have learned that Mike Leach has hired Mike Breske from Montana as his defensive coordinator.
- *New Mexico State:* We have learned that former Colorado State head coach Steve Fairchild is interviewing here for the offensive coordinator role.
- *Hawaii:* We hear offensive coordinator Nick Rolovich will not be retained.
- *Monroe College:* We have learned that former Fordham defensive coordinator Matt Dawson has accepted the defensive coordinator role on Terry Karg's staff.
- *Hamilton Tiger-Cats (CFL):* Buffalo Bills quarterbacks coach George Cortez has been named the new head coach and director of football operations.
- *Abilene Christian:* New head coach Ken Collums has made a couple of hires. Darian Dulan as defensive coordinator and Mark Ribaudo as linebackers coach.
- *Tennessee:* Word in San Antonio last night was that if an agreement can't be reached with Randy Shannon that Baylor defensive coordinator Phil Bennett would be asked to take the job. We'll keep you posted.
- *New England Patriots:* Josh McDaniels has joined the staff.

Figure 3-1. Two-day excerpt (January 8 and 9, 2012) of coaching changes from Football Scoop (cont.)

no stability in college football coaching. There are no givens. You can't go somewhere and say, "We are going to be here a good five years—this will be good." You just never know. Now saying that, we have been here for almost eight years, and we are under an excellent head coach, we have a good program, and we have a great administration that backs us. Yes, we have had some stability and it has been nice, but like I said, when you are in college coaching, that could be taken away tomorrow.

Tina also talked about her experience:

Oh, yes, we've had two different firings. We were at one school and we were only there for a year. The head coach called my husband and wanted him to be a coordinator because their program was starting to go down and he wanted it to get some oomph. The head coach hired him, but B had a feeling and told the AD, "I don't want to come here if I'm going to be gone in a year." He said, "Oh, no, you're safe." And, of course, that was a lie. So, yeah, the head coach got fired, and we knew we could see the writing on the wall. The other time was when he was hired here, but luckily, he was hired here before he was fired. It was the last game, and I knew when the AD came out [that] it was done.

Beth's family had a similar experience, although they've never actually been fired. She said:

We have been fortunate. We have moved, though, to avoid firing. We've heard from other coaches that when the head coach gets fired but you get retained, the next staff comes in and all they do is criticize. So, we've never been fired, but we have come close. We've had friends that have been fired and know how scared they are. And it's public. You know, your whole neighborhood whispers about it and they look at you funny.

Kate said:

We've been close. We've been really, really close. I think it was two seasons ago. My husband really felt like the end of that season that they had a lot of missed opportunities. We had a lot of games where we were in it until the fourth quarter and it would just blow up. And we would end up losing at the tail end. You know, he really, as that progressed, you know we had the sort of husband-wife talk that this could be it. You know he's done so much for the program and made so many changes and it takes time. But I think it is less traumatic as an assistant coach. You'll manage somewhere, I think. Although, if the head coach gets the ax, so do you. On the other hand, if the head coach gets the dream job, there is a good chance he is taking you with [him].

Kate's husband was fired from his job a year after her interview. Snookie also told about her wakeup call:

We have only been let go one time, and that happened because the head coach that we came to the school with was let go. We were at a [Division I BCS] school with great football tradition. Common decency would make you assume that you would be given several years to turn a program around, but for reasons that will probably never be known publicly, our head coach was let go after just one .500 season. During the season, we lost to our in-state rival. Immediately following the game, one of the coach's wives that had already been on the staff when we arrived, said "We are gone." I remember thinking to myself how ridiculous that statement was and categorized her as overly dramatic. Right after the season, our husbands had been called into a meeting and were told by an athletic administrator that they had 100 percent support and that they should get on with recruiting. Three days later, while they were on the road, the head coach "resigned" and the assistant coaches were immediately out of a job.

The Pressure to Win: Losing Seasons Equal Stress

All the instability in football coaching that we've discussed is generated by the pressure to win, which all football programs are expected to do. Justice points out that even a large number of wins aren't good enough for some fans:

> Yeah, 8-4 here and they are calling for your head. You're the worst coach on the planet. I mean, you wouldn't believe some of the things, as successful as our team has been. I mean, [we've won] conference championships. We've been in [Division I] BCS bowls. Well, we haven't won all of them, but you know, there are people that think that there should be a change here. I mean, you've got to be kidding me. So, you went from earlier coaches where you were going 6-5 to [winning conference] championships and people are still going to [complain]. There's just the reality and the nature of the game.

Fans often expect results regardless of the reality of what condition a football program is in. Many head coaches take over teams/program that need rebuilding, but they're still expected to produce wins. One head coach's wife told us:

> It's a no-win situation. If you allude to the fact that you may not have players as good as your competition, you are said to be making excuses. If you build your players up in the media and then they really aren't as good as the competition, then you are labeled as blowing smoke. We've been through several rebuilding coaching situations and they seem to follow the same pattern. You struggle for the first few seasons and are treated like pure crap by the fans and media. You begin to turn the corner in year three and people start warming up to you. Then, in year four, things get righted, you have a great season, and people act like they were in your corner the whole time.

Heidi told us about the effects this kind of stress can have:

> And it's not that we haven't [had success]. ... We went to a bowl game this year, but it wasn't the Rose Bowl and it wasn't the outcome that we wanted. The expectations were higher for us than what we accomplished. I can remember going to the games and being so carefree and then once we had the losing season three years ago, you go to the games and you almost throw up [because] your stomach is, like, twisted and you are, like, oh my gosh, I can't even sit here and you are saying the rosary and you are just about to have an out-of-body experience and you are hearing people say stuff about the head coach and the defense and the offense. Appreciate it when you are winning. Really take the time to enjoy it because it can turn quickly.

The pressure to win seems to increase and the patience with non-winning seasons lessens as one progresses from Division III to Division II to Division I FCS to Division I BCS. It's obvious that this pressure leads to stress for the coaches. In fact, stress in one member of the family affects all other members individually and the family as a whole. This is especially true for coaching families if a team has the misfortune to experience a losing season. According to one wife, losing seasons are "... absolutely no fun. You hurt for them because they work so hard and their lives are controlled by college-aged kids." Several summed it up more succinctly: "Losing sucks." Another wife said that during bad seasons, her husband comes home "tired and cranky."

She's not alone; many other women mentioned that the stress on their husbands during losing seasons sometimes spills over into the family when the men may be short tempered or even "kind of mean." Others tend to become "quiet and distant." One wife shared: "When he loses the game, he is not a very happy camper for a few days. My kids and I have just learned to leave Dad alone during that time." Another wife put it this way: "It's stressful to watch him distressed." Many wives mentioned that they feel they should take an active role in helping their husbands deal with losing seasons and that they often share in his hurt and disappointment. Ann said:

> Honestly, I could say he's only had maybe two losing seasons. He's been very successful at what he's done, but two years, [we had two consecutive losing seasons]. And that ... Not ever having that before, that was hard because he's trying to think, "Man, am I not a good coach" or all these things going through his mind. But yet he had to build a program and start from scratch. That was tough because I wasn't used to it. Yeah, we had lost some games and stuff, but I wasn't sure how I was supposed to handle him and how to help him get through it. Am I supposed to talk to him? Finally, the last couple games of the year, it's, like, just get them over with. We don't ... We know we are going to lose—just get the year over so we can get on.

The "Football Family"

One of the more interesting findings from this study and one that plays a very important part in the wives' ability to accept the instability and adapt to the peculiarities of life with a football coach is their identification with other members of the football program. Football programs often refer to the individuals in their tight-knit group (coaches, players, support staff, and families of these three groups) as their "football family." A number of wives mentioned how much they enjoyed the "camaraderie among the coaching families" and how great it was to have a "football family" to lend support when they needed it. One wife said: "Our staff is like family. We take care of each other, and I think the head coach sets the standard for providing this kind of environment." Ann talked about her head coach husband's staff and their families. She said:

> He's got guys that have been with him 15 years and some that have been there 10 to 13. We have had a kind of continuing relationship with them and their families. When we first started, half of the coaches weren't even married and then they gradually got married and then they started having babies and then it was boom, boom, boom, we have 10 babies.

The collective mentality generated by their seeing themselves as part of the football family allows the coaches' wives to accept the sacrifices they make as necessary for the common good of the program. When the team wins, they all win, and when it loses, they all lose. They see that their individual concerns aren't as important as the collective concerns; they're "we"-oriented—whether as a representative of the university, the team, and the coaches, or as a part of the wives' "team." Our study participants often singled out the wives of other coaches on their staff when they used the words "football family" and discussed the roles that these women played in their lives. They commented that the wives of coaches are a close-knit group and one they can turn to when they need to. These close bonds are based on a shared understanding of their experiences. Their collective identity as coaches' wives comes from their common interests, experiences, and solidarity, and it enables them to withstand pressure and other problems.

Over and over, our respondents mentioned how important their relationships were with the other wives—something one wife called "the great sisterhood I have with other coaches' wives everywhere." The comments the online respondents made include:

- "The wives' support system understands sometimes better than family and friends can."
- "I love that we have a built-in support system with the head coach's wife and the other assistants' wives."
- "What I really like, too, is the coaching staff and how they're really close and the wives are really close. So, his job has allowed me to make new friends, and the support you can get from other coaches' wives is nice."

According to Jamie, these women "… share a common experience that is different from the lives of the people next door and down the street and your kids' friends' parents' lives." She said it's helpful to have someone understand what Friday nights are like at your house and she advises other wives "to try to find good support, try to find a friend on staff, or find someone who really understands what you're going through and talk to them when you have problems. Don't bottle it all in because it can be very lonely if you do." Marissa agreed and said: "Really lean on and know the rest of the coaching staff and the wives because they are your family. They understand what being married to a coach entails." She continued: "If you don't lean on each other, it's going to be a long road because you will be on your own. Consider the football staff your family." Heidi remembered several years ago when her children were young and they lived in a state a great distance from where she came from and where her family lived. She said the other coaches' families became her family. She described how the families were together every day, ate meals together, traveled together, and went to games together. In fact, when the head coach accepted another position and took his staff with him, the wives and children were left to travel to the new place without the coaches, who had gone on ahead of them. They caravanned across half the United States to the new location. Michaela also sees the other coaches' wives as her family. She said:

> Two of the other coaches have wives, and we've been friends for several years. … I love them very much. They're like my family because I'm not really close to mine, and I really care about them quite a bit. I think we are kind of a support group. … I think we do try to support each other.

Looking back over the years, Sarah-Grace said:

> … I think the joys of being a coach's wife are multiplied twentyfold when you feel that you have a strong support staff group and you feel bonded to these other people. It's always the most fun when you have a staff of wives who like each other and who are social, who organize, and who do things together. I think it's an incredible experience. While not all of my closest friends are coaches' wives, the longest, most enduring friendships that I have are with coaches' wives. There is a bond there that is never broken. Maybe because you depend on them in a way that you normally would depend on your husband if he were available. They become more than a friend—they become almost your de facto family in the area where you live.

Many wives emphasized that membership in the wives' sisterhood is not only important for themselves, but they also understand they have a responsibility to get to know other coaches' wives, especially those who are new to their program, to support and encourage them. One wife said she "truly believes we have a ministry, especially concerning other younger coaches and their wives."

Several wives talked about the AFCWA as a good source of support and networking. Beth said: "That camaraderie is where you get all your experience and knowledge. You can usually find someone that's been where you are or where you're going." While the majority of responses about the relationships of the members of the football families were positive, a few wives felt otherwise:

> Other wives sometimes aren't that friendly, and they seem to cause division on the staff that causes distress for me because I'm a nice person and very easygoing. I just don't get the backstabbing and all that goes into this profession. Some of the wives act jealous—like they are superior—and that just really ticks me off. I say "Get a life and let go of the coattail" or should I say coaching shorts, since that's all they wear. I hate the junior high mentality that is displayed by the wives of the other coaches. I hate the power and positioning struggles between the other coaches and wives.

The Head Coach's Wife's Role in the Family

Many of our respondents talked about how important a source of support the head coach's wife can be. Lesley said:

> One of them was really good about trying to get us together. I think that is important too because I had never lived away from home before, except for college, and there are so many wives that were used to having a supportive family and then move halfway across the country and not know anybody. All of us needed to be together. We didn't really know it, but I thought it was an important role of the head coach's wife, trying to keep us together and call each other.

An online respondent had this to say:

> The head coach's wife warned me when we first started dating that the life of a coach's wife is *not* glamorous and it does require extreme patience and support upon my part. Therefore, I feel that I went into this relationship with open eyes and was more prepared for most of the challenges that were to come. She was basically my mentor into the lives of coaches' wives, and I am extremely grateful that she was able to impart some of her experience as a 30-year coach's wife veteran.

Different head coaches' wives have different philosophies about their roles, but several of our participants who are married to head coaches felt it was their job to go out of their way to welcome new wives into the family. Catherine said she thinks that head coaches' wives often get the responsibility of being the welcome wagon, and she wonders if that's fair. She said they help new wives find out where the children will go to school and where to buy a home, and they set newcomers up with a realtor. Claire, the wife of a head coach, said she tries to "… create a network of support for the assistants' wives and to organize playgroups to make sure everyone is happy because I know that the happiness of a wife definitely makes a difference in a husband's happiness." Tina, also the wife of a head coach, said: "They're your family, and sometimes, when you're at a job, that's all you have. So, I try to do a lot with the coaches' wives. And I worry about them." Marissa discusses the wife of her husband's head coach:

> I think here in our situation, we just all love the fact that she is not one to walk around and say "I'm the head coach's wife." That is not her at all. She loves to take us all out to lunch every once in a while—just the girls—and she always insists on paying and things like that. That is just the way she is. She is just a neat person, and she shows that it doesn't matter what position you are in—you can just be down to earth and be a nice person and help everyone out. She helped us on several occasions—whether it's finding things when we first got here—and that is just kind of the role you take on once you've been somewhere. You wouldn't know she was the head coach's wife. She is amazing.

Several study participants told us that the head coach's wife often sets the tone for the expectations of the other coaches' wives on the staff. Some head coaches' wives inform the assistant coaches' wives of team- or program-related events with the understanding that the assistants' wives will participate in events whenever possible, although they understand that other family or work-related obligations may often take priority. One of the wives we interviewed remembered saying to the head coach's wife, who hadn't yet experienced raising teenagers herself: "I need you to respect where I am with my life. I have older kids and different commitments that you might not understand, so just tell me when I need to be at something, when it is important, and when it's not. …"

Some head coaches' wives "strongly encourage" the assistant coaches' wives to attend all team/program functions to which they're invited. Some theorize that the philosophy of the head coach's wife is merely an extension of her husband's philosophy regarding the degree of involvement expected of the wives. As stated before, even though the coaches' wives aren't employed by the university as such, they do find themselves being put in situations where they're representatives of the football program. This is especially true during the recruiting season, where great effort is put into presenting a family atmosphere for recruits and their parents.

Another aspect of the relationship between the wives of the coaching staff is the possibility of a "pecking order"—whether actual or perceived. Just as a head coach, when looking for someone to cover a duty for him, may proceed through an order of assistant head coaches first, coordinators second, and then on to assistant coaches, it appears that the head coach's wife may follow a similar pattern when reaching out to assistant coaches' wives for the communication of pertinent news or public appearance volunteers. One head coach's wife mentioned that she had to be careful not to play favorites among the assistant coaches' wives.

As we mentioned earlier, different head coaches' wives have different views of their role. Two wives discussed their observations of head coaches' wives. The first said:

> I have been on staff with three very different head coaches' wives. One was very sophisticated who ran in a totally different social circle than the assistant wives. Her interactions with us seemed to be done to fulfill her perceived obligations but didn't really seem genuine. An interesting note about this wife: When her husband was fired, the local media was vicious and made some damaging, untrue accusations about her. Even though the assistant coaches' wives did not feel particularly close to her, we all came to her rescue when she was "under attack." We saw a very different side of her during this stressful time and realized she was truly devastated for all of us and carried tremendous guilt that we all lost our jobs under her husband's leadership.
>
> The second head coach's wife was very down to earth and went to great lengths to create a family atmosphere among the coaches' families. Perhaps I have this glowing image of her because we never had to experience being fired together—we always had winning seasons on this staff.
>
> I'm not sure I could even pick the third head coach's wife out of a police lineup. Isn't that amazing? We were only with her husband's staff for one season, and she was rarely around. If there were any wives' functions, she would put one of the coordinator's wives in charge of organizing it. I found this very odd based on my other experiences. One of the other wives explained that she did not get close to the assistant coaches' wives in case her husband had to fire any of the assistants. Personally, I thought that was a major cop-out. Perhaps not so coincidentally, this particular staff was by far the worst staff we have ever been a part of—backstabbing, unprofessionalism, etc.—no sense of family at all.

The second wife said:

> There was one [head coach's] wife who really didn't do very much. She would have us over once a year, but it didn't matter to her if we had a delayed game and it was raining and she was in a box and all of us were getting wet. Since I have been here [as a head coach's wife], I really tried hard to remember the things that were hard for me and help them.

Tina added:

> I always tell them [the wives] the same thing. Well, it's great here because I have a beautiful suite [at the stadium] and I let them come up. When we were here before, the head coach's wife never had the wives up—there are a lot of places that don't. Don't ask me why because I think the wives should come first. You know, I have to have some booster up there too, but … I always make sure there is room for my wives. And I tell them that you guys you come first, you know. Because I think it's important for them to be away from the fans. And you know, here it's not bad though, but there have been places where, boy, you're glad to be up in those seats. But … I tell them if we ever do go anywhere, like, away games and there's some horrible fans from the other teams, you know we just try to keep our mouths shut.

When the "Family" Breaks Down

While much emphasis is given to creating a sense of family among the coaches' wives, the reality is that coaches are fired, and these firings can change the dynamics of the wives' "family." One wife told about the abrupt change of relationships following a firing:

> We have been fortunate in that my husband has never been singled out and let go. The only time we were let go was when our head coach and all of the assistants who had come in with him were dismissed. Almost instantly, the wives of the coaches who had been holdovers from the previous staff (who were probably going to get to stay with the newly hired coach because they were "lifers" that the AD had asked our head coach to keep) no longer talked to those of us who had been let go. They went from being our presumed best friends to blackballing us in a 24-hour period. Then, they buddied up with their new "family."

Several head coaches' wives listed their husband having to fire an assistant coach as one of the most distressing aspects of being a coach's wife. One head coach's wife gives this perspective on the firing process:

> Firing an assistant coach is one of the hardest things that a head coach has to do. In some situations, the head coach is firing a good friend. As the wife of the head coach, you are watching the coach's wife, who may be your dear friend, being put into a state of uncertainty and stress. Remember also that you've spent months or years developing a family-like relationship with these individuals and then overnight that changes. Over the years, my husband has had to let go five staff members. Only one of the five wives involved in these dismissals ever talked to me again.

Summary

In this final chapter of the first section, we discussed job instability in the football coaching profession and the concept of "football families" created by the coaching staffs, their spouses, and their children. Information provided in this chapter provided an inside look at the responsibilities and realities of the life of a football coach and his family, which will enable better understanding of the chapters in our next section: life with a coach.

SECTION II

LIFE WITH A COACH

The chapters in the second section take an in-depth look at common themes that emerged from several open-ended questions in the online questionnaire, as well as from the interviews. The respondents identified both the rewarding and distressing aspects of their lives with a football coach. We discuss the impact on children of having football coaches for fathers, at least from their mothers' perspective. We also explore the effects of their husbands' occupation on the wives' careers, the division of household and family labor, moving, and life in a fishbowl. We conclude this section with a chapter on the rewards our respondents receive from their husband's profession.

4

The National Anthem Gives Me Diarrhea: Life as a Coach's Child

At the time we were sorting through the online responses to see which wives would be available for interviews, Janet had some e-mail correspondence with a wife she really wanted to meet. Unfortunately, she lived in California and an in-person interview wasn't possible. During the correspondence, they were discussing the lives of the coaches' children, and Janet happened to mention how the eight-year-old son of a coach she knew refused to attend any of his dad's games because he was so afraid the team would lose that his stomach become upset every game day. He was scared that his father would be without a job and that the family would have to move again. This wife told Janet that she was very familiar with those kinds of fears and that they haunted her son well into adulthood. In fact, she said that during a recent doctor's appointment for stomach problems, the physician asked her 28-year-old son if he suffered from diarrhea, to which her son replied: "Only when I hear the national anthem." It was stories such as these that told us how important it would be to include in our study information on the positive and negative effects of growing up with a football coach for a father as well as other child-related issues.

A little more than 77 percent of our online respondents have children, and 1.1 percent were expecting at the time of the survey. Almost 37 percent of these participants have two children, 27.4 percent have one child, and 20 percent have three or more. Of the wives we interviewed, one had one child, eight had two children, four had three, and two had four. One of the interviewed wives had no children.

The problem with the data we have—from the online survey and from interviews—is that they're not the responses of the coaches' children themselves but rather the mothers' *perceptions* of how they believe their children feel as well as the mothers' reporting of events in the children's lives. How reliable are these perceptions? We have no way of knowing. Nevertheless, because so many of our respondents mentioned the same issues over and over again and were so consistent in what they had to say, we're confident that the topics in this chapter are accurate representations of their children's experiences. Because of this consistency, it was fairly easy to group the responses into two general categories that were generated by the following two questions:

- Which aspects of their lives as the children of a football coach do you believe your children find the most difficult or distressing?
- Which aspects of their lives as the children of a football coach do you believe your children find most rewarding?

Children's Difficulties

Since the 1970s, a new style of fatherhood has emerged that suggests that "a good father is an active participant in the details of day-to-day child care" (Rotundo, 1985). The long hours football coaches spend at work for much of the year make it practically impossible for them to participate in this kind of fathering. No matter how much coaches want to be home with their children, the demands of their job don't allow it. It was no surprise to us that the lack of contact with their fathers and their fathers' inability to participate in many of the children's activities were the biggest areas of distress for the children. Other major areas of distress that emerged included negative comments by other people regarding their fathers, losing seasons, and moving.

Not Having Enough Time With Their Fathers

As they did for themselves, the wives also identified the lack of time the coaches are able to spend at home as a major problem for the children. The children's ages play a large part in determining when—or even if—the children get to see their fathers, especially during the football season. For very young children, unless their fathers are able to squeeze in some time to visit with them during the day, it might even be impossible for them to get together for days at a time. One wife said: "He is not home when our little guy goes to bed and is usually gone before he gets up during the season." It may be even worse for school-age children during the school year when time together during the day is extremely hard to accomplish, although older teens may be able to see their dads by staying up until he gets home. Julie, a veteran wife, told us: "If you want your children to see their dad, you have to keep them up until what I consider a nontraditional bedtime for children when they are not in school. The result of that is that they turn into night owls and never change." Snookie told about an early morning trip to the hospital:

> I would put my child to bed at around 9:00 p.m., but as soon as he heard the door open (usually between 10:30 and 11:30) as his dad entered the house, he would pop up and the two of them would play for about an hour. On one of those play nights, my child hit his head on a weight bench as he was running for a ball, so we made a mad dash to the hospital at 12:45 a.m. Fortunately, Child Protective Services

was not contacted, but you could just read the expressions of the emergency room staff as they were saying to themselves, "What kind of parents let their three-year-old stay up until one in the morning?" Football coaching parents—that's who.

Not only is the limited amount of time with their fathers a problem but so is the nature of their time together. When the coaches are home, they're likely to be spending time with the family as a whole, with little opportunity for one-on-one time with each child. An additional difficulty is that when the coaches are home, they're often not able to relax with the children as much as they might want to but are still working or else they don't have enough energy to do much of anything.

A number of wives pointed out that the absence of the father from the home means the mothers are essentially single mothers for long periods of time. Not only is this burdensome for the wives, but it's difficult for the children too, as these wives said:

> The children have to deal with me when I am crabby and tired after a long week alone without the help of my husband.

> The kids don't see him enough, and when they do, he is often very tired. Often, it feels as though the kids and I are not his first priority. There is a disproportionate amount of responsibility on me to raise the kids, keep up the house, and maintain relations with school, family, and friends.

Of even greater concern to the wives than their shouldering an inequitable share of the family work is watching and dealing with the effects of the coaches' frequent and extended absences from home on the children. Many wives voiced these types of concerns: "He is missing seeing his daughter grow up and he hates that as much as the rest of us. He spends 90 percent of his time living for the job and 10 percent is left over for the family."

A number of wives mentioned how much their husbands regretted the time away from the family and how much they especially miss being a part of the children's daily lives. One wife's comments mirrored the remarks of many others: "His relationship with our daughter suffers. His demanding schedule and long hours mean that at some times in the year, he will go for days without seeing her."

Several wives mentioned that their husbands spend more time with their players during the season than they do with their own kids. One young wife mentioned that her husband's job demands have even played a role in the decision to not have children:

> My husband has wanted us to have children. I decided against it due to the demands of his job. He is not pleased with that decision. I have no desire to be a single parent, and with his schedule, I would be completely responsible for raising the children.

In his book *All In: What It Takes to Be the Best,* former Auburn head coach Gene Chizik (2011) talked about how the long hours that football coaches work take them away from their children and how he and other coaches try to make their children part of the team to be able to spend time with them. This involves such activities as attending team dinners on Sundays, having the children come to the football complex to eat lunch, and other efforts to make them part of it all. He noted that all the players on his team know his kids' names. Similarly, most of the wives with young children manage to work out ways for them to see their fathers. Marissa, the young mother of four small boys, told us:

> Really, for me, having four little kids, we have to sit down daily and figure out when we can meet. When can we get together. Can we pop in your office at this time? What is a good time if I bring the boys? It takes the two of us to communicate to make our family work. If we aren't in constant communication about when can the boys see you [and] what is going on today, then the boys could technically go three to four days without ever seeing their dad. And for even those 10 to 15 minutes after practice when they can tackle Dad on the field, that just makes the world of difference. If I stop in the office just briefly to say hi [and] bring him a sandwich for lunch or whatever, that is what I have to do to make it work. I'm not going to have our children grow up not seeing their dad for one, two, three days in a row because of his hours.

Heidi, whose children are older, recalled her family's strategies for making sure her husband spent time with the children. She said:

> We have rituals that we have always done since the kids were little because we are so short on time as far as when my husband is home. Sunday night, he always has come home for dinner. Monday, when the kids were little, he would come home for lunch because the coaches would work so late that it would be after midnight before he came home. So, we knew that if he is leaving in the morning before they get up and he is getting home after they go to bed that there would be a couple of days where he quite possibly wouldn't see them when they were younger. Thursday nights, during the season especially, my husband would always come for dinner, and he and our son would always play football, and that was their ritual. Their time. Even when they were little and it was cold outside, they would play with a Nerf inside the house. I think it has been important for our kids to know that on Sunday night, we are going to do this and if possible Monday lunch. If they were both in school, they would come home and have lunch with Dad and then they could catch up with their lives, so to speak. Then, Thursday nights have always been kind of a family night. Sundays and Thursdays have always been a family night when we know we are going to have a sit-down dinner, eat together as a family, and kind of catch up on what has been going on.

However, as children get older, even though they may understand the problems their fathers face, working out time with their fathers becomes much harder because of the children's own activities. Claire, a head coach's wife, said:

> The only thing I have found out, now with my kids and their activities, sometimes I can't come by practice like I could when they were toddlers. When they were little, it was easier. But now, it is harder. And sometimes, he will say you don't bring the kids to practice anymore. I want to, but we are here, and we have this and that, I have to feed them, we have homework to do, and all those things, and it is harder to do that now.

Talking about her teenage son, Heidi mentioned: "He used to go to practice a lot, but I think that is something that changes as the kids get older. They have sports activities and homework. It seems like you gravitate out of that stage." During the football season, Thursday nights seem to be the best nights for many coaches and their families to get together. Kate, the mother of two young children, said: "With all the kids' activities, it's difficult, but a lot of times on Thursday nights, we will come to the tail end of practice and go out to dinner as a family." Claire also talked about the importance of Thursday nights:

> We try to do that as a Thursday night family activity. When the kids were younger, it was very easy and it was very welcoming that the kids and the wives get to come to practice. He always tries not to schedule a meeting for the coaches right away—not to review film—to give everybody some time if their kids are going to come to practice—let them play on the field with their children—and that is really important. That is probably the time that my children value the most on a daily basis—that contact with their father.

When the children are very small, visiting after evening practices doesn't work well. During two-a-days, this is particularly problematic because their fathers are gone during the entire time the children are awake. Jamie said of her 15-month-old daughter: "I took her to practice yesterday for the last 15 minutes and then we ate lunch with my husband. Otherwise, he doesn't get to see her." Even the very small children miss their fathers. Jamie went on to say:

> You know, my youngest is starting to miss him, I think. The other day, she grabbed the phone. She doesn't talk much, you know, but she says some things. I said, "Who do you want to call?" and she said, "Daddy." He hadn't seen the kids for two days because he leaves so early in the morning and comes home so late at night. When she saw him, she ran out on the field and gave him a big hug and things like that. So, I think she is starting to miss him.

One interesting story involving a young coach and his four-month-old son appeared in the *Lexington Herald-Leader* in October, 2009. The article described how Brent and Lexie Holsclaw solved their daycare problem by having Brent keep their baby, Max, in his office at Kentucky Wesleyan College on Mondays and on other days when they had a childcare gap. Other coaches on staff helped out when the need arose—from burping to changing a diaper. Even the players responded to Max's presence by lowering their voices when was around (Suwanski, 2009). It seems unlikely that this level of a coach's involvement with his child at work would have been possible 20 years ago because fathers weren't as involved with their children then as they are today.

An additional issue generated by the extreme hours coaches devote to their jobs is their suffering high levels of stress, which in turn may affect their children. Ellen Galinsky (1999) found in her research on workers who suffer stress as a result of long hours at work that their children are very much aware of the father's stress. They often develop ways to try to mitigate some of this stress or else they find ways to minimize the contact they have with their fathers at those times. This, of course, only adds to the problem, as it reduces the amount of time they spend with the coaches even more.

Finally, the wives' attitudes to their husbands' absence can have a large impact on how the children perceive it. In a 2006 article, Georgia head coach Mark Richt said:

> If your wife is at home and complaining about how much time dad is away and the kids hear that, they can certainly start to think they're getting neglected. If she's with you completely and understands the demands of the job, it's much better. My kids don't know anything different. They don't know it's unusual or strange. The one thing [that] is most important is that your wife and children know what you're doing with the time you do have. (Buchanan 2006)

Dad Not Being Able to Attend Events

The hours football coaches spend at work not only have an impact on the amount of time they can spend with their children, but they also affect their ability to attend their children's school and sports activities as well as birthday celebrations and other milestones. As Wight, Raley, and Bianchi (2008) point out: "Children's educational development is contingent on more than just their classroom hours, including such things parent-teacher conferences, school plays, science fairs and PTA meetings. Many of these activities take place after regular school hours." The coaches' ability to participate in them is severely hampered by their erratic work hours. Julie, the mother of grown children, told us: "The kids just knew that he wasn't always going to be at a parent-teacher conference and that he would be there as much as he could be." In addition, unlike other workers with nonstandard hours, football coaches don't generally have many weekends off throughout the year. This means that the coaches lack the ability to use the weekends to make up time lost with their children during the week as other workers do, thereby imposing further limits on their time together.

Understandably, the children don't like the fact that their fathers can't be there but know that this is just the way it is. Many wives and children are resigned to their absence. One respondent, whose father is also a coach, said: "They are used to Dad and Grandpa not being at their activities, including birthdays, during the season. It is just a given."

Many wives said their children understand that their fathers won't always be able to be around for their actual birthdays, especially if they fall during recruiting and the football season. Special arrangements and adaptations often have to be made. Rachel said this is what her family does:

> Both birthdays fall in the season. We try to plan so he is available, but a lot of the times, he will only be able to pop his head in if we do something. The last couple of birthdays we tried to do on campus—either the climbing wall or the dome—and he was able to pop in. It just depends on when it is. I have one that is at the very beginning of the season and one at the end of the season, so it depends on if there is post-season play or not.

Claire, a head coach's wife, said:

> So, your husband will not always be there on your birthday, he's not going to be there on your anniversary, not going to be there on your kid's birthday. He's not going to be around for any of those occasions. … And even if he is planning to be home, all it takes is a phone call from one of his 90 players who has a problem and that is going to supersede anything you might be doing, and that is just the way it is. That's reality.

The children do understand that their fathers would be at their events if they could and that it's the job responsibilities that prevent their attendance, not the wishes of the coaches. However, the younger ones especially have trouble understanding why everyone else's dad is able to do something or be somewhere and theirs can't. The absence of their fathers may unfortunately result in a lack of closeness between fathers and children. An older coach's wife told us that her children "… don't remember their father as a presence in their childhoods." She added: "He spent far more time with other people's kids than he did with his own."

In addition, some children may grow up resenting football because it takes their father away from them. One wife said that because of her husband's absence from school events, other children in her daughter's school thought her father didn't live with them because they only ever saw her mother there. Another wife, the mother of older children, said her husband "… never made it to their games or knew their teachers. They did not feel close to him growing up. But as adults, they are now close to him because they can relate."

Work hours also prevent coaches from participating in the sports activities of their children in ways that other children probably take for granted. Leslie, the mother of two teenagers and the wife of a Division II head coach, said:

> When our son was younger, I remember he played coach-pitch baseball, and they just get dads to be those coaches. This dad who was our son's coach was an accountant and a great guy, but he could not get the ball over the plate where the kids could hit it, and my husband could, so he did his whole recruiting in the spring around the boy's games so that he could be back in time to pitch because the only way those kids were actually going to hit the ball was if he pitched. So, things like that, he always did.

Rachel, whose children are also active in sports, mentioned that in the summer, for the most part, her husband is still in the office every day, but he's able to get away and has the job of taking the children to their daytime baseball activities. Between them, she and her husband are able to take care of baseball and soccer in the evenings.

Leslie is one of only a handful of wives in our study who said she believes that coaches can participate in their children's activities if they want to. However, we should bear in mind that her husband coached in Division I FCS with somewhat different demands than coaches in Division I BCS experience. She said:

> Well, they [coaches] can do it, and that is what my husband tells all these young assistants that work for him who are having children now. He wants the kids at practice. He tells them, you can find time to be with them. He has been around coaches that say "Oh, I can't make that because I'm too busy," and that is not true because they can if it is a priority.

We also need to consider the attitude of the head coach of a particular football program toward families. He's instrumental in determining the hours he expects his assistants to work, which in turn affects their ability to participate in their children's activities. Pam related her family's experience:

> Well, we were really lucky because when he chose to go to Division I BCS, he chose who he was going to work for, and he knew going in that that man also had strong family values. He was allowed to get away and get to the kids' games when he could and things like that because that was really important to him.

For the wives and children, the physical absence of their father/husband for several days at a time is a great problem, but the extensive work hours and traveling are also hard on the coach himself. One wife said: "No matter how much you hate his being gone during recruiting, he is in a hotel room somewhere wanting to be home with you and the kids, and he is probably hating it more than you do."

Negative Comments About Dad

One of the most difficult aspects of the lives of coaches' children is that they're often exposed to negative (and sometimes downright brutal) comments about their father. No child likes to hear people say hurtful things about his father, but many people fail to take that into consideration when they open their mouths. Claire talked about her young sons' experiences:

> That is hard, especially now that my children are a little bit older and are going to the games. When they were younger, they didn't go to the games—they didn't really know what was going on—but I have my two older boys, who are eight and seven, and [they] are very much aware and want to be at the games. They wear jerseys that say their father's name on the back, and [when] people say [negative] things, it is very hard [on them].

If these negative comments were made solely by their peers, who several women mentioned can be pretty cruel, they probably wouldn't be so difficult for the children to deal with, but quite often, they come from adults. One online respondent said that her children are "[r]eading/or seeing their dad's career in a public forum and then having to go to school and deal with children's/parents' interpretation of their dad's career. Children can be brutal but most often [are] under the guidance (or misguidance) of their parents."

Another wife mentioned that her children have to deal with negative comments about their father and his team from their teachers and coaches—people who should know better. Even though several women mentioned that they and their husbands had made special efforts to teach their children how to handle these situations, this kind of thing can nevertheless be especially tough on the children when the team loses. One older wife said:

> Our children say they didn't suffer anything special, but there are always people who dog on coaches, and they saw their share of that. They loved their dad, and it hurt them to hear that he was a loser when he lost a game.

Evidently, this behavior is nothing new. On October 23, 1948, *The Saturday Evening Post* published an article by Mary Stuhldreher, the wife of University of Wisconsin head coach Harry Stuhldreher, entitled "Football Fans Aren't Human." In this article, Mrs. Stuhldreher said she … "minded for the children because other children taunted them about their father and the letters in the papers, which they once thought a riot, were now getting under their skins." Their sons endured such behavior as their classmates sang "Goodbye Harry" and carried one of them out of the school and dumped him on the pavement. They were also told that their classmates would take up a collection to buy the coach a one-way ticket out of town. However, one of the sons didn't let it get him down and said that if it did, he wouldn't have lasted very long.

He told her: "Gee, Mom. You think a coach's wife has it tough, you oughta be a coach's son." On occasion, children feel they need to defend their dads. Mrs. Stuhldreher talked about the time her youngest son was in a fight with another child. She wrote: "Peter, age ten, came home from church with a bloody nose. Some youngster had told him that his father was a lousy coach and that made Peter mad."

In her interview, Sarah-Grace told us about the experiences of her children during a bad time in her husband's career:

> My youngest son, who played for his dad, had actually graduated and left, so he was experiencing his dad's crucifixion from another university, and he had the hardest time. He was devastated. I worried about him because he just could not understand. He couldn't accept it. My oldest child at that time was a graduate assistant at his dad's football program. He was quiet. He sort of internalized it. He was the one who if someone said something when he was out, he might lose his temper and say something. But it is hard on your children, particularly my boys, when they worked alongside of their dad. But again, I think it made them stronger individuals, but what they realized also is that on the other side of disappointment and pain is a chance to start over.

Tina said this on the same topic:

> I just tell my kids, you know, we've been fortunate. Ninety percent of the jobs have been great. But some fans can be brutal; they think nothing of what they say. They knew they were sitting around me and my daughters and they held nothing back. You know, I don't ever like to get mean with them because that doesn't get you anywhere. I just try to keep my mouth shut, but if it gets really bad, then I'll say something.

Pam talked about her children's experiences and how it differs between divisions:

> So, it was really difficult, and I remember, you know, our kids sitting in the stand crying because we were losing again. And, you know, it was just horrible as far as the family went. But then, it was really refreshing coming back to Division II again, where most of those kids know they aren't going to go to the pros and that they're playing just because they want to be able to continue playing football. And there's a lot less pressure from the administration, for sure, and more wanting them to just graduate good players and good quality people.

Losing Seasons

As we mentioned earlier in this chapter, many coaches' children have to deal with anxiety when their father's team is dealing with a losing season. Not only are they seeing that despite all his hard work and all the hours he's put into his team, but they're also faced with the knowledge that he could be fired, which would mean moving. They know that even if their own father has done a great job individually, he could lose his job if his head coach is dismissed. Pam told us:

> That's the problem we had at our Division I school. Right from the get-go. … We did have one really good season while we were there, but then that just, like, well, who knows what happened after that. And there was just a lot of pressure there. And I remember our oldest son was old enough to be in high school and playing football for a very successful high school program and his good friend was also a coach's son from the same staff. They came to us, the mothers, afterwards and told us: "If there is any way we could trade any of our victories for one victory for our dads, we would do it in a heartbeat." And you hear stuff like that, and it just breaks your heart. The kids feel so bad for their dads and see how hard they are working and it's not paying off and you know people being evil and putting for sale signs in the yard and things like that. You know it's just cruel.

For some coaches' children, being in the public eye at all is a problem. Their mothers say that always being "on show" at public events becomes burdensome. A real lack of privacy exists in some communities because everyone knows who they are and what their dad does; they feel as if they're always being watched. This does depend to some extent on community size, and living in a larger town helps the children maintain some degree of anonymity more easily than living in a small town. Lisa Berry, the wife of University of Louisiana at Monroe head coach Todd Berry, was quoted in an article in *The Miami Herald* as saying they taught their daughter at a young age that "our family is in a fishbowl and that being a coach's daughter has its privileges, but it has disadvantages too" (Kaufman, 2006). It's also easier to stay out of the public eye in communities where football isn't so important to its residents. Being the coach's kid is especially difficult for boys, as they're often expected to be good athletes simply because of who their fathers are.

Snookie pointed out that the media have begun to treat coaches' children in the same manner as they treat coaches and players. Negative behavior by these individuals tends to find its ways into the headlines. She and her husband had many discussions with their son concerning the fact he must make good choices because his mistakes were much more likely to become public knowledge than the mistakes of his friends.

Moving

Having to uproot and move somewhere else or even the possibility of doing so creates problems for many coaches' children. The wives mentioned how difficult it is for the kids to leave their friends, grandparents, and other extended family members behind. They also told us it's often difficult for the children to adjust to new schools, new houses, and new churches each time they move. We were told that the instability created by multiple moves is very tough on some children and may result in feelings of insecurity. Several wives told us that moving a lot also creates learning gaps for their children, as they have to contend with different school systems, and others reported that in some cases, their children are far ahead of the students in their new schools.

How well the children adapt to moving varies according to their age. Our respondents agreed that moving gets harder as the children get older. They play on teams and participate in school activities, and some of them may even have serious romantic relationships. Several of the wives we interviewed had a lot to say on this topic. Julie told the following story:

> Probably the hardest age for us to move a child was in junior high— even harder than high school. My daughter said that going into sixth grade was horrible; she said I don't know how you ever got me out the door the second day of school because I was kicking and screaming. I don't remember that, but she says it was true.

Pam said:

> For our kids, they've been fortunate because they were born and raised in one area, and they moved once when they were just starting middle school. And then, they didn't have to move again until later high school or early high school for some of them. Well, if you ask them, especially my daughter because she had to move the second time when she was just a half of a year into high school, so that was hard for her.

Sometimes, a move means one child has to remain behind to finish high school. This is what happened in Pam's family, but she believes it "worked out okay," although it wasn't an easy thing to do. Ann also had some adjusting to do in her family when they had to move from one end of the state to the other. This is how they handled the situation:

> We have a daughter that's 17 and a daughter that's 20. Our 20-year-old is going to be a junior in college, and our younger daughter will be a senior in high school, so I stayed there until school was out. Our daughter was pretty excited about maybe moving. We told her it was going to be her decision because we didn't want to someday down the road have her say, "Well, you made me move." You know, we said "No, you've got plenty of time. You know, December through June, you can think about it. See what you want to do." First, she wanted to move. Then, all of a sudden, she's like, "Mom, I don't know. I want to graduate with my friends." You know, we've been here seven years. It's pretty much their home—our girls' home. So, she's like, "No, I think I'm going to stay here now." So, we aren't far enough away that we can't work it out. But it's really hard because she's 17. … I mean, the 20-year-old,

yeah, that's hard too, but we've lived with it the last couple years because she was in college and we know she's not going to be with us, but a 17-year-old …

For children, moving can impact confidence, create anxiety, and affect social relationships. The sex of the children is also a factor in adjustment to moving, with girls appearing to have a harder time than boys. Tina talked about her experiences with her daughters:

I think that [moving] is the toughest part of it all, especially with girls. You know, so many losses, and that's what's tough about it. So many tears and emotions, and, of course, they [the coaches] take the job right, away so they're gone. And the wives are left back to sell the house, do the packing, and, you know, deal with the kids' emotions. So, that, I think, to me is the worst part. But whether you're upset or not, you have to appear positive to the kids. Always stay positive because they are going to feel it if you don't. So, you know, they … Yeah, there have been a lot of tears, you know, and I cry right along with them. But it's just amazing to see how things fit into place so quickly after we moved. You know, the only one that didn't was our oldest daughter. When we moved, she was just devastated. It was just awful. That was the worst move ever regarding our kids. They just loved where we were living and had great friends, and she was going into senior high school. But we left, and she was just devastated. And our daughter had always been very popular, the leader of the group, and involved in everything in school, but when we moved, she wanted as little to do with the school as possible. Girls can be brutal, you know, especially if you're pretty. They were very jealous, and none of them wanted to accept her. I think it is harder when you are popular because all of a sudden, you move and you're nobody. And, of course, the boys are always easy. They have their sports.

At what point in the school year the move takes place is also important. Most parents who are faced with having to move their children believe that waiting to do so until the end of the current school year is the best idea so the children can start a new year in a new grade with other new children. However, Pam explained this may not always be the best thing to do:

He left us probably a couple months to finish up the school year and then we all moved down where he was. That was a really rough summer because all the ball seasons had already started, so the kids had to just sit there and just watch everybody else … and my kids all played sports, but they couldn't participate. And I said, "We are never moving at the end of school year again." So, next time we moved, he left in December, and we ended up moving at spring break in March.

That way, the kids could finish the last three months of school, and they actually made a lot of friends, were able to play summer ball, and had things to do in the summer.

The size of the school to which the children go as well as the size of the school they came from also make a difference. Beth talked about how her girls, who had been popular in their original small schools, had a difficult time adjusting to a school that was three times larger where nobody knew who they were. It can work the other way too; going from a large, more impersonal school to a much smaller one can make for an easier transition.

Because frequent moves create so much upheaval, the one constant in children's lives becomes their family—creating a stronger bond. Several of our respondents talked about how important it is for the parents to provide a positive attitude toward moving and that a strong family unit is important when they move. One online respondent said: "We always moved with the attitude that we were all in it together." Another wife said she and her husband always try to prepare their children for the fact that life is full of changes. In that way, she said, moving isn't as traumatizing as it could be. But, she noted, her children still talk wistfully about the friends they left behind.

The coaches themselves are well aware of the problems moving creates for their children. In *All In: What It Takes to Be the Best,* Coach Gene Chizik talked about this and told how all three of his children cried when they learned they'd be leaving Iowa and moving to Alabama. He said: "That's one of the tough things for kids in the world of college coaching dads" (Chizik, 2011).

Summary

In this first section of this chapter, we examined the perceived distress that's experienced by coaches' children. This distress is often the result of characteristics of the coaching profession that have been or will be discussed at length in other chapters in this book: long hours away from the home, a "fishbowl" existence, and the emphasis on winning, which can often result in a move for a job promotion or a move as a result of a job loss. Study participants acknowledged that the coach's hours cause him to miss valuable family time, but they gave suggestions on creating opportunities for family time or creating positive attitudes about the coach's long hours.

While study participants marveled at how cruel "fans" can be and discussed the impact these unsportsmanlike behaviors have on their children, most took the position that they must manage what they can control, which is their response to these behaviors. Study participants discussed their personal decisions about moving and the ramifications of those decisions. Although opinions differed, it was clear that the children's ages, children's gender, the time of year the moves were made, and the family's attitude toward the move were factors that had to be taken into consideration.

Children's Rewards:

Our respondents identified several aspects of their children's lives that those children enjoy by having football coaches as fathers. They love feeling a part of their father's team and the relationships they have with the players and other coaching families, and they're very proud of their fathers. In addition, the wives believe their children enjoy living in a college community and benefit from the opportunities to develop excellent social skills. They note that several of the rewards their children enjoy are advantages that most other children never get to experience.

Feeling a Part of the Team

A large number of the wives mentioned how much their children enjoy feeling as if they're a part of the team. Not only that, but they feel part of their fathers' job in ways that few other children do. They love wearing the team jersey on game day, cheering for their father's team, and all the other fun aspects of football. They relish the competition and the victories and the opportunities to be at events that would be unavailable to them if their fathers weren't coaches. One wife said:

> For my sons, they loved getting to accompany their dad on the sidelines at practice or be the ball boy or ride the bus to away games or interact and establish relationships with the team.

And Pam noted:

> When the kids were little, I would always take them to watch practice, and they would get to go eat once a week at the cafeteria. So, that was a really nice thing to do in August because there would always be air conditioning in there.

Other wives pointed out that the children can go to their dad's work and get to see him during the day—something that children with fathers in more conventional occupations seldom manage to do. For some children, helping with the team has been a very important part of their lives. This is true for boys as well as girls. Pam said of her sons:

> They loved being on the field. I mean, they couldn't wait until they were old enough. … That was back when they had cords on the headsets … when the boys got to hold the cords. Yes. Oh, I mean that was a huge, huge thing.

One of Ann's daughters had similar experiences:

> And our oldest daughter actually was on the sidelines with him for seven years. She started out at seven holding his cord. When they introduced wireless, it almost killed our daughter because she did it for

four years and loved it. She knew more about football then. I mean, she was only seven years old and she was right there. And you know, as my husband said, it was good to actually have her there because the coaches kept their mouths clean and the players were real good around her and always very polite. And I mean, she saw all of them as big brothers, but when they took that cord away, she was devastated. I mean, she was really … "What am I going to do, Dad?" The first year or two after that happened, he still had her down there, and she would hold his board or something just so she was able to be down there. And then finally she was getting a little older, and she said, "There's not really much for me to do." At one time, she actually got hit. Her dad always told her, "You have to keep that cord and you have to follow me wherever, and whatever you do, just don't let go of my cord." Well, one of the players was coming at her, and I mean, he just rammed her, and she went right down on her back. And she just kind of laid there, and she got up, and, of course, her dad's like, "Oh, come on, you know you're not hurt." … So, she didn't cry until she came up at halftime and then she was bawling, but when she went back down, she was fine.

A number of wives told us how much their children love football because of their involvement in their fathers' job. Beth discussed how this is the case for her three daughters:

They enjoy it—they love football. They know the game very well. I mean, he [my husband] has three girls and my father-in-law says he is the luckiest man in the world. He comes home and he doesn't have to ask if ESPN is coming on. It's already on. They are watching it. And they love the colorfulness of the game and the staff and the people they meet. They go to the football complex whenever we can. More so when they were younger because they now have their own demands—their own athletic stuff they have to do. Oh, yeah, I think that's a positive in the job. I think it's where kids can be very much a part of things. … I mean, you have to be reasonable. But kids can go and see what their dad does for a living. Not all kids get to do that.

Relationships With Players

According to their mothers, coaches' kids tremendously enjoy spending time with the players and getting to know them. They love having all the big football players around and really look up to them. As Claire said: "They love that. And I think it is a huge thing for our children to not be shy and go up to people who are four times their size and say hello to them and talk to them and not be intimidated by them." An online respondent noted:

Having 80-plus big brothers that love to hang with them, throw them on their shoulders, and provide them with great role models, our boys are very fortunate to grow up around football. I feel it will only make them better humans and more family oriented in their own lives.

Another wife said: "They have the whole football team to play with. They love the whistle. They love tackling Dad and the players." In her interview, Justice said:

Our son knows all the football players. I mean, he helps his dad during spring ball feed the balls to the running backs and goes up there and runs with them. And when we are at the bowl games, you know, he'll go play in the players' hospitality room and play video games with them.

Some wives noted that their children really like it when they have the players over to their house for dinner, birthday parties, and so on. Many of the wives mentioned how good the players are with the children and how they seem to have a way of making the kids feel important. One mother of a four-year-old said that her son "… does like the players, who are very sweet to him." Several times, we were told that the coaches' children have developed some special lifelong relationships with some of the players. This type of interaction isn't just limited to boys. Girls participate too. For example, Pam talked about her children's contact with the players and said: "It really expanded their comfort level around different types of people and even our daughter too. She would get to know some of the players, and that was good for her." Ann said her girls were like little sisters to some of the players. And it's not just something for the older kids—even the little ones get player attention. Jamie told us about her children, who are both under two years old: "They [the players] come over, and they always play with the kids when we bring them there and they're just so good with the little kids."

Although the children themselves, especially the younger ones, might not identify this as a benefit, their mothers said how important it is for them to learn about diverse cultures, and their interactions with the players allow them to do this. Others mentioned the important role models the players are to their children. One wife said her children "… have a great relationship with the players on my husband's team. The players are really kid friendly and are great role models for them." Marissa said:

After practice, the boys go run around the field with the football players and Daddy. It is like they have 80 to 90 big brothers, and they love it. If I come to practice for some reason and I don't have one of them— say, one of them has school or is at an event—they will be like, "Where is G.? Why isn't he here?" The second practice is over—if they don't have somewhere to be, the players are over there high-fiving [and] playing catch with them. Just the opportunity for my boys to grow up with that is amazing. The opportunities they are allowed being around these boys, the experiences, [and the] cultural backgrounds—a lot of the players are different from what they are used to [being around]. It is nothing but positive.

Coaching Staff as Family

The closeness of coaching families to the other families on staff creates several advantages for the children. One of the online respondents said: "When we move towns, we have the built-in 'coaches' families' to have as friends right away." Because most of the coaches' children share similar experiences, they can easily relate to the adjustments and transitions that the new children are experiencing. Even when moving isn't an issue, a bond is often created with other coaches' children as they spend time together at games, practices, and other team-related activities and experience the same advantages and disadvantages. The wives tell us that great camaraderie usually exists among coaching families—all of whom look out for all the kids. One wife said: "Our boys love being around the other coaches; they have so many people to look up to and love and who love them too."

Pride in Dad

A large number of our respondents talked about how proud the children are of their father and how much they admire them. They love to see their dads on the field and watch them on TV or listen to them on the radio. Several said the children take great pride in their father's dedication, accomplishments, and success. They seem to understand the importance of knowing that the coaches are achieving their dreams. Of course, it doesn't hurt that much of the time, the children's friends are intrigued and impressed by their father's job and think it's really cool. Rachel talked about this in her interview:

> Oh, yes, I would say both of them were very excited. I would say my younger child was probably more excited about it only because he is determined to be an NFL football player. He has a goal and he has got some talent. Obviously, both children have received some athletic talent from their father, and that is a good thing it wasn't from their mother. They both enjoy football. I think for my younger son, it was a little bit more of a status thing for him than it was for my older son maybe because those kids have been around for a long time. When we moved here, my oldest was starting kindergarten, so he has been with the same group of kids for seven years now, and they all know who his dad is.

In her interview, Kate said about her young son:

> You know, all of their friends know what dad does. We did a fundraiser for their elementary school—the elementary school night at one of the games. And it was so much fun, but you know, that morning, it was a Friday night game, and when my son went to school that morning, everyone was so excited. "We are going to your dad's game tonight." He nearly had a breakdown.

Ann's daughters are very proud of their dad being a head coach and have found that being the coach's kid makes it easier for them to make friends. She said:

> They like their dad being the head football coach. It's actually helped us when we move. I mean, kids seem to kind of … I mean, they know about football coaches and they seem to take to our girls and bring them in easier. If he's down, sometimes he goes "Well, I think I'm going to get out of coaching and go sell insurance or whatever." And, of course, I know that's not ever going to happen, and the girls are like, "No, Dad, we don't want you to be that. We want you to be a coach." So, but, yeah, they love having their dad be a head football coach.

Some of the coaches' sons have decided to go into the same occupation and some even work with their father. Tina said:

> He's [our son] coaching our quarterbacks. My husband thought he should pay his dues like everybody, but he has full responsibility for the quarterbacks. So, he's so excited, he loves it, and the kids love him, so, you know. And, of course, he knows his dad's system better than anybody because he's been around it all his life.

Pam talked about her son's decision to go into coaching:

> He has seen his dad coach in college and has always … The kids have always hung around at the programs, so that's something he wants to give it a try. So … he's putting in his time right now as a [graduate assistant].

Pam also talked about her daughter's choosing to be on the field:

> What really surprised me, though, is that she always wanted to be down on the field with Dad or in the locker room, but she never could. She always got stuck sitting with me in the stands, which is a hard job because she's felt like she has to keep me calm and all this stuff. And she says that's the toughest job. But then about … when she was maybe her sophomore year at college, she's been going for a couple years now, she just out of the blue said that she was going to help out with the training staff. And so, she's been, like, an assistant trainer for a couple years, which she hates anything to do with medicine or blood or anything, but that was how she got into it. Both her brothers play football. She wanted to be there. So, for our son's last year, she was there too. So, we would all get on the bus together and go to away games, and it's kind of cool. We just didn't bring the dog—that's all.

College and Community

The children enjoy many advantages because their fathers are college and university employees, according to their mothers. Again, we believe some of the advantages may not have been those the children themselves necessarily would have identified if we had asked them directly, especially the youngest of them. Their mothers say the biggest advantage for many kids is their ability to go to college free if they go where their father coaches. Not all institutions are able to offer this benefit to the coaching staff, and in some cases, it's only the head coach's children who enjoy this perk. In some instances—for example, St. John's University in Minnesota—the coaches' children have a choice of where they go to school as long as they choose to attend either St. John's, the College of St. Benedict, or one of the schools that's a member of a consortium of participating institutions. Some children, of course, would rather not go to school where their father coaches. Beth talked about this in her interview:

> Being a coach's kid, she wants to go to a school where her dad does *not* coach. She wants to go to football games and not have to worry about the outcome of the game affecting her future. She can choose to tell who she wants that her dad's a coach—or not.

If tuition remission is a part of a coach's' employment package but his children choose not to go where he coaches, Beth thinks this might be misunderstood by some people. She goes on to say that her daughter "… is just looking for some anonymity and she deserves it. And I guess I just hope that everyone at our university and our staff understands that is our decision that we have made with her. But sometimes, I think the expectation is that you'll just dive in and think all of this is wonderful, but they don't really understand that you have to make these different choices when you don't necessarily have any security for your future and you don't know where you're going to be."

Several wives mentioned the opportunities their children enjoy living in a college community, such as excellent public school systems, performing arts events, the chance to interact with students, and being a part of the college environment. Having access to the sports facilities, such as swimming pools, gyms, and tracks, were also frequently mentioned.

Social Rewards

A number of the wives mentioned how football coaches' children have benefitted socially from their fathers' occupation. For example, although we've discussed at some length the disadvantages of frequent moves, the mothers find it can actually have some advantages. Each move gives the kids the opportunity to meet new people, which exposes them to a variety of cultures and enables them to interact with many different kinds of people—all of which increases their confidence in social settings. They learn very quickly to become adaptable to new situations, and in many cases, they develop outgoing personalities and social skills they might not have otherwise. One wife said:

We had to move so many times that our two children are very outgoing. They are comfortable in almost any situation. They love meeting people and have learned to adjust quickly and easily when we move.

Another mother said: "Our children didn't like all the moves, it has made them better and more welcoming, caring people in life." Other wives discussed their children's experiences living in a variety of geographic areas, which exposed them to different cultures and communities. Julie told us she's talked about this to her adult children: "They can't imagine having lived in the same place forever. They see moving as a real positive thing. They have friends all over the country." Aside from the travel involved in moving, some coaches' children have also opportunities to travel to away games and bowl games and to enjoy many activities organized for the coaches' families at bowl games.

Discipline

We've discussed at length the advantages and disadvantages of being a coach's kid—at least from their mothers' perspective—but we need to address one more child-related area that was raised many times by our respondents. They told us that having to deal with discipline issues when their husbands aren't around creates some problems but also results in some interesting solutions. Leslie talked about this:

> During football season, it is awful. I can't stand it. When my husband would come home, I would say, "This is what happened today and this is how I handled it." We would talk about it, and if I felt there would need to be Dad input (this was mostly with our son because he was very headstrong), then he would chime in.

Not having the children's father available when disciplinary issues arise can create problems too. This was the case for Heidi:

> It was hard for me not to call my husband and say what had happened because he is doing his job and he is working and I couldn't disrupt him because they are so busy on Sunday nights. At the same time, it also was just one more time when you are like, "It sure would be nice to have had your husband there to help with the parenting because you don't really know what to do or say." And, obviously, when he came home later that night, I did tell him what had happened.

Jamie, whose children at the time of her interview were too little to need much in the way of discipline, nevertheless relies on her husband's support. She said:

> I guess I just do what I think is right. And, you know, my husband is very supportive. He would never question me. He would never question the decision I made. He would just go with it. Sometimes, I would try to call

before I would make a decision. But if I feel it needs to be made, I'll just make it. He'll support me.

Like several other wives, Heidi told us she really needed input from her husband when dealing with her son:

> Our second child, the boy, is not as easy, and there are times when it is hard to come up with discipline—come up with ways of getting him to do the things that you want him to do, such as homework, for example. It is difficult sometimes, especially since he is a boy, not to have a dad there. There are times when I have had to call my husband at work and put him on the phone so that he could give him a what for or threaten to come home or whatever—but not terribly often, although it certainly does happen.

Most of our respondents who talked about discipline issues noted they're the primary disciplinarian in the family simply because they have no alternative. Justice told us:

> I'm the primary disciplinarian. We do spank our kids. I'm not … I don't have a problem saying that. I think that's what's wrong with half of these kids today. They have grown up in that generation where everyone has got to feel good and we are not going to damage our psyche. Yeah, I think that's what's wrong with a lot of them. So, I'm the primary disciplinarian. I would never say "Wait until your dad gets home" because that takes away all the authority I have and [it] makes him the bad guy. They would much rather their dad disciplines them than me because I by far spank them harder and am probably tougher on them.

Research by Pietropinto (1986) looked at 400 physicians and their relationships with their wives and children. This study found that those doctors who work extremely long hours—much like football coaches—tend to be very demanding of their children. Claire's comments seem to support this finding: "My husband is very good at being a heavy hander. He is a very good disciplinarian and can be very, very hard on them. I think he is very hard on them in general." Tina also noted that her husband was a lot stricter than she was and that he was a real disciplinarian. Sometimes, she said, she thought he was a little too harsh, but he kept the children in line, and they are happy for it now. Ann discussed disciplining her girls:

> … [B]ecause I felt like I need to be a friend sometimes more than a mom, but I got to where I had to draw the line. It's, like, because with him not being there, I felt like I needed to make up for that, I guess. But he was always the one. … I'd kind of let them do things, and he would come home and be the disciplinarian, and he's like, "Why do you always let me do that because I come home and have to be the bad guy?" But all he had to do was just raise his voice.

The kind of discipline Marissa's husband uses can sometimes create problems, she thinks. She said:

> I think the only thing that I find—and I don't know what the word is—maybe frustrating at times—is sometimes he forgets it is not his players but his children that he is talking to. Sometimes, he brings home his coaching voice, and I don't think he realizes it. He just has this loud, booming voice, and sometimes, he is disciplining the boys, and it is so loud. And I'll say, "You need to quiet down. You are scaring the children." For the most part, I do most of the disciplining because I am there the most. He will chime in if we really need to put a foot down or something. Usually, Daddy's voice will get them to behave.

Heidi also had something to say about the impact of her husband's voice:

> And I think both of my kids have a great respect for my husband (not that they don't have respect for me), but they have a different respect for him. I wouldn't say that it is a fear, but they truly don't want to let him down. They don't ever want to look bad in his eyes. They want to look good in my eyes too, but I think there is more of that with him. I don't know that if it is because he has been gone so much and that they just want his praise when he is there. So, they don't want the negative.

Several wives shared discipline strategies that work well for them. Beth said:

> I deal with things as they come up, but they know that there are times when I'll say "I think that will be okay, but we need to discuss it with your dad." Usually, he and I are pretty good about trying to deal with conflict without them around.

Kate also tries to deal with discipline issues as they arise:

> I deal with mostly the on-the-spot sort of discipline issues. But we definitely try to talk about the more … the bigger issues. Sometimes, you know you just want an extra hand. You just want to say "Wait until your father gets home." Well, that will be midnight, so that's not going to work.

Pam is also opposed to the "Wait until your father gets home" idea:

> You know, you always hate being the heavy, but you couldn't really say "Wait until your dad gets home" because it wouldn't be for a while. But I think for the most part, you know, I guess I just worked through them and that kind of thing. And I'm sure discipline-wise, when you are the only one there all the time doing the disciplining, it's not as effective as when you have a backup.

Summary

The perceived positive rewards for coaches' children mirrored many of the experiences that were identified by study participants as their own personal positive rewards: an opportunity to develop close relationships with players and families and pride in the job the coach does. Like children of other college employees, coaches' children may enjoy cultural opportunities and tuition advantages. Although moving was discussed as a cause of distress in the lives of coaches' children, it also brings about the opportunity for exposure to different parts of the country and was perceived by many study participants to have created more "outgoing" personalities in their children. Our study suggests that, in most coaching families, the wife is the parent who spends the most hours with the children; however, the philosophy of discipline seems to be very much an individual family decision.

5

The Coach's Wife as a Career Woman

Snookie's Story

I received a degree in education. Because I was married when I graduated from college and my husband had one more year left, I took a job as a store manager because I could not find a teaching job. My husband was student teaching at this time and had been promised a coaching/teaching position in a southern state. We had already purchased a mobile home that was located on land convenient to both jobs. When he graduated, the "promised" job did not come through and he ended up taking a job with a school system in another southern state. I took a position in the same town at a drugstore because of my prior experience at the store. When a paraprofessional job at the local high school (the same one where my husband was coaching) came open, I took it to get my foot in the door with the school system. The next year, I was hired as a teacher at an elementary school and kept the position for three years.

Our time in this second state ended when my husband was hired as a GA [graduate assistant] at University A*, where I was awarded a graduate assistantship in the education department. We sold our house, quit our jobs, and moved back to the first southern state. Even though I hated giving up my job, it was a great opportunity for my husband, it moved me closer to my family, and it gave me the opportunity to complete my master's degree free of cost and in a condensed time period. I did not realize it at the time, but this was giving me experience teaching at the college level that would play a role in future employment. Once my husband completed his graduate

*To preserve anonymity, universities have been labeled as A, B, C, etc.

assistantship, he was offered an assistant coaching position at the same school. I looked for and found a job at a private K–12 school as a full-time teacher. I taught at this private school full time until the birth of our son and then I taught there part time. When my child was about two years old, I began teaching full time at a public school. During this time, I taught a night class in pedagogy at University A.

After we had been in this state for 10 years, my husband's head coach accepted the head coaching position at University B in a southwestern state. My husband accepted an assistant coaching position there. I left my public school job at spring break. In this southwestern state, I was able to get a five-month job as a full-time substitute teacher. I actually made comparable money as a part-time teacher and as a full-time sub. Unfortunately, my husband's head coach was let go at the end of the first season. My husband was then hired as an assistant coach at University C in a western state.

Because towns in this western state were few and far between and not very populated, a person's chances of getting a teaching job were slim unless someone retired, got pregnant, or died. I did manage to get a job as a teaching assistant, but it paid $30,000 less than my previous full-time job. I only worked there one half of the school year because my husband's head coach took the head coaching position at University D in a Midwest state and took his staff with him.

When I first arrived in the Midwest, I did substitute teaching for one half of a school year just to get my foot in the door and bring in income. The next school year, I was able to get a part-time teaching position. I learned that the education department at the university was looking for someone to teach some classes. I probably should have inquired earlier because I found out that this university was very open to spousal hires. Again, I did this to get my foot in the door. The next semester, I was asked to take a full-time teaching job that lasted four years. Then, my husband took the assistant head coach position at University A (again). I was asked to teach full-time at this university. After one season, my husband was hired as the head coach at University E.

We moved back to the same southern town that we started out in. I took a full-time job teaching in a public school. It quickly became apparent that demands on my husband as head coach were much greater than those as an assistant coach. With a son in the critical middle school years and a husband who had taken on a job that was going to require a great deal of work (even in football profession terms), I made the decision to resign from my job and I assisted my husband with his job for a semester. Because we were in a familiar town, I had connections and I inquired about teaching some general education courses on a part-time basis. I was told this would be possible, and I continued to assist my husband and work part time for three years. When my son was a senior in high school, I began teaching classes on a full-time basis. After five years at this school, my husband accepted the head coaching position at University D—again.

When we got back to University D, the first person I saw as I was going into the press conference announcing my husband's hiring was my former department chair. He asked if I wanted to work full time again, but I told him that I needed to get a feel for the responsibilities and demands of a head coach's wife before I made the decision. I decided to go back to teaching part time—teaching the same class I had taught when I left six years earlier. I am currently teaching this class on a part-time basis.

At this point in my life, I am watching people I taught with in my earlier jobs getting ready to retire after an entire career in the same school system. Although I may be jealous for a minute, I consider myself blessed in my career. I never stayed put long enough to build up a decent retirement account in any state because of my husband's jobs, but because his jobs have provided a comfortable living and have enabled us to save money, these retirement accounts are not necessary. I may have had to take some pay cuts and some jobs that were not really in my field and I may have had to "start over" numerous times, but I always managed to find employment. I take pride in the fact that both my husband and I have been employed at some institutions more than one time. I believe that this is a testament to having worked hard and done a good job when we were there the first time. Quite honestly, we could have always survived on my husband's salary, but I do value my professional life, and during the few times that I was totally out of the workforce, I was not completely happy. Part-time work seemed to come along during times that worked best for my family. However, as you can see from my story about resigning when my husband took his first head coaching job, when I have to choose between my job and my family, I choose my family.

Snookie's 30-year career history may not be typical of the work experience of all the employed wives in our study, but it certainly isn't unusual. When we began this study—and knowing as much as we did about the lives of coaches' wives (which wasn't as much as we thought we knew)—we anticipated that the majority of our respondents wouldn't be employed or, if they were, they wouldn't be employed full time. This wasn't the case. Of the 16 wives we interviewed, 11 were employed. Seven were employed full time, two part time, and two worked out of their homes. From the online survey, we found that 71.8 percent of the wives were employed outside the home, and of those women, 73.2 percent worked full time and 23.9 percent worked part time. In view of the football-induced complications and responsibilities in the lives described in earlier chapters, it's difficult to imagine how these women, especially those with children still at home, are able to pursue careers, but they do. Our online respondents were employed in a variety of occupations in the following categories:

- Educational/training (42.1 percent)
- Business/management (13.7 percent)
- Healthcare (12.2 percent)
- Sales (5.1 percent)
- Office support (5.1 percent)

The remaining 21.8 percent were employed in a variety of professions, including architecture, law, and engineering, as well as in such occupations as daycare operator and pre-school personnel and various service occupations. The issues we most wanted to understand have to do with the effects of the husbands' occupation on the wives' employability, their choice of careers, their career advancement, their ability to manage their careers in light of their other obligations, the importance of their careers to their families and to the wives themselves, and their husbands' support of their careers. We also looked at some former career women who talked about their decisions to forego paid employment—at least temporarily.

Wives' Employability

One of the biggest issues with which the women in our study have to contend is the impact of their husbands' occupational moves on their own careers. Given the number of times many of them have moved because of their husbands' work, it's not surprising that in a number of cases, their own careers have suffered in a variety of ways. Despite many of the wives being highly educated and highly qualified professionals, they've often found that obtaining work in their areas of expertise isn't easy. Many employers are reluctant to invest time, energy, and funds in employees they believe will only be around for a relatively short period of time. One wife told us she's known "… so many coaches' wives for whom it's been very difficult to obtain positions because employers realize that there is a certain finality to their time. … They know that coaches will move." Tina told us that "… at most of the jobs, I don't let them know who I am—that I'm a coach's wife. I'm afraid it's going to prevent me from getting a job." Sarah-Grace, an experienced teacher, mentioned that even though she was always able to get teaching positions when they moved, there were still problems. She said:

> It wasn't until the kids started school that I went back to teaching, but we moved so much—seven times in nine years—and I was always the new teacher—always the one getting recertified—which made it difficult.

One of the most often noted disadvantages is that the wives have to settle for a series of jobs rather than a career in their chosen field because of the frequent moves and their having to start over each time. Snookie related in the first part of this chapter an occasion in which she worked as a teacher's aide despite having a master's degree because this was the only job available at that location at that time. Several wives told us about similar experiences. One woman said that all the moving meant she hadn't been able to finish her degree, which also contributed to the difficulty of finding jobs each time they moved. For Tina, another effect of her husband's occupational moves has been that she hasn't been able to stay in the same field from location to location but has been employed in a number of different capacities:

> I was an executive assistant to the CEO of a company. ... I worked in a law school in the career development office. Everywhere we went, I've had something different. I've been in the legal field, the medical field.

We learned it was often too difficult for many wives to settle into their own careers because of the instability of their husbands' occupation. Several women mentioned that their careers had suffered because they had to turn down jobs or had to leave jobs to follow their husbands' careers. Many told us they knew they'd be following their husbands' career around the country regardless of how successful the wives were in their own occupation. They said they had no doubt that what they did for a living would always take second place to what their husband did and that the family would never move if they were to get a promotion or a better career opportunity, although they would if their husbands did.

Wives' Choice of Careers

Many of our respondents indicated that they would certainly have chosen different careers if they had known they were going to marry football coaches and if they had been aware of the impact his career would have on their own. Heidi told us how her husband's career had influenced her own career plans. She said:

> I wanted to go into business. I wanted to work for a big company and carry a briefcase and do all the things that a businesswoman would do. That is what I initially thought I would do. Because of my husband's job, it really never happened. Sometimes, he will say to me "When are you going to get a real job? When are you going to go and do what you really want?" And I don't know if I ever will because there just isn't the time for me to go and do it—at least not right now.

However, some occupations do seem to be more compatible with life as a coach's wife than others. As we noted earlier, teaching and nursing are the careers mentioned most often by the wives in our study. Marissa, a young mother of four small boys, said she believes teaching is a great profession for a coach's wife because when she worked, the summers off allowed her to spend more time with her husband when he actually had a couple of weeks off and she didn't need to worry about having to take time off work. She went on to say: "Being in special education, there is a chance that I can get a job just about anywhere we go. Special Ed is in high demand, so I'm not worried." Leslie, the wife of an Division I FCS head coach, looks at the ways in which her husband's career has had an impact on her work history very positively. She said:

> It has really impacted me in a positive way because I have met so many fabulous educators. We have lived in six states. Every school that I have ever taught at, I have gotten things from that school and brought them with me. I feel like I am a better teacher because of all the places that we have been. It is hard to leave friends, but I can take from the other schools, and it has made me a better teacher.

Teaching does have its drawbacks, of course, such as poor pay in some areas and never being able to establish seniority or achieve tenure. In addition, licensing requirements must be dealt with when teachers move, as many states require them to become recertified, and this is more difficult to accomplish in some states than in others. One wife told us she holds teaching licenses in three states. In addition, the availability of teaching jobs is currently affected by budget cuts in education as a result of the foundering economy, and wives who previously found it relatively easy to find employment in education may find that this is no longer the case.

Other occupations also appear to "travel" well. Those wives who are nurses report that they've always been employable, although again, they find it difficult to advance in their careers because of the frequent moves. Pam, a physical therapist married to a head coach, has also found it relatively easy to find jobs whenever she's moved because, as she pointed out, "therapists are in short supply most places." She did have to go through new licensure procedures when they moved to Indiana, but fortunately, they haven't moved too many places. Jobs in health-related fields are expected to stay in fairly good supply as the country's population ages.

Wives' Career Advancement

One of our respondents said that each time her husband changes jobs, she has to either start from scratch or take a step backward, and she isn't unusual in this regard. Others noted that they've found it to be impossible to build any seniority and that their frequent moves hold them back from moving up in their careers. Others noted that their careers haven't progressed in a linear fashion, and were it not for the constant moving, they believe their careers would have taken them in more successful directions. One woman, a college professor, commented that instead of being able to apply for tenure-track positions, she's had to work in adjunct positions, which pay far less and which often have few benefits and no retirement plan. Rachel, a mortgage banker, described her career trajectory:

When a full-time coaching career became available for my husband, it was a very difficult family decision to pick up and move. I had worked for a company for 10 years and had worked my way up in positions and would have to start all over again. After we moved, it was very difficult to find a job for a professional female that would have the flexibility that I needed. It took about six months in our new community [until] an opening came up, and it has worked out very well. It wasn't probably what I saw coming out of school anyway because I thought I would be with the company I started with forever. It was a good company to work for. You just kind of roll with it, I guess, and things change, and you have to change along with them.

Justice, a lawyer, noted that if her husband were to take a job in another area, she would have to take the bar exam there because no reciprocity exists between states for attorneys with fewer than five years of practice. However, on the positive side, she said that because her husband is the primary income person in their family, she's been able to change from civil law, which she found boring, to practicing criminal law, which she enjoys. Now she wants to get up and go to work and is excited about what she does. Her husband's occupation and earnings have given her the freedom to change the nature of her work without having to worry about the financial consequences.

The Importance of the Wives' Careers to Their Families

Many of our wives understand that their careers are important to their families on a number of levels, even though they're not necessarily enthusiastic about working or about the particular jobs they hold. One wife said that if she didn't have to work, she believes her life would be much better. For many, especially those whose husbands are in the early (and not-very-well paid) years of coaching, their income is essential to the family's survival. One wife said: "My job is very important because, since he is just starting out, he barely makes any money. I have to support us until he is able to make a name for himself." Another noted: "For years, my salary was the thing that allowed us to survive. He made such poor pay—and, actually, so did I as a teacher—that we *both* had to work to live." Michaela told us that in five years of marriage, this is the first time that she hasn't made more than her husband. She believes that she currently provides about one-third of the total family income, whereas before, she always made significantly more than her husband.

A number of wives in our online survey said they provide more than 50 percent of the family income and that their earnings are necessary to make ends meet. Overall, from this part of our study, we find that on average, the wives who are employed provide almost 30 percent of the family income. One woman said she's the major earner in the family and that without her income, they would have very little. Others mentioned that their earnings are imperative for the family to afford its lifestyle and that they couldn't live where they do (especially in the more expensive housing markets) or enjoy many other things if the wives didn't work. Several respondents mentioned that their financial contributions paid the bills, which allowed their husbands to live their dreams.

As far as benefits are concerned, several women noted that their jobs provided the health insurance for the family and also allowed the wives to contribute to their own retirement plans, although the constant moving often meant they were never in one place long enough to become vested in a system.

Strategies for Managing Careers With Other Obligations

Several of our respondents told us they've been able to maintain their careers by making adjustments and compromises and through the use of technology. One of these strategies has been to choose occupations that allow them to work from home. Claire has been able to conduct her business from her home regardless of where home happened to be. She said:

> I knew I wanted to be able to have a business I could work at from home and one that would have some geographic flexibility. With the Internet, it has just been wonderful. I've been able to do it from wherever we lived, and there was never a glitch in my career. It has been wonderful. I knew all along that I wanted to have a career, and with having children, I wanted to be an at-home mom and have an at-home career, but I felt it was integral to be able to establish that career before I had my children. I think many people start to want to have an in-home job after they have their children, and I think it is too hard to get into that routine as well as to establish respect for having an at-home business. If they can start it before at home and then have children, then it works better.

Another work-from-home wife told us how important it was to her to be available to her children while providing some of the extras for her family. She said: "Working from home allows me the opportunity to instill family values, disciplines, etc., into our children and mold them versus someone else doing so." Ann, a head coach's wife in her first year at their new location, was excited because: "My bosses where we were before are actually going to put me on remote, and I'm going to be able to do the billing and stuff through the computer." At other times, Ann has adjusted her hours to work part time, and before her latest move, she was fortunate enough to have a job where she worked Monday through Thursday and was off on Fridays. In that way, she could travel with the team and could also attend their events. Many other women have made adjustments to their hours to accommodate not only the needs of the football team but also the need to be able to attend their children's functions and sporting events.

Heidi mentioned how the amount of flexibility in the hours of a job was one of the factors she always considered in deciding whether to take it. She said that in her situation, she didn't feel she could do everything she needed to do for the family, the team, and her husband and still work 40 hours a week. Sarah-Grace's experiences are a testimony to her flexibility and creativity:

> I was in school when we married, and I finished, then I taught for the first four years we were married. Then, when we moved to his first full-time college job, I had two babies: one was two and one was seven months old. I worked at odd things. I delivered newspapers, I cleaned apartments, I worked at the bookstore at the university—anything I could do that would allow me to stay home with the babies and make a little bit of money. When my youngest baby was seven months old, I had my own kindergarten at the little church where we went, and my neighbor kept him. Then, I stopped and stayed home until he was three and then I went back to work at a church so that I could go with him. I'm a big believer in staying home with your children if you enjoy it, and I did. I really didn't work full time again until after they started school and then I went back to teaching.

> But we moved so much. We moved seven times in nine years at one point. I was always the new teacher on the docket, so I was at different states getting recertified so that I could teach in that state, and I was always in the pink zone—the apprentice teacher. We lived in Texas before we moved to Arizona, and I had the best teaching job I ever had. My husband called me at 10 one day in April and said, "Can you get somebody to take your classes?" I said, "Are you crazy? It is 10. What do you mean 'somebody to take my classes'?" And he said, "Well, I've been offered a job in another state and they have to have an answer by 2." I said, "Well, when would you leave?" He said, "This afternoon." And I said, "Well, let me see." So, I got somebody to take my kids, and I got home and he said, "Come on in and follow me back to the bedroom." And I said, "Why am I following you back to the bedroom?" And he said, "Well, I've got to pack." I said, "What do you mean 'you have to pack'?" He said, "I took the job, and I have to be in Houston to catch a plane at 6:30 tonight." I said, "You are kidding me? I thought we were going to talk?" He said, "Well, what is there to talk about? You always tell me that if I thought it's what I ought to do that is what I should do. And this is what I need to do." So, we took him to the airport at 6:30 that night. I told him on the phone, "I can't continue to invest myself in these children and then get torn out from them in the middle of the year." This particular situation was just so good, and I said, "I can't teach anymore. I can't do this. I've done this for seven years out of the last nine, and I can't do this." And I said, "When I finally get out there, I'm not going to work for a year or so."

Justice is another wife who has experienced a number of job changes before settling on a career as an attorney. She said:

> I signed up to do Mary Kay when I was nine months pregnant. I'm kind of one of those people who will try anything. I did that and made sales director and made senior sales director, but it wasn't really my thing. I resigned when I started law school. I worked at the university here in athletics up in the academic part. When we were at another school, I was the tutor coordinator for the football program. I've either been in school or working other than I think the first six months after our son was born.

According to Rachel, flexibility is the key:

> My job is flexible because we are fully commissioned. If I'm not working, I'm not earning any money. That means that I work some weekends and I work some evenings, and we have laptops and I take that home and work at night and I work when I can get that in. We do have obligations, such as meetings and things, that we need to be there for.

Some wives mentioned that they've turned down jobs that they would've liked to have taken because of their husbands' jobs. Beth, a registered nurse, mentioned that if she wanted to stay in hospital work, she would have to be able to work all kinds of hours and all the days of the week and "No football coach's wife wants to work on Saturdays." She said she had to fit the kind of nursing she does to accommodate the demands of her husband's career and the demands of her family because she's "the glue that holds everything together."

A couple of respondents had some less conventional ways of adapting (or not) to the demands of their husbands' occupation on their own careers. A wife from the online survey said she recently decided not to move with her husband to his new job out of state because she loves her current job, her home, and her community. Another said: "I will not give up my career just to be at his side at all times."

The Importance of Their Careers to the Wives

Many of the wives in our study value their occupations highly and often stated that they've invested a great deal of time, energy, and money to get where they are. Echoing Snookie's earlier comments about valuing her professional life, one woman said: "I have built up a life for myself that is independent of my husband's. I went to school for a number of years, and I take a lot of pride in what I do." Some mentioned that their careers were their passion and gave them a sense of contributing and that they believed what they were doing was important in the lives of others. Others said their work gave them a great sense of accomplishment and fulfillment and they loved having the opportunity to be of service to others and to shape their growth and development, especially when it came to working with young people. Several of the women on the online survey said they believed what they did for a living was every bit as important as their husbands' work. This woman's comment is typical: "I work for a nonprofit women's organization serving victims of domestic violence. I believe my position is just as important as that of my husband."

Several of the teachers in our study said that teachers make a huge impact on society's youth and that they have the opportunity (like their husbands) to influence young people. One wife said she views her position as a teacher as a ministry and finds the time and dedication she spends on her work very fulfilling. The nurses also told us about how important their careers were to them. They obtain a great deal of job satisfaction from taking care of patients and helping to bring them back to health. One woman believes she's performing a great service as she works in a labor and delivery unit on an Indian reservation and sees her job as very important to the well-being of the community.

Husbands' Support of Their Wives' Careers

The majority of the career wives said that their husbands were supportive of their employment and recognized how important their work was not only for the contributions to the family finances but also to the wives' happiness and fulfillment. One woman said: "We are both individuals that are driven to succeed, and we love and support everything the other is doing." Another said that her husband hasn't taken jobs he's been offered if she might not be able to find a job in her field in the new location. Other wives mentioned that their husbands understood that the social interaction the wives have through their work is important, and they very much appreciate and respect the time and effort their wives put into their careers and what that effort and time produce for the family.

Some Wives' Decisions to Forego Their Careers

A number of coaches' wives have worked outside the home for much of their married lives but have at some point decided to take time out of the workforce. Tina said:

> Well, we moved here and we got settled, [it took a lot to get settled in] and then I got involved in a lot of charity organizations, volunteering, and I don't know. It just seemed like there was so much going on, I just had no time to think about working.

Like Snookie in the opening of this chapter, Tina finds that being the wife of a head coach has increased the time she spends on team-related activities and responsibilities and decreased the time she has available for paid employment. She said:

There are so many things that you have to attend with him, so it makes it hard to work. You know, there are always things going on that you have to be at and there are trips that he takes now, you know, that include wives, and I wouldn't be able to go with him if I was working.

Other wives have changed their occupations. A respondent to the online survey gave up her career as a speech therapist because she couldn't cope with the demands of her job, motherhood, and her husband's full-time-plus schedule. She decided to stay home with her children and do daycare for the extra income it provided. She accepted that her career came second to her husband's but said she didn't regret it, even though financially, it was difficult for many years. Another wife said that when she was a teacher, she believed her career was every bit as important as her husband's, but now that she "just works as a receptionist in a doctor's office," her job is just that—a job. She gave up her career to advance her husband's. Career disruptions also cause loss of earnings. One wife said she experiences "financial despair (I drop in salary every time we move) and loss of self-esteem because I'm not financially contributing much."

Summary

Prior to our study, we had theorized that two aspects of the coaching life—high time demands and frequent moves—would make full employment for coaches' wives the exception rather than the norm. However, our findings indicate that a majority of coaches' wives do work full time for a variety of reasons. While some wives work to provide necessary income, others cite valuing their professional life as the deciding factor in having a career. Although some wives in our study have been able to consistently maintain employment and even continue to advance in their chosen professions, many others pointed out that their frequent moves have often required them to "start over" in their careers or alter their career choices, and in some cases, those changes in location led them to decide to forego a career altogether.

We've already established that due to the great time demands on the coaches, their wives almost always assume most of the responsibility for the home and family. This fact of the coaching life plays an important role in the wives' decisions to work or not to work, the number of hours they work per week, and other career choices.

6

The Division of Family Labor

Whenever we asked our respondents about the division of family labor* between them and their husbands—whether it was for the online questionnaire, in the interviews, or during presentations at the AFCWA—the most common response was an incredulous "What division?" followed by a great deal of laughter and some very interesting, often amusing, and occasionally unprintable comments. Probably, our favorite quotation comes from one of the interviews when a wife was asked to talk about who does what in her family. She said: "I do it. I do everything. Who wouldn't want to be married to a coach's wife?"

Do the Wives Really Do It All?

It's apparent from our sources that the answer to this question in a majority of cases is a resounding yes. According to one online respondent, coaches' wives are strong women. She said:

> We can hold our heads up high when all things are crumbling around us. We can pack, load, and unpack our house on short notice. We can attend school programs, meetings, tailgates, and football games while wearing one outfit and providing food for each event. We have to be strong and intelligent.

Some variation occurs according to the level at which the husband is employed, his position, and the time of year, but overall, football coaches' wives are doing all the traditional female household and child-related tasks as well as those tasks that in most non-coaching marriages would be the responsibility of the husbands. Being well

*Family labor includes all tasks, chores, and responsibilities that serve the needs of families and their members. These include but are not limited to cooking, cleaning, laundry, outdoor work, household repairs, child-rearing tasks, errands, automobile maintenance, pet care, and financial tasks.

organized and having excellent time management skills is an essential quality for these wives if they're to successfully manage and handle all the details of their family lives without their husbands' help for a good part of the year. Rachel, the mother of two children, said that through the whole year, unless something is specifically delegated to her husband, she's the one who will take care of it. She said she can make a nice home, raise the children, and hold a full-time job and that her husband knows the majority of it falls on her and that she's able to do it. In addition to performing all the family work and child-related tasks, Claire, a head coach's wife, supervised the construction of their new home. She said people compliment her husband on their home all the time, but he didn't make a single decision about anything that went into it. Beth, commenting on her ability to do it all, noted:

> It's very independent. It's kind of an irony kind of deal. He wants you to be there and be supportive at the games and all that kind of stuff. Be at recruiting dinners. But yet, you have to function so independently as head of the family and really be proactive. I mean, you have to in our relationship anyway. I take care of the house, the yard, the kids, the dog, and the cars most of the time. A good 10 months out of the year. He counts on me to make good decisions. So, you really have to be very independent. But yet, sometimes you do feel that it's a throwback.

In this chapter, we look at how the wives feel about having to bear so much responsibility and how they deal with it as well as the tasks that some of the husband do assume. We explore differences according to the wives' ages, their husbands' rank and level, and whether the wives are employed outside the home.

Doing "Men's" Work

We were amazed by the traditional male jobs related to the house and family that the coaches' wives on the online survey and the personal interviews undertake on a regular basis. These include taking out the garbage, cleaning out the garage, and washing and maintaining vehicles. As far as house maintenance is concerned, the wives do all manner of repairs, deal with service people, change lightbulbs, do plumbing, paint, put up shelves, and do electrical work. In the yard, they mow, rake, shovel snow, and pick up dog poop. They pay the bills, do the taxes, and take care of investments. Miscellaneous tasks include putting up outside Christmas lights, assembling bikes and other toys, mending toys and electronic equipment, taking pets to the vet, and making all decisions regarding the buying, selling, and building of homes and moving.

Marissa, the young mother of four boys and the wife of an Division I FCS assistant coach, said in her interview:

> To be perfectly honest, I do everything. You have to remember, my husband grew up a New York City guy. He grew up right outside the city, and I grew up on a farm in Iowa. I mow the lawn, and that is mainly

because I give him a break there. He has grass allergies, and if he mows, he breaks out. He breaks out in a rash and he is sneezing the rest of the day, so I give him a little bit of a break there. I love to mow. For me, it is exercise and I love it. For snow removal, we actually have a very nice neighbor who has a huge snow plow and he always does our driveway. But if he didn't, it would be my job. My husband has done that before, but the problem is that snow removal is in December and January, and that's when he's recruiting in Florida.

Yard work is something a number of the wives do on a regular basis, and many of them said they enjoy doing it because it's such good exercise. Pam said this about her Division II head coach husband:

I was my dad's only "son" growing up, so I was used to doing yard work. We just had all girls in our family, and my sisters would prefer to do the inside work and I always preferred to do the outside work, so it wasn't a huge deal. It's not something I complain about having to take over in August when he is basically gone.

Buying and maintaining the family automobiles is a responsibility that men often assume in families, but this isn't the case in Heidi's family. She's the one who gets the cars serviced and who buys the new vehicles. She said her husband "… has never bought a vehicle or a house ever. He wouldn't have a clue."

When we looked at the male chores our online respondents do, we expected to find the younger wives would be less bound by traditional roles than the more mature wives, but no clear differences emerged. We were fascinated by some of their comments. In the 25 to 34 age group:

[I do] everything—taking out the garbage, changing toilet seats, fixing gutters, mowing the lawn, snow blowing, killing bees' nests, wrestling with our son, paying the bills, financial planning, hanging pictures, changing the oil….

—An assistant coach's wife

Where do I start? Mowing is my job, fixing things around the house, landscaping and any outside tasks are mine. Anything that needs to be put together, glued or screwed together, has directions for installation, etc., is my job. I wouldn't let him do it anyway.

—An assistant head coach's wife

[I do] everything: yard work, home improvement (I'm an engineer, so I like it), oil changes/car maintenance. … Heck, I just designed and built the house we are living in. I communicated with the contractors and dealt with the issues, not my husband.

—A Division III head coach's wife

Wives in the 35 to 49 age group had similar things to say. For example:

> We live on a lake, and I can do about anything from taking care of the dock, boat, and yard. I have learned many male tasks over the years, and my husband doesn't own a toolbox.
>
> —A Division II wife

> I do all of it. I have completely renovated a 106-year-old home by myself without his help.
>
> —A Division III wife

The senior wives (ages 50 to 64) were no exception:

> I do yard work on a regular basis. I also do most of the upkeep in the home. The toolbox belongs to me; it even has my name on it. Most odd jobs around the home—inside and out—I take care of.
>
> —A Division II head coach's wife

> I am the husband and the wife in our family. I have always fixed the things that needed to be fixed, paid the bills, taken out the garbage, painted rooms, whatever needed to be done.
>
> —A Division I FCS head coach's wife

How Do the Wives Feel About It All?

How the wives feel about the division of household work is determined in part by the era in which they were raised. Older wives are of a generation that saw their mothers live traditional lives, taking care of the home and the children and making it possible for their husbands to succeed in their chosen occupations. These women were raised to see such responsibilities as appropriate and expected for wives, while participation by their husbands wasn't. Even when they were employed themselves, women of this generation expected their occupations to take a backseat to the husbands' careers. They assumed employment in addition to their other responsibilities. Conversely, men in traditional marriages "expect more instrumental spousal support from their wives than egalitarian men do" (Mickelson et al., 2006). It's not hard to see why many of our older wives have been able to accept and even flourish despite handling all the traditional female responsibilities as well as those traditionally assigned to the husband

Julie, who was in her late 50s at the time of her interview and who didn't work outside the home, told us that as far as indoor things were concerned, her husband has "… never done anything. Zippo. … And I'm okay with that. It's whatever your strengths are. And mine were in the home—inside and out—so it worked for us." Rachel, who's a few years younger and employed full time, was a bit more bothered by it all and said:

Sometimes, it bothers me, and I just have to blow off steam with him. The other day, he came home and told me about how much stuff he had to do and all these emails that he had to do and there wasn't enough time in the day, and I said, "Well, you know what, I have all those same things and then I'm deciding what is for dinner and getting the groceries so we have food for dinner and paying the bills and making sure the kids' clothes are clean." It was just one of those "Here is the deal: You can complain, and I understand that you have to blow off steam too, but you shouldn't be complaining to me right now because I'm doing all of that and more."

And Ann, who was in her 40s and worked from home when she was interviewed, said:

It used to bother me a lot more than it does now. It used to bother me because I used to feel sorry for myself. … I think most coaches' wives kind of feel sorry for themselves sometimes—like, why am I here doing all this. I guess I've just gotten to where he's the breadwinner and I'm the one that's … It's just kind of been my role to be the one. … Now, there are nights that I'm like "OK, you know I'm here, and I've got to do this and I've got to do that," but for the most part, I've been pretty good about it. Like I said, I don't make that much money or work that much, so I should be able to do what I do.

Marissa, a stay-at-home mother in her mid-30s, also had occasions when she wasn't very happy with the arrangement:

I would say it maybe bugs me at times when I've had a really long day or week and sometimes I will lash out a little bit and say it would be nice if I had some help. Or if I'm going somewhere, I'll say it would be nice if I come back to a picked-up house. I would say sometimes it does, but at the end of the day, I'm kind of a little bit of a perfectionist and I want it done my way anyway, so even if he does help out, I go back and redo it. I need to stop doing that, but I don't think it will ever change.

Michaela, in her late 20s and employed full time, agreed. She said: "I would rather do it than have him do it, especially the laundry." However, not all the younger wives are as accepting. The imbalance in the sharing of family responsibilities is often difficult for them to deal with. They grew up in an era where equal participation by both spouses and parents is an expectation. Wilcox and Nock (2007) note that "… in marriages where wives typically work, husbands do markedly more housework and childcare than they did 50 years ago and most spouses expect that they will share, at least to some degree, the domestic, emotional and market work associated with maintaining a family." We found the following comment from a 34-year-old wife particularly insightful:

Much of the struggle I have had with the profession stems from gender issues and the 1950s structure of coaching families. It just continues to strike me as odd in this day and age that this is the only profession that I can think of where there are no football coaches' spouses, only wives. I often think that if I were an accountant married to an engineer, we would both simply be professionals on an equal level—married but partners. I've had to get past a lot of my own self-imposed stereotypes to find a place for myself where I truly feel equal to my husband.

Finally, Claire told us she doesn't believe her husband really understands everything that's involved in running a house, raising four children, and being responsible for everything that has to be done. She said:

Sometimes, the house is a chaotic mess, and I like knowing that I have a couple of hours where I can clean it up. Although sometimes, it would probably be better for him to come home and see how it really is and how we really have to live when we are racing off to baseball and basketball and this one needs a tutu and they are changing here and there is underwear on the floor. And it is often that way. There are four children in different activities. It really is. I think one of the difficulties is that I make it look too easy—that it is a piece of cake. I don't think he sees my challenges.

How Do the Wives Keep Everything Running Smoothly?

We thought that some of the strategies the wives would employ to make sure everything that needed to be done was done would include hiring other people to do some of the work, recruiting the children, and sometimes simply letting things slide. Many wives did say they hired outside people, and a handful mentioned that their children were old enough to pitch in, but not one person admitted to lowering her standards. Rachel, like many others, hires someone to help with the housework. She explained:

I hired a cleaning lady, and I hired her specifically for the fall because Saturday was my cleaning day, and when we are gone every Saturday at a game, it was cutting into Sunday, and Sunday was the only day I had to do everything else that didn't get done on Saturday. I have relinquished a lot of those for dust duties. I still do all the laundry, and I take care of all of the bills and what the meal is going to be.

Justice, who is employed part time, also has help with house cleaning:

Every other week, I have someone to do a full clean. But as far as keeping it picked up, you know, our house is always the hangout for our son's friends. I mean, it's nothing to have five, six, seven, or eight boys over there. So, there is a lot of picking up that has to be done.

Claire's household help does a great deal more than clean. She said:

> I have a babysitter—like a nanny person who helps me about 20 hours a week. I have to have her. She knows how to keep up laundry. There are no toys on the first floor. When you have toddlers, I'm sure you know, with kids, they are playing with the Tupperware and playing with this, and that is how kids are supposed to be. And it doesn't really concern him how it gets done either, which is interesting. And he thinks because we have help, it is easy, but it is not because you are the mom and you are still the mom. Sure, I have help with the laundry and the bathrooms, and that is a huge help. The cleaning and keeping up with the laundry itself is a huge help. And I can give her a list of errands, and she can run around town and do a couple of errands.

Pam, who didn't have household help until she returned to her full-time career, said:

> When I went back to work full time, we actually did get help in the house. It was my husband's birthday present to me—the birthday present that keeps on giving. He researched it when we moved back here. He researched cleaning ladies, and he actually arranged for me to interview one because he knew I would never do that on my own. And … and I was able to have a cleaning lady every two weeks, so that's been nice.

And Jamie, the young mother of two small children, looks forward to having a cleaner house:

> Now this year, since we have two kids, he promised me a cleaning lady. So, we'll see if I get it. And that's what we're going to try this year because with my having a job and then coming home and trying to get everything done with the two little ones, it just … I think I would be really stressed.

Yard work is another area in which the families sometimes get help. One of our online respondents, the wife of an assistant at a Division I BCS school, said she runs the household and her husband works outside the home, and that's the way they want it. However, they've hired a person to do their yard work because when her husband is home, they prefer he spend what little time he has with the children and not working in the yard. Kate told us that her family doesn't even own a lawn mower. They have a teenager cut their grass, and they have a snow removal service in the winter. Heidi has her son help with the yard work:

My son, now that he is older, he cuts the yard. He has a lawn mowing business—he has several yards that he does. He has gotten to be quite good at it. I like doing yard work, and I'm kind of fanatical about my yard as far as I like to bag and trim it, and he certainly has taken after me. He likes the yard to look nice because he does these other people's yards, and he wants their yards to look nice. He is a big help with that, and it helps tremendously.

Even though many of our wives are very adept at doing many household repairs, a number of them said they use other people for this type of work. One middle-aged respondent said: "I call repairmen for anything major because my husband has no electrical or mechanical inclinations *at all*—he only knows football."

What *Do* the Husbands Do?

In the same way in which we asked the wives what traditionally male tasks they did on either a regular or occasional basis, we also asked them what traditionally female tasks their husbands did either regularly or occasionally. From the online survey, we identified several areas in which husbands participated:

- *Child-related tasks:* changing diapers, helping with homework, child-related errands, dressing kids, watching kids, bedtime routines, getting up with kids
- *Laundry:* folding, ironing, doing own laundry, sewing
- *Cleaning:* floors, kitchens, bathrooms
- *Dishes:* loading and unloading dishwasher
- *Food-related tasks:* cooking, making lunches, and grocery shopping
- *Other:* Making beds, picking up, errands, pet-related tasks

However, it's important to note that 24 percent of the wives on the online survey said their husbands did none of these tasks and that many of them did very few. Interestingly, the one task that coaches do seem to do around the house when they don't do anything else is laundry. About 50 percent of the wives answering the question concerning the tasks their husbands do on a regular basis said he does the laundry. This is almost certainly because it's something that can be done late at night when many of them finally come home. This is true in Kate's family:

> He does laundry—and especially when I was working because, you know, somebody has to do it. It was constantly throwing a load in on the fly and folding when you watch whatever at 11 o'clock at night and taking it upstairs. And especially … I mean … I kind of get into a routine doing it during the season when I'm not used to having the help and then … then … it's almost like when he's there to help, it kind of throws me off. But then I quickly remember that I'm not going to say no to help, so he'll jump in.

However, this isn't the case in Heidi's marriage:

> I don't think he has ever even done a load of laundry. He did try to iron the other day, and he was ironing a pair of shorts, and I came in and he said, "I don't know why, but these don't look any bit different," and I went and checked, and he didn't have the iron on. So, we of course thought that was hilarious. He said, "Oh, it was on. It was on." But there was no way. It was cold—you could put your hand on the iron. So, I don't think he had the iron on.

Justice's husband is the complete opposite:

> You know, believe it or not, he probably does close to as much as I do. He's not the norm. Like I said, he's very … he's just … he's anal. I mean, if there are four T-shirts in the laundry, instead of waiting until there is a full load, he's got to stick it in there, and I'm just like ok. He's constantly doing laundry. That's his big thing.

Jamie's husband does laundry some of the time. She said: "He does try to help with the laundry because I don't like doing the laundry. So, every once in a while, he'll go down there and do it." And Beth told us about a recent development in the laundry department in her house:

> I have to tell you, it's been a funny a year. We have been married 22 years, and he came home a day before us from vacation because he had to be in the office on Monday when he started back. And the girls and I flew home on Monday, and you know, within an hour of being home, you're thinking "I have to get the laundry started. I've got to get to the grocery store. I've been gone for a week." I went downstairs, and he had done all the laundry. I came upstairs and said to the girls, "Are you sitting down?" And they said, "Well, Mom, he went to the grocery store too." And I thought, 22 years, and when I saw him yesterday, I kissed him and said "That's better than any birthday present you could buy me." You just don't get it. It's like … thank you. I mean, he doesn't do it. Well, I really appreciate I didn't have to ask him. It was a big moment in our house yesterday.

Several wives talked about their husbands' participation in house cleaning. Leslie told us her husband could clean better than she could. She noted that on their "… hardwood floors, he will get on his hands and knees, and he'll scrub them. His mother is like that—a real clean freak—and I'm like, 'If you can't see it, then it's not there.'"

Cooking is another area in which the coaches participate, especially in the off-season. Justice said that her husband isn't really a cook, but "[h]e'll make breakfast though. Like on the weekends or like today, he's home with the kids, [so] he may have gotten up and made pancakes. I don't know, he likes to do stuff like that." One of the online wives said: "He cooks. No one likes this because he always cooks the same thing." Others mentioned that when they had the time, many husbands, like Ann's, cook during the summer. A couple of wives mentioned that their husbands' rank made a difference in the amount of cooking they were able to do. For example, Leslie said: "My husband grills and he cooks a lot more than I do when he is home. It has been easier now that he is a head coach because he can kind of set his own time schedule." Kate had similar comments to make:

> You know, in the summer time, I pretty much plan on putting some sort of meat out for him to take to the grill, and we'll fix a salad. We like to do that. This winter, I was real sick, and he was home more of the time, but I mean, we were joking it was March before I cooked a meal. He really stepped up because I needed to be on bed rest and all that kind of stuff. So … And that's where the flexibility of being a head coach really is helpful. You know, he can kind of say, "You know what? I'm going to be at home today."

Pam's husband, a Division II head coach, does a variety of tasks around the house. She said:

> He's pretty good about pitching in around the house. He's always helped out with the dishes. He figures if I'm cooking, he can do the dishes. So, my kids' friends are always amazed that he'll pitch in that way. He's not so much about cleaning bathrooms—he doesn't really like to do that. … But there are certain parts of the household that he doesn't mind doing. He's a wonderful vacuumer but not so much on the dusting. So, we just pick out what he's good at and what he doesn't mind doing, I guess. We've always had the rule [that] whoever is the last one out of bed makes it, so that's been a good rule. If you want to lounge around, then you have to pay for it.

One of the older online respondents, the wife of a Division III head coach, told us that her husband "… makes my coffee for me every morning and brings it to me while I am getting ready for work. He makes the bed every morning. He is a neat freak and cleans out closets all the time. He sweeps the kitchen floor in the morning and unloads the dishwasher for me. He does the grocery shopping whenever he can. He will also do the ironing for me when he is down in the family room making recruiting calls or he will throw a load of laundry in." It's interesting to note that this wife said her husband unloads the dishwasher and does the ironing "for me," which seems to indicate she views these tasks as hers and that he's only helping out rather than participating in shared tasks.

Figure 6-1, which is compiled from online responses, shows that one-third of the husbands of those wives who are between 50 and 64 don't do any traditional female household work, and this is the case for almost as many husbands of the wives in the 35 to 49 age group. One-fifth of the husbands of the youngest age group don't do any traditional female work in the family.

Wives' Age	(N) (Percent)
25 to 34 years (N = 110)	24 (21.8%)
35 to 49 (N = 124)	39 (31.5%)
50 to 64 (N = 48)	16 (33.3%)
65-plus (N = 4)	—

Figure 6-1. Percentages of wives reporting that their husbands don't do any traditional female household tasks (by wife's age)

No clear pattern emerged when we looked at the same issue by husbands' rank (Figure 6-2). The largest percentage of husbands who don't do any traditional female tasks occurred among the head coaches (32.3 percent), but the assistant coaches were also well represented at 28.8 percent.

Husbands' Rank	(N) (Percent)
Position Coach (N = 66)	19 (28.8%)
Coordinator (N = 60)	15 (25.0%)
Assistant Head Coach (N = 23)	5 (21.7%)
Head Coach (N = 96)	31 (32.3%)

Figure 6-2. Percentages of wives reporting that their husbands don't do any traditional female household tasks (by husband's rank)

Finally, we explored differences by the NCAA division in which the husband coached (Figure 6-3). Not surprising, when we consider the hours coaches in Division I BCS work is the finding that a large percentage (43.4 percent) of coaches in this division, according to their wives, don't do any traditional female tasks. What did surprise us was the small percentage in Division II (18.4 percent) who did none of this work.

NCAA Division	(N) (Percent)
Division I BCS (N = 99)	43 (43.4%)
Division I FCS (N = 51)	20 (39.2%)
Division II (N = 49)	9 (18.4%)
Division III (N = 69)	20 (29.0%)

Figure 6-3. Percentages of wives reporting that their husbands don't do any traditional female household tasks (by husband's division)

Do the Coaches Get to Do Any Guy Stuff?

We have explored the type and extent of traditional female family responsibilities assumed by the husbands, but we were curious to know if they actually got to do any of the traditional male tasks and, if so, which ones and how much. We also wanted to know if position and division made a difference. The same factors we discussed in the preceding section also affect how much time the coaches are able to devote to performing the traditional "male" tasks around the home: the yard work, the snow removal, the home repairs, and so on. Julie talked about her husband's enjoyment of working outside when their children were young:

> Well, in those days, he loved to do yard work, which was good because we had a large yard. At one point, we had three-and-a-half acres, and at another point, [we had] an acre and a half, and another time, we had two acres. We both worked at it. I love to garden, so we had huge gardens. It was a very healthy lifestyle. We lived within a mile of town, and the children had free rein of basically seven acres because the neighbors had children identical in age and they had three-and-a-half acres and we had three-and-a-half acres, with no fence down the middle. We mowed an alfalfa field for them, and they played ball out there, and they did all kinds of creative, crazy things and always had a horse handy or a mule or something. It was good living. Coming home and doing the yard work was relaxing and enjoyable for him. The only time he didn't cut the yard was in the fall.

Several women told us their husbands enjoyed mowing when they were able to do it, and they also mentioned that the men found it therapeutic. Rachel told us that her Division II head coach husband does all the yard work and pretty much all his car care, although she takes care of her car. As soon as fall camp starts, then she gets the yard work. Her husband does the snow removal unless he's off recruiting, in which case, if she needs to get out of the garage, then that's her job. Heidi also said the one job her husband does is the snow removal if he's home. They don't have a snow blower, but he just loves to do the shoveling, she said. She really finds that helpful because that's a job she really doesn't like to do.

Another task that's traditionally often handled by husbands is taking care of finances. Beth said this is something her husband does. He does the financial planning, watches the money, and sets aside funds for vacations and special occasions. She said this is his forte and something he enjoys doing, and she appreciates that he does it.

Does the Division of Labor Cause Problems in the Marriage?

From what we've written so far, it's evident that the division of family work in coaching families is unequal—to say the least. We don't mean to suggest that the coaches wouldn't do more if they had the time or that they don't regret that their wives shoulder most of the responsibilities for much of the year. According to the wives, neither they nor their husbands like the way things are, but they realize they can do very little about it. On the online questionnaire, we asked the wives to say whether the inequality in the division of labor causes problems in their marriages, and we looked at their responses by age, husbands' rank, and his division. We believed the younger wives would say it caused problems in their marriages more often than would the older wives. Wilcox and Knox (2006) state that wives' tendency to believe the division of housework is fair is shaped by their husbands contributions to housework and other tasks, including breadwinning but also by the wives' subscribing to either gender equality or traditional beliefs. In addition, these writers suggest that "more traditional-minded women, women who do not work outside the home and women whose husbands earned more than two-thirds of the family's income all reported that they were happier in their marriages." We also thought that because of the large number of hours Division I BCS husbands work that more of their wives would report problems. We suspected we also would find differences by the husbands' ranks. No matter which of these subgroups we looked at, the most frequently given response was that they disagreed "occasionally."

Does the Wife's Age Make a Difference?

Figure 6-4 shows that the percentages of wives who say they fairly often, often, or very often disagree on the allocation of household tasks is quite small. We do see some differences by age, with almost 30 percent of the 25- to 34-year-old wives, 23.3

percent of those aged 35 to 49, and 4.5 percent of the 40- to 64-year-olds saying this was the case. It would appear, then, that the younger wives and their husbands do disagree on the allocation of household tasks more often than their older counterparts. However, we should note that the percentages of wives who never disagree or only do so occasionally are very high in all age groups.

Wife's Age	Never	Occasionally	Fairly Often/ Often/ Very Often
25 to 34 (N = 108)	27 (25%)	49 (45.4%)	32 (29.6%)
35 to 49 (N = 116)	32 (27.6%)	57 (48.1%)	27 (23.3%)
40 to 64 (N = 44)	15 (34.1%)	27 (61.4%)	2 (4.5%)
65-plus (N = 4)	3 (75.0%)	1 (25.0%)	

Figure 6-4. How often husbands and wives disagree on the allocation of household tasks (by wife's age)

Does the Husband's Division Make a Difference?

As shown in Figure 6-5, when we look at the percentages of wives (by the husband's rank) who say they and their husbands disagree on the division of household labor fairly often, often, or very often, it's interesting to see that the percentage is lowest in

NCAA Division	Never	Occasionally	Fairly Often/ Often/ Very Often
Division I BCS (N = 89)	30 (31.6%)	46 (48.4%)	13 (14.6%)
Division I FCS (N = 54)	20 (39.2%)	25 (45.1%)	9 (16.7%)
Division II (N = 43)	9 (20.9%)	25 (58.1%)	10 (23.3%)
Division III (N = 73)	15 (20.6%)	28 (38.4%)	20 (27.4%)

Figure 6-5. How often husbands and wives disagree on the allocation of household tasks (by husband's division)

Division I BCS at 14.6 percent and becomes a little larger in Division I FCS (16.6 percent). Then, quite a jump occurs in Division II (to 23.3 percent) and, finally, 27.4 percent in Division III. This isn't what we expected to find, given the number of hours coaches in Division I work in comparison to the hours of coaches in Divisions II and III. Perhaps the wives in the lower divisions believe their husbands' hours should allow them more to time to do family work or perhaps those wives in Division I know nothing can be done about it and therefore they don't bring it up.

Does the Husband's Rank Make a Difference?

No clear patterns emerged when we looked at disagreements about household work by the husband's rank (Figure 6-6). Looking just at those who said they disagreed fairly often, often, or very often, we find that the percentages for position coaches is 20.8 percent, 22.7 percent for coordinators, 25 percent for assistant head coaches, and 22.7 percent for head coaches.

Overall, we expected that the wives would report more disagreement than they did, particularly in view of their responses to another question that asked: "If husbands and wives both work full time, they should share household tasks equally." Looking at the total number of usable responses (261), we found that a mere .07 percent strongly disagreed with the statement, 7.7 percent disagreed, 18.4 percent neither agreed nor disagreed, 45.2 percent agreed, and 28 percent strongly agreed. It would appear, then, that for many of our respondents, the reality of their lives may well be at odds with their personal convictions.

Husbands' Rank	Never	Occasionally	Fairly Often/ Often/ Very Often
Position Coach (N = 72)	16 (22.2%)	41 (56.9%)	15 (20.8%)
Coordinator (N = 66)	21 (31.8%)	30 (45.5%)	15 (22.7%)
Assistant Head Coach (N = 24)	9 (37.5%)	9 (37.5%)	6 (25.0%)
Head Coach (N = 97)	25 (25.8%)	50 (51.5%)	22 (22.7%)

Figure 6-6. How often husbands and wives disagree on the allocation of household tasks (by husband's rank)

Most Coaches Do Participate When They're Home

A large number of our respondents as well as the wives we interviewed said their husbands will do family work when they're home and in the off-season, but otherwise, they don't. As Beth put it: "It's not because he's not willing or he thinks he's too good. It's just that he's not home enough." Many of the husbands, like Leslie's, do the cooking when they can. She said:

> My husband cooks more than I do actually, so whenever he is home, he cooks. When football season starts, he would tell the kids, "I won't be able to cook," and they would go like, "Oh, no, it is Mom's turn to cook." … I have about three to four recipes, and my kids get tired of eating them.

Michaela, one of the younger wives we interviewed, said her husband is a very good cook, and they eat really well in the summer time, but, of course, he doesn't have time for cooking during the rest of the year. The younger wives on the online survey made some interesting observations. One wife of a Division II assistant coach said:

> During the off-season, all chores are non-gender-related. My son and husband both know how to wash clothes, do dishes, and mop. During the football season, I become quite familiar with the lawn mower, rake, and shovel. If we don't have set chores but do what is needed at the time we are available, then our household flows much better. Everyone is so busy, so everyone needs to help when they can. Some can do more than others at different times of the year. It works for us.

A young wife of a Division I BCS assistant also noted that her family runs along different lines. She wrote:

> We don't look at household chores in the old-fashioned traditional way. When he is home, he does it all—cook, clean, bathes, diapers, dishes. Everything except nurse the baby, and if he could, I'd make sure he did that too. When he is not home, I do it all—including but not limited to looking for leaks in the attic, buying real estate, investing in stocks, building shelves, and minor car repairs. I don't get [upset] about doing these things because I don't see them as "man" jobs.

A number of respondents wrote that their husbands are happy to help when they can but often have to be asked. One wife of a Division II assistant said: "He is always willing to cook, clean, and do laundry when necessary. He usually needs to be asked, and I try to mostly ask out of season. His hours are way tougher than mine for that period of time." Rachel said of her head coach husband: "He would be more than happy to help if and when he can be there and I can delegate it to him." One young wife noted: "I pick up the slack during the season and recruiting. He helps whenever he can (and when I just can't)."

Looking back on the division of labor over the course of their long marriage, Ann said:

> I think I might have maybe had him help me a little bit more, but I don't know. … Kind of like they do now. I just always did everything myself because like I said, I didn't have a big career. I mean, I worked every day, but maybe if we would have started out sharing a little bit more in the earlier stages and as the kid got older and stuff like that didn't bother me as much, but I would say maybe that. You know, when the young couple gets married in this profession, even though he's working as he is, the wives are working too. And maybe to make sure you share a little bit more with the things, and I think it would be a lot easier on both because I didn't do that. I mean, I did everything just because I thought that's what I was supposed to do.

Summary

It's obvious from what we've learned that by no stretch of the imagination can the division of family work in coaching families be described as equitable, but then, equality in these marriages isn't something the wives realistically expect to occur. We believe it's not whether the division of labor in coaching families is actually fair that's important to the wives' happiness; rather, it's the wives' *perceptions* of fairness under the circumstances. In addition, earlier research has established that emotional support from the husband is a stronger predictor of marital happiness than is instrumental support (Erickson, 1993.) Similarly, Bird (1999) noted "… among married women, those who feel loved and supported may not perceive an unequal division of household labor as inequitable."

These earlier works tie in well with our findings in Chapter 10, in which we note the theme of strong commitment to their marriages on the part of both partners. Such commitment, according to Rogers and Amato (1999), "seems to generate a sense of trust, emotional security and a willingness to sacrifice to one's spouse on the part of couples, all of which lead to happier marriages for women." The ideal for coaching marriages, then, isn't to have family labor equally divided down the line but for the partners to be in agreement with whatever division works for them.

7

On the Road Again: Moving for a New Job

"Coaches' wives often begin many of their sentences by saying, 'If we're still living here this time next year ...'"
—Snookie

One of the most frequently mentioned negative aspects of their lives as football coaches' wives in our study is moving. Moving for a better job for their husbands, moving because a coach has been fired or because the head coach for whom he worked has been fired, moving from state to state, and moving across the country have all been part of the lives of many of these women. Although some of the younger wives and some wives whose husbands are in Division II or Division III have been spared the nomadic existence of their sisters in Division I, most of the others have moved a number of times as a result of their husbands' career changes. Among the veteran wives, experiences like those of Sarah-Grace aren't unusual. She said:

> We moved 15 times from city to city or state to state. We have moved 37 times from physical residences to physical residence. It wasn't until move number 12 that I even thought, you know, I ought to be really ticked that I'm having to relocate all the time.

In her book *Moving for Work,* Anne Hendershott (1995) discusses the phenomenon of trailing spouses (i.e., spouses [almost always women] who follow their husbands from place to place as they look for success in the business world). She suggested that in the corporate world of today, the ideal trailing spouse of the past—as the term was traditionally understood—no longer exists. This spouse, according to Hendershott, is "... self-sacrificing, nurturing, supportive and most importantly *transportable.* She is ever-ready to cheerfully pack up and follow her husband wherever his career dictates. And, at every new location, she immediately meets new neighbors by inviting them over for tea, readily joins the PTA and becomes active in many community organizations so the family can feel at home at once."

While increases in women's labor force participation have meant that these women have all but disappeared from the sides of their husbands in corporate America because of their investment in their own careers, it appears to us that some are still alive and well in the form of football coaches' wives. Many of our respondents, as we've discussed in an earlier chapter, have made enormous sacrifices in their own careers to follow their husbands'. However, it's also clear to us from our interviews with the wives and from what our online respondents had to say that their constant and sometimes unexpected and unwelcome moves might appear to be accomplished seamlessly but aren't without cost.

Moving Is Stressful

No doubt about it: moving for anyone is stressful—not only from a physical perspective but also because of all the decisions that have to be made: what to keep, what to sell, what to donate, and so on. It's stressful finding a new home, getting settled in a new community, and having to find new friends, schools, and churches. Even if the move is a good one for one family member, it doesn't necessarily benefit everyone else in the family. Spouses, children, and extended family members who are left behind may all suffer in a variety of ways. The emotional cost of moving can be significant. Moving is expensive, and the greater the distance and the more possessions one has, the more expensive it is. Even when the actual moving costs are reimbursed, other expenses are involved in moving from one region to another.

Moving can be experienced in several different ways by coaching families. Sometimes, the family has to separate temporarily because most coaching moves take place in late winter or early spring, which doesn't coincide with the end of the school year. This means the husband often moves to his new position while his wife stays behind so the children can finish the school year and she can sell the house. Much of the success of a move, as we discussed in Chapter 4, depends on the age of the children. Generally, the younger they are, the easier it is, according to our respondents.

How well coaches' wives deal with moving has much to do with their personalities. Some look at it as an adventure that gives them the opportunity to see other parts of the country and to meet new and interesting people. Others note that it's essential to retain a sense of humor. A wife from the online survey said: "I swore I would never marry someone in the military because I didn't want to move around. Ha! The Lord had other plans—and a sense of humor. I didn't marry someone in the military, but I move more than a lot of people in the military."

Even when the logistics of moving are handled well, the instability of the coaching profession and its links to frequent relocation also generate what several wives called a sense of rootlessness. They said that frequent moves are stressful because just when they get settled and make connections in the community, they move again, which results in their never feeling established in the places they live. Reimer (2000) discussed the importance of home for people who move—the idea that one's self-concept is linked to a "sense of home." He found an emotional link formed by individuals' attachment to place—the good memories and the social relationships with family and friends. Relocating, he suggested, can effectively sever people's sense of home and leave a gap in their lives. An older wife's experience is a case in point. She said: "The football profession is one of change—coaches are always changing jobs. I want to have a place that feels like home, especially now that we are getting older." Despite her numerous moves, Snookie feels that her family found a place that feels like home:

> Our first home purchase was a mobile home that was placed in a town where my husband was going to coach football at the local high school. Unfortunately, that job opening did not come through due to budget cuts, so we ended up renting this home to various families for several years. Eventually, we found a lake lot to put this mobile home on, and it became our plan B home—if we got fired, we always had plan B, which was a bit comforting. This mobile home came to represent so much more to our family than the starter home we thought it would be when we first purchased it. Through the years of moving and job changes, this lake place was our constant. No matter how chaotic our football life became, we always had the lake. We watched our child grow from summer to summer there. Twenty years after the initial purchase of the mobile home, we replaced it with a small cabin that will be our retirement home.

Moving After Being Fired

The experience of moving by choice and moving because a husband has been fired from his job—regardless of the reason—is very different. Snookie said:

> We have been very blessed because of our 16 moves, only one was the result of a job loss. All of the others were moves that we chose to make either due to a great job opportunity or a home upgrade. There are marked differences in giving up a home when you choose to leave it and when you are forced to leave it. When you choose to make a move, you begin to mentally prepare yourself for the move as soon as the new opportunity is presented (even before it is secured), whereas the move that was the result of a job loss blindsided us. When you choose to move, you spend days researching the area that you may be moving to in order to help you make a decision, but when you lose a job and need another quickly, you may end up moving to a place that would not normally be a good fit for your family. (We were fortunate that we ended up in a great town after our job loss.) The home immediately becomes a house with a bad memory that overshadows

the good memories. In addition, the hurt and emotions caused by the job loss can follow you to your new house and hamper your adjusting to the new town.

As Snookie alluded to, employment decisions sometimes have to be made in a hurry, and in places where limited job opportunities are available, problems may arise. Pam said:

> And you know if you are looking for a job and you have a job, it's a much different dynamic than if you are desperately looking for a job and you have nothing. And I think that's when a lot of coaches just take something just to have income coming in and it might not be a wise or good fit and they move on again. That's when you see those multiple moves.

What makes moving as a result of a firing especially hard on the coaches' wives is that so much is out of their control. It's not their decision to move and it's not even their husbands' decision to move, and the couple may have very little choice in where they move. Dealing with the emotional aftermath of a firing is also difficult, and knowing that if the next move isn't a good fit, then almost certainly they'll soon be on the road again.

How Moving Decisions Are Made

Apart from moving decisions made as a result of a firing, the decision to take a new job in a new location is arrived at in a variety of ways in coaching marriages. According to Rives and West (1993), moving usually represents a joint family decision, and the wife's labor force commitment plays a role in such decision. However, this isn't often the case in coaching marriages. We don't mean to suggest that all coaches make career moves without regard for their families. For example, former Louisville and Tulsa head coach Steve Kragthorpe said when discussing moves, "The first thing I'll look at is where my family would live. … If the situation is not a good situation for my family, I don't care how good a job it is, my family is more important than football is" (Evans, 2006). Many of our respondents were unhappy at having to live in places not of their choosing, and one wife said:

> How many jobs are there where the husband accepts a position without even visiting the community and oftentimes the wife has no choice in the matter? You just hope to have a seat in the musical chairs game each year, and it isn't a reflection of how hard you've worked whether you do or don't have one.

Other wives did tell us that decisions were made only after discussion. Justice, whose husband has been in the same position for a number of years, talked about how they approach job offers in her marriage. She said:

But he has been offered positions at other schools. In fact, he was offered a coordinator position recently, but I mean, they are paid so well here, the family is close, great staff, great working hours. Unless somebody offers you a coordinator's position that has a significant value over this, it's basically a no-brainer for us. It's not worth it. What they're offering has to be a lot—yeah, has to be amazing for us to leave here.

Heidi talked about her husband's decision to move up from Division I FCS to Division I BCS: "Sure, we talked about it. It was a step up—it was a move up in his career. We were very excited about it, and at the time, our kids were younger, we just had the daughter then, and we could move her easily." Tina and her husband also discuss possible moves:

Yes, we sit down and talk about it. Most of them have been pretty easy decisions because each one has been another step up. Some I fought him on. Like I did not want to move one time—I just … I just didn't have a good feeling about it. It turned out I was right. But it's so hard sometimes because you know when they dangle that money in front of you, it's very hard to turn it down. So, he basically doubled his salary to go there. And now, looking back, it was a good year. You know, because in each town, when we look back, it's, you know, it's always been a move up. So, it's always worked out.

Jamie and her husband look at these decisions in much the same way:

Just this last year, when the old head coach left and everyone was debating "Are you going to go with him or not go with him?" you just kind of sit down and talk about his career. Would it have been a good career move for him? And then, you bring the family in. What is a good move at that time for our family with two little kids and things like that? I guess you just … I don't know … You just talk about family and then his career if it's a good move and if it's time for him to leave the school that he's at.

Beth looks at job decisions in a different way. She said:

Well, I did agree when we married that I would follow him. We did have that discussion, even though I didn't know what I was getting into. And I think, you know, you have to have a good enough relationship that you can tell each other. I mean, as hard as this last move was for us, we had to do it to avoid being fired. Fired was going to be a pretty negative experience. And then you don't know where you'll be. You don't know what will happen to you. So, I think, you know, it depends on your relationship. You have to talk about it—you have to—and you have to agree.

Rachel feels the same way:

> I made a commitment early on that I knew my husband wanted to be in the college coaching profession full time and that I was going to follow along with that wherever we needed to go. It was a heck of a lot easier moving when the kids were little than it is now, so the opportunity has to be pretty significant for us to pick up and move at this point.

Marissa told us how she and her husband deal with moving decisions:

> He has had some interviews in the past few years and some close calls, and every time, I basically tell him that "Whatever you feel in your gut is right." We pray on it, and we talk about it, but I basically leave it up to him. I'm up to anything that he feels is going to be career advancement for him, he feels it is a step up, he feels it is a great situation that our family would really benefit from. I would never say "No, I'm not going there." I would never say that.

For Pam, the career moves her husband has made have been good choices as far as not picking up a job that wasn't stable just to get to the next level. This has meant they haven't had to move very often. Ann's husband not only discusses any possible job changes with her but also includes her in the process of deciding:

> If he kind of knows something's happening, we will talk about it before that. If not, like this move came suddenly … [we] didn't really know what was happening. … He and I will talk to do our pros and cons and then we will have our girls get involved because it's a big part of their life too. So, we always sit down and have a little family discussion and decide what's best for us. Do we want to stay here? Because there have been a couple times that we haven't moved. He's had opportunities, and we didn't think it was the right thing. … I've always gone with him on the interview and he'll always ask me, and he says "Well, how do you feel?" Every time we've moved, I've always felt it was what we needed to do. It's always like a right time to move. We've been very fortunate because everywhere he's been, … the least amount was two years. And the rest have been like four or five.

Adjusting to the Move

In her book *The Trauma of Moving*, Audrey McCollum stated that "moving is women's work" because they're the ones who assume the major responsibility for planning and carrying out a move as well as the responsibility for reconstructing the household at its new location. Even when the move is paid for and arranged by an employer and the packing and physical move are handled by professionals, other details must be taken care of. Finding a place to live, getting utility services arranged, locating the best places to shop, choosing a bank and opening accounts, and taking care of changes of address are all tasks that usually fall to the wives in coaching marriages, and all of them add to the wives' stress.

When Husbands Move First

The stress of moving and relocation is intensified for those wives whose husbands go on to the new place ahead of the rest of the family, although as Snookie points out, the husbands may also feel stress about having to move before their families can join them:

> Regardless of whether the move is your choice or not, many times, husbands have to move immediately and the wives join them later after finishing jobs, letting children finish the school year, etc. This is hard on all family members, but I believe it was harder on my husband when he moved ahead of me than it was on me and our son. We were still in the comfort of our home and in our same routine, whereas he was in a new city, with a new job, in temporary housing, and lonely.

As anyone who has dealt with a state-to-state move knows, infinite details need to be attended to before and after the move, and having to deal with all of them by oneself makes things even more difficult. However, even under these difficult circumstances, some coaches' wives find ways to make it work. Reporter Beverly Bartlett in a 2002 article said that Peggy English, wife of veteran coach Wally English, often found that the cities she most dreaded moving to were the ones she ended up liking the best. What helped her was when Coach English would move ahead of the family and would find good neighborhoods and good schools before the rest of the family got there (Bartlett, 2002).

Getting settled in a new place is often more difficult if the wife isn't employed because it's then harder for her to get to know people in a new community. In addition to the loss of structure provided by her job, she won't have the opportunity to meet new people and make new friends in the workplace as would be the case if she were employed. This problem is intensified when the coaches are starting new jobs that require them to spend more time at work than they may have done before at a time when the wives and children are feeling lonely and in need of company. Mothers of young children may find it particularly difficult to become established in a new location if they're tied to the house much of the time. Several of our respondents mentioned the loss of identity they've experienced in new communities where they're seen primarily as the coaches' wives. In these situations, "husbands move to something while the rest of the family move away from everything" (Hendershott, 1995).

Catherine talked about a move she found difficult even though it was an excellent career move for her husband. She said:

That was my hometown [we left] plus my husband and I had gone to undergraduate and graduate school there and then to move here and to go to the grocery store and not know anybody was quite shocking. There are going to be many times you'll experience that, but it was very difficult.

What Helps Make the Transition Easier?

The initial stress of relocating can be reduced by the help of similarly situated people, which is why the wives of new coaches are grateful for the help of the head coach's wife and the wives of other coaches on staff. Some schools have programs to help the coaches' wives relocate, while in other places, most of this responsibility falls on the shoulders of the head coach's wife. Catherine talked about her recent move:

> There is a contact person to help out with the moving. And I think the head coach's wife sometimes gets the responsibility of being the welcome wagon and helping new moms or the moms with children find out where they go to school, where are you going to buy your home, setting up a realtor. …

Finding and becoming involved in a new church is one way in which our respondents said transitioning to a new location is easier, although this isn't always as simple as it sounds. Catherine described her experiences:

> You know, I'm still personally struggling with finding a church where I'm fully comfortable as a Lutheran. I have tried a couple, but I have not found that here. So, I go to church with my husband now. I've also talked about converting and doing all that too, so there's a lot of things that I still need to research.

The difficulties of settling into a new location are intensified for some wives as they find it hard to juggle the demands of their husbands' career with their own career in a new location as well as the logistics of their children's school and other activities without the support of family and friends. Until social networks are established, such problems as finding someone to take care of the children at short notice or to pick a child up from school, and so on, are challenging.

Moving away from family and friends is also difficult from an emotional perspective. Many of our online wives mentioned loneliness and not having any friends in the new location as being a major problem not just for themselves but also for the children. Although moving for Snookie has become less traumatic over the years, she told us about the first move she experienced away from the area where her parents, siblings, and extended family were easily accessible to a state a couple of days' drive away. She said:

As with any move, it is sad to leave behind family and friends. When we were getting ready to leave for my husband's first out-of-state coaching job, I remember standing in my parents' driveway with my mom, dad, brother, and sister and all of us bawling like babies. I cried through many of the first moves, but it got easier to say goodbye to people with each move because I began to realize that it's easy to stay in touch (especially with today's technology). I often wondered if I was becoming hardened because I no longer cried when we moved—I just methodically packed up and left. My family began to see my moves as an opportunity to go visit another part of the country, so I think they see my nomadic life as a plus.

One of our online respondents looked at family issues in a different way. She said: "I also get frustrated that family and friends who aren't in the business and have long-term roots established in communities think it's a breeze to relocate every few years and feel they can weigh in on our decisions." Several wives talked about how they've learned to make friends over the years. Beth said she makes friends "really through the kids right now and through work. I find a lot of camaraderie through work. So, those are healthy things for me. I … When the kids are gone, I am very aware that when the kids are gone, I'm going to have to find new ways. Church can be a big way to do it. Get involved in the church." Julie, whose attitude toward moving is more upbeat than most, sees the friendships she has made over the years as a real plus. She said:

We have wonderful friends from coast to coast. I was very excited to move from the West Coast to New England because I knew I was never going to see fall color unless he was retired or we moved there for a job. So, that was really exciting, even though I was leaving my family and my children were very small at that time. You also know that it is not forever in this profession; sometimes, it is longer than you think it will be and sometimes shorter than you think it's going to be, but you always know it's not forever.

Buying and Selling Houses

One of the most difficult aspects of moving is the buying and selling of houses. Pam talked about her experiences:

That's not something I enjoy at all. I stress about that a lot. We actually had pretty good luck. We did have a house that didn't sell for over a year, so that was really tough. And eventually, we got renters, which I think actually helped us sell it. She [the realtor] was really good as far as showing the house and everything. But I know that I've got one family on our staff now that still has a house that they lived in another town 16 years ago. And you know, they've rented it—rented it for a long time—and went back to check on it, and it was in horrible condition. So, they've been kind of rebuilding it. She [the wife] doesn't think it will ever sell. I was just talking with her this week. It's now in a really bad area of town. So, she's hoping they will be able to rent it again, but they've had such bad luck before. We've never had trouble like that, so we've been really, really fortunate.

Some wives move right away with their husbands rather than staying behind to sell a house. Leslie said:

It was always more important that our family stay together than it was that our house sold. I just did not want to keep our kids away from their father. They are away from him enough. He didn't want to be away from us, so we would just go and sometimes we would have a house that didn't sell and we were renting, and we decided to build a house where we were, and we would have three payments, credit cards, and that kind of thing.

Jamie told us about another coach's wife and her views on moving with her husband:

When my friend moved to Kansas, she tried to stay and finish her year out, and she's like, "It's just not good," and that was her advice because when we were almost going to go … that was her advice to me. She said, "Leave with your husband. Don't try to stick it out and sell the house. Leave with your husband, and everything else will work out." Even though they're not home a lot, at least they come home at night, and you can see them and still have that hour or so that you have with him that night.

Tina told us that within the space of a single year, her family bought and sold two houses. Luckily, at that time, the housing market was in better shape than it is now and they were able to sell quickly. Snookie shared her moving experiences:

During 30-plus years of marriage to a coach, I have moved into 16 different residences, including two stints in married student housing (when we were first married and 20 years later when we were having a home built), a mobile home, two apartments, two rental houses, one long-term hotel stay, and seven houses that we owned.

We have actually been quite fortunate when it came to selling homes. Twice, I sold a home to a neighbor without ever having to advertise it. The sixth house that we owned was the first one that we struggled to sell because that was during the housing market slump of 2009, but it did sell after two years.

I recall in my younger coaching wife years having a "seasoned" wife tell me about some of the places she ended up living in. She told me that she disliked one particular residence so much that she would turn the dryer on every time she left in hopes that it [the residence] would burn down while she was gone.

While I never felt quite that way about the places we lived in, there were some interesting stories along the way. We lived in a *remote* western town for one coaching stint where the number of houses to rent was very limited. There was a footrace between the new coaches coming onto the staff for the best rental houses. Somehow, I don't think we won that competition. The house we rented had shag carpeting that rivaled Graceland's. It was so bad, I wouldn't let the kids lay down in the floor without something under them. I worked out a deal with the landlord to do minor repairs to the deck and spruce up the landscaping in exchange for him replacing the carpet. Following suit, the second time we were in a rental house, I went to great lengths to make the yard and flower beds look nice, prompting my neighbor to tell me that "we were very clean for rental people."

Once, my husband moved for a job and I stayed behind to finish out the school year. There was a story in the local newspaper about my husband taking this new job. Perhaps not so coincidentally, my house was broken into twice soon after. Eventually, I moved our possessions on to the house that my husband had purchased in the new state and stayed with a relative until the end of the school year. This new home was the only time my husband was ever involved in the purchase of a home, and he literally picked the house and purchased it without my ever seeing it. He did an excellent job because this has always been my favorite house of all the homes we've lived in.

Our second stint in married housing was quite different from our first stint when we were young newlyweds who thought it was great to live in a 400 square feet apartment. Our second experience included a child and six guinea pigs who screeched every time we opened the refrigerator door.

Advantages of Moving

Are there any advantages to the moving that coaching families typically have to do? Some wives did find bright spots. One woman told us: "Moving has been a huge stress, but again, I've learned what I'm made of. I never knew I had it in me." Michaela, the youngest of the wives we interviewed, sees moving as an adventure. She said:

This is our third move in five years. I love it. I think it's very exciting. I don't really want to be in any place more than five or eight years because there are so many other places out there.

Probably after reading Michaela's comment, many of the older wives and those who have moved many times will shake their heads and wonder if she'll still feel that way after a few more moves or when she has children.

Summary

Whatever the reason, moving is a reality in the coaching profession—particularly at the higher divisions. Whether the move is made for a positive or a negative reason, it brings with it a host of decisions to be made and actions to be taken. In this chapter, veteran coaches' wives shared their experiences of dealing with the separation of families, the importance of a positive attitude toward the move, how the circumstances leading to the move can have an effect, and their thoughts on settling into their new locations.

8

Life in a Fishbowl

Mary Stuhldreher's 1948 article (mentioned in Chapter 4) chronicled the behavior of the public toward her, her husband, and their children during one not-so-good season. Some of the things she discussed included nasty and, of course, anonymous phone calls (this was before caller ID), insulting remarks about his father from children at her son's school, the refusal of a sales clerk to wait on her, and negative comments about her husband's coaching ability from their yard man as well as from many friends and acquaintances. Mrs. Stuhldreher said that at one point, things were so bad she "… forgot that I was a coach's wife and had to take it. I buried my face in my hands and wept." Are the wives of football coaches today experiencing the same types of behavior from the public some 65 years later? From what our respondents have told us, it would appear so, although because of advances in technology, the ways in which the public conveys its messages has changed.

Not many occupations are subject to the constant public scrutiny that football coaches endure, and few occupations cause people to aim their vitriolic comments at families as well as the worker. One respondent said: "People have no idea that it isn't just a game. It is a career. They have no idea that the whole family sacrifices, and it drives your life." Heidi, who is the wife of a Division I BCS coordinator, had this to say:

> I think that is what in this profession just shocks me. How people can be so critical and they don't know that much in many situations. They don't know the circumstances, they don't know, and they don't care. If IBM stock drops, I don't go running over to my friend who works for IBM and start screaming at her because their product was bad or whatever. Yet, they feel because they buy a ticket or that they are "fans" that they can say whatever they want. It is open game, open territory. Like I mentioned earlier, when you are winning, it is great and everyone is happy to see you and everything is going great, but when the times aren't so good, that it is very hard to take.

Life for many coaches and their families is like living in a fishbowl. It's not just the coaches' performance that's subject to public judgment, but this also extends to the demeanor and appearance of their wives and to the behavior of their children. In addition to the disadvantages attached to being—for all intents and purposes—"public figures," football coaches and their families must also learn to cope with the often irate behavior of fans, ugly postings on the Internet, negative comments in the press and on the radio and TV, harassing phone calls from people who don't give their names, and vandalism of their homes. The worse the season, the more of these types of behavior there are to contend with. As one wife pointed out: "They [the fans] can get you fired; they have a very powerful voice." The wives in our study tell us that the fans and the media can say anything they want—whether it's true or not—and that coaches and their families have no recourse. As Beth, another Division I BCS wife, said in her interview:

> Well, you know, it's always been my philosophy that you are always proud of your team. I mean, that's how I deal with it. And you can't … We can't win as coaches' wives by being ugly back because we are so visible. And we do represent the school. I mean, I would never want my husband or the university he works for to be embarrassed by my behavior in public.

Many of the wives in our study suggested that if the public really understood what coaches' lives are like and the sacrifices that these men and their families make, they might be less likely to indulge in this kind of behavior. Although most of the remarks and comments our respondents made concerned the negative aspects of living in the public eye, we believe it's also important to talk about the advantages that some (although not as many) of the respondents identified. We also believe it's important to note that a number of wives pointed out that their experiences with the public differed according to the level at which their husbands were employed as well as the size of the community in which they were located. The major areas of public life that emerged from this study include fan behavior, public image and behavioral expectations, and the media, including the Internet. In addition to the online respondents and the wives we interviewed, we're grateful for the input for this chapter from a number of wives who attended our session at the 2010 AFCWA meetings in Orlando.

Fans

Teams have always had "fair weather" fans, and that's still the case today. However, in addition, the stereotypical 21st-century fans expect instant and consistent success (wins) from their football coach, and if this success isn't delivered when they want it to be, they often begin calling for him to be fired. The direct impact of the fans' comments on the career of a coach is debatable, but nevertheless, they create great stress in the lives of coaching families. In general, our respondents see their exposure to negative comments from fans as an almost normal feature of their lives. The wives don't like it, of course, but over time, most of them learn to put it in its place.

Fans in the Stands

Much of the negative fan behavior occurs in the stands during home games, especially when a season or a game is going poorly, and it takes a variety of forms. Hearing everyone's opinion about what the team is doing wrong, listening to fans say mean things about the players and coaches, and dealing with criticism and complaints from fans who think they can do it better are tough situations to handle. Several wives mentioned that what makes it even worse is that the fans often don't have any idea of what goes into coaching. In a *Sporting News* article, Rita Rodriguez (wife of Rich) said: "It hurts your feelings. Sometimes people will walk by the box and they won't yell anything directly to you, but they'll say things very loudly so you can hear them" (Rodriguez, 2005). Heidi agreed:

> Oh, gosh, the fans can be so horrible. They really can be ugly. When you talk to older coaches' wives (I'm 45—I'm getting older)—the ones that have really been in the business a long time—they always say that you can't listen to it. But I think it is so hard not to take it personally. I think that is the biggest con when things don't go well and they take it out personally and they take personal potshots against your husband. It is hard, it hurts your feelings, and you hurt for them. I think you hurt even more because you know how much goes into it, and you know there isn't anybody besides your son or your husband who wants to win more besides the kids. … With the players, the game is over, and they go and they do what they have to do, and the coaches, it never stops for them. It is not a four-year stint and they are done. It's a lifetime experience.

A few of our respondents mentioned that the husbands often have no idea of what life in the stands is like. Beth told this story:

> … [W]e just saw one of our best friends over summer break. And he coaches at the University of Missouri. He and his wife got to see Iowa and Michigan play. And they were up in the stands, and the Michigan fans were yelling at Lloyd Carr and the Iowa fans were swearing at whomever. He said, "I told my wife, I can't handle this up here, listening to them berate these coaches." And she was like, "Well, honey, this happens all the time."

How the Wives Deal With Fans

Many of our respondents said that coping with negative comments and behavior from fans in the stands is easier if the wives are somewhat removed from the fans and if they're surrounded by other wives. Justice, whose husband coaches for a Division I BCS team, said in her interview:

… [A]ll of our wives are in one area together. Now they are on my actual row, and I've had the same seats ever since I've been here. It's actually all wives for a considerable way down. And then behind me are wives and in front of me. There are other people sprinkled in. … So, we don't hear a lot just because … I mean, we are in the middle of the stands, but we've got so many wives together. And I think a lot of the people have been there for a long time because they're season ticket holders, so they kind of know.

Jamie, the young wife of a Division II assistant coach, agreed. She said:

We do sit in the stands, and we're kind of off to the side, so we aren't around a lot of disgruntled fans, I guess. We're kind of blocked from those. I know there are fans out there, and it's frustrating, and some things are hard to hear. They get mad and just think they could be better coaches—just like that.

Pam, whose husband is a Division II head coach, recalled a time when her husband was coaching at the Division I BCS level and his team was not doing well:

Some of the wives wouldn't even come to the stadium or they would come in but they wouldn't sit down or they wouldn't sit in our assigned seats. Most of the time, I avoid confrontation and just move. If they [fans] start talking loudly in my direction, I'll just get up and move.

For others, it's helpful to give themselves a little mental reminder that the fans don't know the roles or the players, that they're often not as knowledgeable as they think they are, and that they're in the stands, not on the field, for a reason. The wives do acknowledge that the fans have a right to their opinion, but they do their best to stay out of the way of negative comments, although at times, it's very difficult. One of the online respondents said:

I have heard my husband's name called out from the stands with awful things shouted after it. I want to take my little ones up to those people and say, "Would you like to say that in front of his three daughters?" I guess it's just ignorance, but it's still frustrating.

For others, not letting anyone know who they are works well, as this online respondent said:

I also do not like it when the fans talk about the defense negatively, although I do make it a point not to be known to the parents and spectators in the crowd. … After all, it is my husband's career and not mine. I would rather keep it that way.

For most of our respondents, trying to ignore the comments seems to work much of the time, although sometimes, it gets too difficult not to say something. Tina, the wife of a head coach and also the mother of a college quarterback, said:

> You know, I don't ever like to get mean with them because that doesn't get you anywhere. But if it gets really brutal, I just might make a comment. I just try to keep my mouth shut, but if it gets really bad, then I'll say something. Usually, I try to ignore the negative criticism at games. I did, however, one time turn to the guy behind me (whom I knew) who had been loudly critical of the quarterback and said, "How would you feel if you were at [your daughter's] dance recital and people kept screaming at her every time she messed up?" He grinned sheepishly and said, "You're right."

While most of our respondents said they try to ignore the negative comments, Justice, a Division I BCS assistant coach's wife, said:

> … I am very outspoken. My husband is one of those people who will stand up on the bench and start telling the fans to get up. Because I don't know if you know about our fans, but we think they're horrible. I mean, you're expected to win by 20. And then it's just, like, yeah … that's great. And if you don't, then you did a [terrible] job. And our fans aren't … You know how some places, even though the football program might not be that good, their fans are so into it and supportive. Some of the SEC schools have, like, all these chants that they do and all this stuff. Not here. You're lucky … I mean, I had people behind me [complaining] because I stand up. "Sit down. You're blocking our view." That didn't go over very well. I said, "Go home and watch it on TV." So, I'm very outspoken. I mean, if I hear something … There were people sitting in front of me one time saying, "Well, who does he think he is? Is he the cheerleader?" Because he was saying "Get up and yell" so that the kids hear that you're into it and it motivates them. I said, "Maybe if you'd get your [butt] up and cheer, he wouldn't have to stand down there and do that."

The Impact of Fan Behavior on Children

What many wives find really hard to deal with are the fans who hurl insults and heap abuse on their husbands in the presence of the children. As Beth said: "… and that's when I come out like a bear." One of our online respondents said that even when rude fans aren't considerate of her children, she still tries to ignore them, but sometimes, people don't think before they speak and they can be so mean and say things that upset the children.

Children are also exposed to negative remarks about their fathers in other places. As we mentioned in Chapter 4, several women noted that their children have had to deal with comments from their peers, teachers, and even their own coaches. Even a coach's home isn't off-limits, and in fact, it's often targeted by disgruntled fans. Stories of "For Sale" signs being placed in the yards of coaches abound. Heidi told us the following story:

> A couple of years ago, it was the first losing season we had had since we have been here, and I remember specifically there was a really bad loss, and I can't remember who we lost to, but the defense had played very poorly, had given up a lot of yards, and couldn't stop anybody, and people were very critical. I remember pulling up in the driveway on a Sunday night, and it was dark, and there were some high school kids jogging by, and they yelled out as we went by, "The defense sucks." My son was so mad, so enraged, that he started to take off after them because he was upset.

Tina also mentioned her children's reaction to negative comments from fans in the stands. She said: "… [S]ometimes, the older children want to say something. My one daughter was ready to take them all on. I tell them, 'You guys just have to close your ears. This is a part of it, and there is nothing we can do about it.'" Another wife with younger children deals with the issue this way:

> Sometimes, I'll have the babysitter take the kids home if the game isn't going well. Other times, they'll stay home at the start of a game and I'll have the sitter call. If things are good, I'll tell her to come with the kids. We worry about the feelings of our children.

One head coach's wife secures additional tickets to her suite for game day. She distributes these passes to the wives of the assistant coaches so that, if necessary, they and/or their children can find a refuge from the fan criticism.

Divisional Differences

Several of our respondents whose husbands had coached in various divisions noted that negative behavior in the stands is much worse in Division I than in either Division II or Division III. Pam said:

> Well, when we were in Division I, they [the fans] were awful, horrible. I mean, we had … Unfortunately, we had the longest losing streak in the nation at that time. And you know, people were really, really cruel when they found out they were sitting by coaches' wives. They just let us have it. You know and … It was pretty nasty there. And my husband always tells me if somebody starts complaining to me about how their kid is

not getting playing time, I'll just say my husband always says it's how they practice is whether or not they get to play. But most of the time, I just avoid confrontation.

There's no doubt about it: Many fans are intense and truly care about the team, which can be positive. But they also have a sense of ownership and entitlement, which they believe justifies their negative behavior.

Fans as a Positive Force

However, a number of wives mentioned how much they appreciate the loyalty of so many fans—loyalty to the program, the coaches, and the players. They see them as representatives of the team who can add so much to the positive atmosphere at a game. Several mentioned that fans can be a great source of support for their husbands because of their personal and/or financial involvement. Some wives had suggestions for reinforcing positive fan behavior, such as complimenting them and thanking them personally for their support whenever possible and always trying to stay positive in their contact with fans.

Local Celebrities: Behavioral Expectations for Coaches and Their Wives

Living in the public eye is stressful for the coaches, the wives, and the children. Ann, the wife of a Division I BCS head coach, shared what she told her daughters as they were growing up:

> With our kids, we always tell them that they are on display here. They've got to do what's right—showing people what's right because if they get in trouble, everyone's going to know. They're going to be on the front page of the paper. You can't keep anything private.

Another wife said: "Because it is so public a life, it has been very difficult at times on our children. Not many children have their fathers criticized in public (TV, newspaper, at school, in the town's stores and restaurants) for their jobs." Other wives noted that people think they "know" you and demand your time and attention. Heidi told us that in her community, "… some people know who you are or, like, there is name recognition and some are just oblivious. It is like anything else: When you win, it is great for people to recognize your name, and they are like, "Oh, gosh, the defense did this or that, and we are going to the Rose Bowl." But then, when you are not doing as well, I think then you are a little bit more paranoid about it. I think you are more paranoid that they are recognizing your name with being negative and maybe they are not. But you have a tendency to think that they might be." Even going to the grocery store isn't without its problems. Catherine, the young wife of a Division I BCS assistant coach, said:

It's hurtful when you're in the grocery store, and I might be hearing stuff about the head coach, and that is also indirectly about my husband. That's your bread and butter, and sometimes I say to people, "It's my child's future."

Claire, a head coach's wife, agreed:

Even if it is not football season, people just go crazy. People look at what I have in the grocery cart, people look at me in church, people look at me with the kids, and that has been an adjustment for me to realize that people are always watching what I am doing.

As we mentioned in Chapter 1, coaches' wives are expected to make public appearances, to attend all games, and to be perfectly turned out at all times. Communities often place expectations on how they should act or dress. One woman noted that she has a hard time dealing with her family about dressing up to go to a football game:

They don't understand that as the head coach's wife, I need to present myself a certain way. Although I'm going to watch a football game, I'm also going to my husband's job site.

Another said she "… must always be on good behavior and professional. I can never just run out in a hurry in my 'scrubs.' That's always when people recognize you. You kind of hate getting caught at the grocery store in your paint/work/yard clothes—no makeup, hair a mess." Another wife commented: "I usually try to wear at least a little makeup when out and not have on ragged clothes. You always have to be aware that you are representing your husband and your school and will what you do embarrass either of them?" But even if you're caught in public looking less than perfect, as one wife said, it does at least let people know you're a *real* person with feelings and ideas too. One very important piece of advice mentioned by several wives was to never be seen in the opposing team's colors regardless of how good you look in them. As Claire said in her interview:

Being aware of what my kids are wearing—that they can't wear the other color of the school we are playing that week. We are constantly aware that if they are playing Nebraska, we can't wear red. We have basically given all of our red away. We don't have red anymore in the house at all. I remember once that I wore red to the football office, and it was the week we were playing Nebraska, and I didn't even think about it—it was just a red jacket that I had—and my husband got so upset and said that I just can't do that. … It is kind of crazy.

Snookie told a similar story:

Red was the team color of our hated in-state rival. I made the mistake of wearing a red sweater to an athletic department Christmas party our first year at this particular university. (Isn't red a Christmas color?) Anyway, I had numerous persons at the party point out to me that I should "never wear red if we're going to coach here."

Living in the public eye and having expectations for their behavior and appearance is difficult for some women who are by nature private people. One woman said: "I'm on the shy side, so it's stressful for me to play that role." Another said that she finds it hard "… to be gracious when you really don't want to be." Along the same lines, still another wife said it's not easy "[h]aving to be 'on' when you don't especially want to be or don't feel up to it. There are times when you are not feeling up to being a role model or whatever." Still another online respondent said: "You can be a fun person, but you can't appear to look cheap, loose, or to be consuming too much alcohol or the public will make judgment calls on your character." She went on to say: "Keep in mind that perception is reality. It doesn't matter if you are a 'church lady' with the highest of morals. If the public sees you as questionable, you might as well be questionable." Several women mentioned wives should never, ever cry at games. Fans in the seats may perceive crying as instability and that wives should try to put the loss in the proper perspective.

It's Not All Bad

However, positive aspects to being in the public eye do exist. Several wives mentioned that coaches' wives "… show a professional appearance that complements the football programs and shows loyalty to their husbands and the teams." Others mentioned that it's a role they can take on and be proud of and be happy to do and that they can be a positive example for players and fans. In addition, several said that the wives "get to attend a lot of great functions and be an ambassador for the university."

To make this aspect of their lives as wives of football coaches easier, a number of wives recommend trying to remember their position and everything it involves. They say it's good to set a positive example—to be excited about their husbands' jobs and to always appear supportive of the coach, the team, and the coaching staff. But at the same time, they're never able to forget that they're always in the public eye. Several told us how important it was just to be oneself—in public and in private. If the wives are natural and comfortable with who they are, then that will take the pressure off. In addition, they noted that it doesn't hurt to be the first to laugh at oneself.

Community Size

Without a doubt, dealing with being in the public eye is far easier in a larger community than it is in a small one. Catherine points out that if she lived in a larger (and less football crazy) community, she believes she would enjoy more separation from the public. She said that in a smaller community, you just hear it more. Other wives agree that a great deal of talk occurs in a small town and that someone is always watching you. One wife said she has had to learn to keep her mouth shut because people do listen in a small town and that she's been misquoted.

Beth has experienced life as a coach's wife in small and large communities. Currently, they live in suburb of a major city, where she said it's possible for her to go to the mini market in old clothes because nobody knows who she is. Julie, whose experiences have been similar, said: "You don't tell everyone who you are or what your husband does for a living. We have chosen not to do it that way. In small communities, you don't have a choice. Here, I can pretty much remain anonymous. This is a big enough community." Kate, whose husband was the head coach at a regional university overshadowed by a neighboring Big Ten powerhouse institution, said:

> I try not to look horrible because, yeah, when you least expect it, you'll be recognized. It's not as bad here as in other places. … I always try to look at least presentable. I love the anonymity. Sometimes, I think I do have to be careful to not assume that anonymity as much as I do.

The Media

The media have always played a role in the lives of football coaches, but the ever-increasing coverage of sports has thrust the coaches and, in some instances, their families into the limelight. Twitter tracks the hour-by-hour behavior of coaches. Facebook accounts create a sense of personal relationships when, in fact, none exist. The media's task of filling 24-hour sports channels and fan websites often results in trivial incidents in the lives of the coaches being reported in overblown proportions. Personal information regarding the coach and/or his family is often reported instantly to millions of people via the Internet. Life can be particularly difficult for the coach and his family if the team is having a losing season. Negative or not-completely-accurate information abounds, statements made to the press by the coaches can be misinterpreted, and critical and speculative articles about the coach's future appear on a regular basis—all of which are difficult to not take personally. One wife said: "The media circus and the backlash that goes along with every loss—and even victories sometimes … it affects our entire family."

Sarah-Grace recalls a time when the head coach of her husband's team was in imminent danger of losing his job (which in many cases also means loss of their jobs for the entire coaching staff):

> The head coach's wife said, "You need to hunker down and bring the family close. You don't read the newspapers, you don't listen to talk radio shows, and you don't get on the Web. You keep on doing what you have always done, and that is supporting him and believing in him and not letting other people have negative influence on your life. That is how you handle it." I did every one of those things. I quit taking the

newspaper, I quit listening to the talk radio, I never unlisted our phone, but if I didn't recognize the number, I didn't answer it, and I stayed away from places. … I tried purposely to keep away from situations where there were rabid fans or avid football supporters of the university. …

Other wives shared some tips about managing negative media, which include never talking to reporters, stop reading or listening to comments, and always remember that the media take great liberties with how and what they report. Interestingly, several wives mentioned that the media can be valuable in giving good publicity to the program and the players and that reading positive comments about the coaches and the families is gratifying. They also mentioned that the media can be a great help in shaping public opinion. Some of the ways the wives have found to strengthen the positive effects of the media include developing good relationships with reporters and commentators. The idea is that the more they see you as a person rather than just a name, the less likely they are in many cases to be as scathing in their comments. They also mentioned the importance of being complimentary about coverage by saying things like "What a great article" or "You really told it like it is."

In addition to newspaper articles and radio and TV commentaries, another source of frustration and pain for the wives is the Internet. While most people would agree that the Internet is a wonderful tool for staying in touch and staying informed, the coaches' wives tend to see it as a blessing and a curse. One of the questions we asked on the online survey was "What is the worst part about being married to a college football coach?" and one of the most common responses had to do with the Internet. Many wives said that the problem with message boards, blogs, and chat rooms is that they contain so much negative information—much of which is nothing more than rumor and conjecture. Other drawbacks include having details of their private lives made public as well as their husbands' salaries and bonuses.

During the season, especially if it's not a good one, many of our respondents simply stay away from it. For example, Julie said: "I don't read the Internet … because nobody has to be accountable. They can say horrible things. They can say whatever they want to say and there is no accountability for it." Similarly, Marissa, the wife of a Division I FCS coach, said:

> I need to follow the head coach's wife's lead; she does not read a paper during football season or the Internet. And that is tough because I'm so into it and I want to know what is going on, and I like to read the paper because I like to read the articles about the players, and I like to read the positive things, but it's hard to stay away from the negatives. … You just have to let it go though and not dwell on it.

Despite knowing her husband doesn't want her to look on the Internet, Claire still does it because, she said, "I feel like I need to prepare myself for what is coming. I need to know what people are saying out there." Surprisingly, some wives mentioned the good things about fan websites and message boards, which include the fact you're loved when things are good and that the popularity of websites does increase public exposure to the team. Of course, this is only a good thing when the comments are positive. One veteran wife offered the following advice to cope with negative comments. She said: "Help your husband to keep them in perspective and remind him that it is very different calling a play in 25 seconds than it is having three days to think it over." This wife also mentioned how she and her husband laugh and then they envision other jobs being performed in front of the public the way that coaching is.

Summary

Being a coach's wife means your life includes hearing criticism of your husband in the stands, seeing criticism in newspapers and on the Internet, and having to appear presentable and "be on" when you leave your home for any reason. While a few of the wives in our survey can be outspoken, most pointed out that their responses to these situations are often based on the underlying premise that they're representatives of the schools at which their husbands coach and they're expected to display professional behavior. Because of this, the wives have a variety of plans and philosophies to deal with these situations. Several wives point out that while the fans, media, and Internet are often seen as negative factors, they can also be advocates for a coach and his football program.

9

The Best Things About Life With a Coach

In previous chapters, we discussed the various sacrifices wives often make for their husbands to pursue careers in football coaching. But to ignore those aspects of their lives they find rewarding would be to paint an incomplete picture. The rewards we discuss in this chapter are those they receive directly and indirectly from their husbands' occupation and not those they receive from their own achievements—whether personal or professional—or from their marriages or family lives. The top responses to the question "Which aspects of your life as the wife of a college football coach give you the greatest rewards?" are the following:

- Relationships with coaches' wives and families
- Husband loves his job
- Positive impact on young people's lives
- Proud of husband
- Success and winning
- Coaches' children given opportunity to be involved
- Meeting new people
- Getting to travel
- College atmosphere
- Notoriety/perks
- Living in different places
- Sharing husband's football experience
- Games
- Friends all over the country

We've discussed some of these advantages in other chapters. In this chapter, we'll focus on the enjoyment the wives derive from seeing their husbands' success and happiness; seeing how the coaches affect young lives; being part of a shared mission; getting to know the players; getting to know the players' families; and the joy of winning.

Indirect Rewards

Their Husbands' Success and Happiness

Many of the wives' rewards from their husbands' profession come to them by way of the pleasure they receive from seeing the coaches happy in their work and knowing their husbands are doing what they're passionate about. One wife told us: "I am rewarded by being my husband's wife because he is the person he is. Nothing about his job as a college football coach rewards me directly—other than having him happy from the work he does." Several said what a wonderful thing it is to see their husbands look forward to going to work every day, while still more mentioned that coaching football is their husbands' dream job and his passion, and they can't imagine them doing anything else. Some told us they knew their husbands wouldn't be happy without football and that the coaches are fulfilled and excited by their careers.

Our respondents reported that they derive immense satisfaction from their husbands' individual career success, and because they and their husbands are so heavily invested in the team, they also experience great satisfaction when the program itself succeeds. This satisfaction isn't just confined to the team's success on the field but also occurs when they see these young men succeed in their personal and professional lives. We suggest that these are key factors in the wives' ability to withstand many of the hardships we have already identified. The following sentiments are typical:

> In reflecting on some of the things I have written, it sounds depressing. It can be—but the rewards always have a way of springing up and being worth it all. My husband gets paid for doing something that he truly *loves* and that usually makes him *very* happy—that is a good thing.

> I love the fact that my husband goes to work every day with a smile on his face because he loves coaching football and working with such bright young men.

> I know that this is what my husband loves to do, and I support him wholeheartedly in it. I love watching him coach and seeing how proud he is of his players. I wouldn't want him to even attempt another career.

The Coaches' Impact on Young Lives

One of the most frequently mentioned and meaningful rewards for the respondents is seeing the effect their husbands have on the lives of young men. This is particularly true in cases where the players come from disadvantaged backgrounds. The following sentiments are typical:

> I get great pleasure out of witnessing the impact my husband has on his ballplayers. I really believe that some of his players have been successful in their lives because of his involvement with them. I am truly proud of him when I witness the admiration and respect the players have for him. He has dedicated his life to the success of his players—not just on the field but also off the field. So many of these athletes do not come from stable families or from families that are actively involved.

> His job is a ministry, and he touches the lives of those young football players every single day.

> Watching my husband build respectable men with character and knowing that he is making differences in so many lives makes me love what he does as much as he does. Some of my greatest rewards come from being a part of the lives of the young men who play the game and seeing my husband not just teaching football but teaching them how to succeed in life.

> Listening to his athletes talk about what they have learned from him and what an impact he has made on them as students, athletes, and as young men. I am very proud of him.

Some football players' families live too far away for them to be frequent visitors to campus or to regularly attend their sons' games. For these students, the coaches become father figures and hope their involvement makes a difference in the lives of the athletes. One wife said her husband takes great pride in helping young men accomplish their goals, especially when a player turns his life around for the better. Another said: "Witnessing my husband's positive influence on a young man's life is incredible." Long-term relationships with their players are another benefit for the coaches and their wives—watching them grow up into responsible, hardworking men, marry, and sometimes go on to careers in the NFL. A respondent said her husband is happy when his players come back and tell him how important he has been in their lives. Another said:

> The coaches are not only teaching someone how to play football—they are teaching them how to be a person, getting them through school. For a lot of them, he's their father. I mean, a lot of the guys don't have dads, so, you know, these coaches are their dads and are raising them.

Direct Rewards

Being a Part of a Shared Mission

One of the more interesting findings from this study and one that plays a very important part in the wives' satisfaction is that they see themselves and their husbands as a team—that they and their husbands are on a shared mission. As Ann pointed out: "You have to have a team at home too or it doesn't work." Husbands and wives share common goals in that both want the team to win games, but they also want boys to grow into men and graduate. The wives recognize the important role they play in the coaches' careers and often stated that they (and their husbands) know that some of the coaches' success is because of the wives' contributions and support.

Several wives commented that in a business as competitive and unforgiving as football coaching, they're the only people their husbands can always count on and that the wives are often the only people who provide the coaches with truth and perspective. One wife said: "He values my input and support—whether in good or bad times. He recognizes my contributions to his career successes." Another said: "I have a responsibility to support and respect my husband in his career—acting as a sounding board, etc. It is very rewarding to be needed in this way and to have the close relationship with him that is necessary to make marriage and coaching work." And a third said: "As you live through the ups and downs of coaching, you discover really all you can count on is each other. No one knows exactly how you feel except the two of you." Another wife said: "Knowing I'm helping my husband in his career does have a trickle-down effect. We truly believe we have a ministry, especially concerning the players, the younger coaches, and their wives."

Additional insights include:

> I play an important role in his career, and I feel some of his success is because of me. I've put up with a lot (firings, low pay, moving 11 times in 31 years, etc.), but I honestly feel that God blessed him with the ability to coach—and coach well.

> I am happy that my husband has achieved many of his goals and that I helped him reach them.

> I know that I am enabling my husband to be successful in not only coaching but mentoring boys into men. We share the same vision. We have confidence in each other that we are working toward a common goal.

The wives perform a number of functions as part of their partnership with their husbands. Some are active in promoting the team within the community and fundraising, while others plan football activities and socials. One wife reported:

I actively support him at every university function not limited to social but also attend every time prospects are in town. I belong to the parents' group and actively speak a minimum of five hours a week to parents by telephone.

The following comment shows how much the wives enjoy feeling involved in their husbands' work in ways that wives married to men in other occupations are seldom able to do:

[I love] the excitement of participating on Saturdays to be a part of the work he does all week long. I love being able to watch my husband in "action." This is one of the only jobs that a wife is able to see the fruits of the labor.

Sometimes, it's not just the husband and wives that see themselves as part of a "team," but members of the public seem to do so too. This excerpt from an article by Warren St. John in *The New York Times* exemplifies that theory:

Usually the criticism is directed at players or the coaches, but occasionally, the wives themselves are targeted. Mrs. [Mack] Brown was caught up in an unruly mob of fans when her husband was the coach at North Carolina and [she] received a black eye. In the middle of a dismal three-win season at Penn State in 2003, one sports columnist blasted Sue Paterno for not talking her then 76-year-old husband into retiring. "Sue Paterno is the real villain," he wrote.

Getting to Know the Players

A great many wives told us they derive great satisfaction from their personal involvement with their husbands' players. While they're very proud of their husbands' role in helping the young men succeed on and off the football field and while they receive great pleasure from hearing the athletes talk about what they've learned from the coaches and the impact the coaches have had in their lives, it's their own personal contact with the players that the wives find even more rewarding. They enjoy being involved with the team and express great affection and appreciation for "… those guys who give so much of themselves to the game." Some say they see the players as being like a second family, and they come to love and care about them. They feel great pride in seeing the young men grow and succeed, and the players and coaches' families form attachments that in some cases last a lifetime. One wife told us she enjoys "watching the lives of young people change because of your relationship—watching them grow up and mature and being a part of something greater than yourself." Another told us how important to her is "[g]etting to know his players, developing lifelong relationships with them, watching them mature, get married and play in the NFL, and being invited to their weddings, children's baptism etc., even after they leave us." An assistant coach's wife said that each year she "… adopts 10 or more players as her own," and another said she loves being their "second mom away from home. I feel like I have a hundred kids that are my second sons, you know."

Several other wives also mentioned how much they enjoyed watching their own children interact with the players. This one believes her children benefit from their exposure to the players:

> I enjoy being a mom to the players and providing a family atmosphere for them in our home, especially for those who don't have good home environments. It has also provided a great learning environment for our daughters around the acceptance of diverse cultures and a lot of "life lessons" as a result of some player situations/problems and in learning how to maintain your composure under difficult circumstances.

Many wives enjoy being able to do things for the players—from watching them play to having them over for dinner or baking cookies for them. This wife said: "I love to cook and bake, so the players tend to love him [her husband] for all the food they get." Another recalls a time when "[o]ne player was hurt and his mom could not afford to fly in, and he asked me to give him a hug because he really needed a mom and since his couldn't be there, I was the next best thing." Another was quite vocal in her feelings for the players, saying: "They are just an extension of my children, and you'd better not mess with any of them. I come to their defense as fast as I would my own children." Several wives talked about their great pride in the academic success of the players. Kate, the young wife of a head coach, told us:

> There are a lot of challenges for them down the path, no matter how hard you try to help them to actually graduate and get a degree. But, boy, when you do, you think, "OK, job well done." You know we've done something worthwhile. So, yeah, that's very cool.

Marissa, another young wife, had this to say:

> I just think it is important, I have always believed—and this is my belief—that it is important for the wives to be involved, like I said earlier. I go to all of the games, and the only reason I'm going to miss a game is if we can't fit all of the boys on a plane or if something in our lives interrupts it. I think it is very important to attend the games—to support them. If you are not involved in those 11, 12, 13 weeks, I just don't think that is right, and that is my personal belief. It frustrates me when I'm the only wife at a game that is only four-and-a-half hours away. To me, it is important—and not just for my husband to see me supporting them but for the players to see me too. You get to know those players, they are at your house, and they are playing with your children. You get to know their parents. They are like an extended family. For them to see me, and they come up to me and they say, "We know that you are at

all the games and we appreciate that," and lots of times, I feel like I am their mother away from home. They do call me the team mom, which I think is so hilarious. I'm 32 years old. I'm like 10 years older than them and I'm the team mom. One of our players broke a foot and everybody was out of town. I went to Walmart and got him some groceries and brought them back to him. Just little things like that that I think is important being a football wife. It also makes me feel good to help them out.

Getting to Know the Players' Families

For many wives, another rewarding aspect of their lives with a football coach is getting to know the players' families. Sometimes, because many families live in distant states, the wives' contact with them takes place only during recruiting or at occasional games. However, other families live closer and are able to attend many of the games and have a considerable amount of contact with the coaches' wives and families. One wife said that she loves getting to know the players' parents and said: "We are like a big family."

The wives' contacts with families are especially important during the recruits' campus visits. One wife said: "I truly enjoy meeting them especially during the recruiting process. You form a bond with them, and some will be forever." Another wife said: "I help with recruiting and entertaining parents and making them realize that their son is coming to a great place." Heidi also stressed how important she thinks it is for coaches' wives to meet parents during recruiting. She said:

> I think it's really important to have the wives there and to have the kids involved so that the parents coming in with prospective athletes can see that and can feel comfortable about their kids going there even though it's 1,000 miles away from home.

Several respondents described a number of ways in which they work to create relationships with the players' parents and family members. For example:

> I send parents newspaper articles about their son. I take pictures during the season at events and send [them] to parents. I create a unique Christmas card collage for the parents of their sons. I always assure them that our home is always open for their son to come over for a home-cooked meal or just to have a "homey" feeling if they are homesick. My husband also assures the recruiting parents of the same thing in all his talks with them and tells them that his wife takes the freshmen players under her wing to help with their homesickness.

> My husband makes a commitment to those parents, and he tells every single player and their parents that he will be in charge of your child and he will make sure that they stay on the right track. He will make sure they stay out of trouble, and he will take care of them when

they are away from home. I feel like I am an extension of that. I am the coach's wife, and that is also a job for me to handle. I will make sure your child gets a home-cooked meal every once in a while. I will help them if they need something.

The Joy of Winning

As we discussed earlier, the effects of losing games—in the long term and in the short term—can be devastating for the coaches and their families. By the same token, the joy and excitement they experience from a winning season or even from winning a single game in which their team was the underdog are reasons for celebration. Probably half of our online sample mentioned the joy and excitement of winning games. Others talked about the benefits and experiences they enjoy when the team makes it to a bowl game with all the entertainment that's provided for the team, the coaches, and their families.

Other Rewards

Other rewards for the coaches' wives may include good game day parking passes, car allowances, travel to parts of the country they might not otherwise have the opportunity to see, participation in community events, recognition, public admiration and respect, and reduced or free college tuition for themselves and their family members. Many wives enjoy the special events they get to attend and the opportunity to meet many new and interesting people. They enjoy the college atmosphere and living in and raising their children in a college town. Employment at a university often means good benefits and retirement plans.

Several wives who are married to head coaches mentioned a number of extra perks that come with being "the first lady" of football, such as traveling to all away games with the team or often having your own suite at the stadium. Perks may vary with different teams and levels. Some wives may or may not choose to take advantage of these perks, and as we discussed earlier, the head coaches' wives may or may not share these perks with the wives of the assistant coaches. The comments this wife made reflect the feelings of many of our respondents. She said:

> I have always enjoyed the travel, the games, and the fans. I travel to every game and try to help my husband any way I can. I feel being involved—just addressing envelopes or proofreading a letter—helps me be a part of his life. Being the wife of a football coach is not the ideal life, but I enjoy it. I truly believe being a coach's wife is just as much a calling as being a coach. I thought long and hard about the "life" before marrying my husband. I am so proud of him, and I love being allowed to invest in football players, their girlfriends, and other students that come across our paths. I truly don't think we would be as happy anywhere else.

Summary

It's interesting to note that so many of the responses identifying the most rewarding part of being a coach's wife tend to be intangible concepts, and these responses were consistent from wives across all levels. Where "perks" of being a coach's wife, such as going to bowl games or having a game day suite, may not be available at all levels, all coaches' wives (regardless of level) have the opportunity to be proud of their husbands' positive impacts on young men, their successes (that may not always be measured in number of wins), and their love for their jobs. Wives note that they share the football experience with their husbands, taking equal pride in the successes of the young men on past and present teams; developing close relationships with other coaches, players, and the players' families; riding the highs after a win; and commiserating the losses together.

SECTION III

MAKING COACHING MARRIAGES WORK

The third section takes a realistic look at coaching marriages. We discuss the good things about them and things that are difficult. We identify the characteristics of the spouses that contribute to their marital success, and discuss coping strategies and attitudes that the wives have developed to make their marriages work.

10

The Characteristics of a Coaching Marriage

"Our lives are different from individuals' in other professions.
We have learned what it takes to make the marriage work.
It takes commitment, compromise, and love."

—An online respondent

Many Americans say that having a happy marriage is one of the most important—if not the most important—goals in their lives, and numerous studies have shown marriage has many benefits, especially financial, health, and emotional. The more we study the responses from all our participants—the online respondents and those we interviewed—the more compelled we are to try to understand how, in light of the demands of their husbands' job, they could possibly experience the great happiness and satisfaction in their marriages that so many of them report. We want to understand the benefits to these women who for much of the year perform not only the traditional female household and child-rearing responsibilities but also shoulder most of the traditional male tasks in the family. Above all, we wanted to confirm what we initially believed to be the case: that the ways in which spouses treat each other is a major factor in explaining the durability of coaching marriages and the satisfaction that so many of our respondents derive from them.

We use social exchange theory as a way to provide insight into the costs and benefits these wives encounter in their marriages. Briefly, this theory suggests that partners in intimate relationships, such as marriage, are rational beings who make decisions that will minimize their costs and maximize their benefits (Becker, 1991). For example, in traditional (i.e., employed husband, stay-at-home wife) marriages, women make the rational decision to exchange household responsibilities and child rearing for the benefits of a man's earned income (Cherlin, 2004). However, this theory goes on to suggest that when the pain suffered in such a relationship outweighs the pleasure or the benefits of leaving the marriage exceed those of staying in it, then the partner who believes he or she is paying too high a price will abandon it.

The information contained in Chapters 1 and 2 suggests that from a purely rational perspective, the benefits the coaches' wives receive from their marriages are far outweighed by the costs. Diana Tucker (2001), in her study of coaches' wives, concluded: "We are never really given a good idea of what those benefits are beyond her husband's winning record or just the 'privilege' of being married to him." Compared with wives with husbands in less demanding occupations, these women don't enjoy many of the rewards that more conventional marriages bring, and in fact, they also incur responsibility for a number of the obligations that most husbands would generally assume. As one wife pointed out: "It takes a certain type of woman to be a football wife. It is definitely not for everyone. What people don't understand is that it is not a *part* of life—it is a *way* of life." Similarly, a number of wives pointed out that the demands of coaching also deprive the coaches themselves of many of the benefits that husbands and fathers normally obtain from marriage and family life.

Overview

The mean duration of the online respondents' marriage is 13.5 years. The range in number of years married is newly married to 52 years. A little more than 8 percent of husbands and wives had been married previously. The statistics for the wives we interviewed reveal a mean duration of marriage of 19.1 years, with a range of four to 42 years. Only one of the 16 wives had been married previously.

From the online survey, we found that only 25.2 percent of the wives said they were dissatisfied or neither satisfied nor dissatisfied with their marriages. When asked to respond to the statement "My marriage is no longer as important to me as it used to be," 87.9 percent of these respondents disagreed with this statement. We didn't ask specific questions about marital satisfaction of the interviewed wives or about the importance of their marriages to them, but these topics did come up in almost all the interviews as the wives provided an in-depth look at their marriages. The following two questions on the online survey were designed to give us a picture of the respondents' perceptions of the best parts of their marriages as well as the worst parts:

- Please list the characteristics of your marriage you find the most personally satisfying.
- Please list the characteristics of your marriage you find the least personally satisfying.

What Are the Most Satisfying Characteristics of Marriage to a Football Coach?

Four areas emerged: being married to their best friend and feeling loved, appreciated, and cared for; total commitment to each other; humor and fun; and religion and spirituality.

Being Married to Their Best Friend and Feeling Loved, Appreciated, and Cared For

A large number of respondents told us how lucky they felt being married to their best friend. One wife said: "We're best friends; we bring balance to each other." Another said: "My husband is my best friend. I truly enjoy spending time with him; he is very loving and genuine."

Several wives told us they feel very much loved in their marriages. One wife said: "I know that my husband loves me more than anything. I know he would rather be with me than anything else." Others enjoy the feeling of unconditional love and support, and they stress the importance of saying they love each other every day. One wife explained: "Loving him and knowing that he loves me helps a lot. His acknowledging how much I have given up for his dreams is essential." And another one said: "I married a wonderful man, and it has still been a difficult life, but I did agree to it when we exchanged vows. I can't imagine how hard this would be for a woman if she felt her husband did not love her and care about her." A young wife said: "I am awestruck at the depth of our love for each other."

Feeling appreciated and having mutual appreciation for each other is another quality of many coaching marriages. Other features of their relationships that are particularly rewarding to them that fall into this category include a genuine liking for each other, sharing common interests, being attracted to each other, enjoying each other's company, and having a spouse who's thoughtful and attentive to their needs.

Total Commitment to Each Other Through Trust and Respect

Another very positive aspect of the marriages of these coaches' wives is the total commitment the spouses have toward each other and their dedication to the marriage. A study by Stanley, Markman, and Whitton (2002) found that "… a clear and consistent commitment allows both partners to feel secure" in the relationship. Earlier work by Nock (1995) reported that "…wives who believe that their husbands are committed to the marriage respond with greater personal commitment … and express greater marital happiness." Several women mentioned that they and their husbands are committed to staying together through good and bad times. One wife said that her husband's "… commitment to me is undeniable. I know that I am the most important thing in his life."

Other women talked about how they and their husbands are very supportive of each other and that their marriage thrives on mutual respect and admiration. One wife said: "We are both so supportive of each other and celebrate accomplishments together." Being able to depend on each other is also important, as another wife noted: "Knowing that I am the one person my husband can always count on and rely on is important. I have to be his truth and his perspective sometimes." Another wife said: "We are respectful of each other and both derive great pleasure from giving to the other in whatever way possible. He doesn't take me for granted, and I don't take him for granted." Finally, trust was mentioned by several wives as a positive aspect of their marriages. One wife said: "The most important quality that makes our marriage a success is that there is 100 percent trust between us. I completely trust that my husband wants to be with his family as much as he can, even though it's not possible sometimes." Research by Wilcox and Nock (2006) confirms the importance of trust in marriage, saying that it "… makes women happier about the current state of and future prospects for their marriages."

Humor and Fun

Other often-mentioned positive characteristics of coaching marriages are the importance of humor and the ability of the couple to have fun together. Many wives talked about how their husbands made them laugh and how much laughing together means to them. Some even mentioned the importance of also being able to laugh *at* each other. Despite the lack of time together and the constraints imposed on the relationship by the coaching profession, a number of women did mention that they're still able to have fun and enjoy some degree of spontaneity. One wife said: "We have fun and try to be content, even though it's a challenge at times." Others mentioned that despite the difficulties, they've managed to maintain their sense of humor. This comment is interesting: "A sense of humor is important; it makes you love him even when he is pouting like a four-year old." In her work on coaches' wives, Diana Tucker (2001) confirmed the importance of humor, saying: "In order to be a good football coach's wife, it would seem to be imperative that one has humor—the wife is supposed to laugh at her situation instead of getting angry or trying to change it."

Faith and Spirituality

A strong commitment to faith is associated with marital satisfaction (Hughes and Dixon, 2005), and a large number of respondents indicated that their faith and the faith of their husbands are instrumental in their ability to sustain their marriages even when things get tough. A little more than 76 percent of the online respondents said their religion is important or very important to them, and 69.2 percent of them said the same thing about their husbands. One woman said: "I truly believe we have been successful—at marriage and coaching—because God is our first priority. Once you put God in charge, everything else will take care of itself." In fact, 72 percent of the respondents and their husbands are of the same faith, and a number of them talked about the importance to their marriages of a shared spiritual bond and their participation in church activities, prayer, and Bible study together.

What Are the Least Personally Satisfying Characteristics of Marriage to a Football Coach?

Without a doubt, the demands of a football coaching career take a huge toll on the marriage relationship itself. We were able to identify four major aspects of their marriages that our respondents say create the most problems for them: lack of couple time; communication issues; lack of attention, intimacy, and affection; and lack of social life and couple friendships.

Lack of Couple Time

It's very clear from the online survey as well as the interviews that the wives would like to spend much more time with their husbands than they do, and many wives indicated that their husbands felt the same way. Lack of "couple time" was frequently mentioned as the hardest part of their marriages. One online respondent said:

> My husband works six to seven days a week 80 percent of the year. We have little time to do the small things, like go out to dinner, take in a movie, or go shopping on a whim. We cram every spare minute he has free into enjoying only a portion of the things I would be happy doing together.

The respondents mentioned over and over how they have to work hard to make the most of the limited time they do spend together. Several said they purposefully schedule time together, which helps, but it also tends to eliminate any kind of spontaneity in their activities. The small things that husbands and wives are able to do together, which are taken for granted in most marriages, aren't things coaches and their wives can do for much of the year. They have little time to go out to dinner together, go to a movie, or go shopping. For some wives, the inability to spend much time doing things together makes them feel as if they don't have a real partnership. One wife said: "We both have incredibly busy schedules and have to work hard to carve out time to spend together." Another commented that the amount of time they actually get to spend with one another is kind of depressing, although they do try to make up for that when he does have some free time. Sometimes, we were told, it's very difficult for wives to be alone when they see other couples spending time together. Loneliness is an oft-mentioned problem, and maintaining a marriage in which the partners spend so much time apart is extremely hard.

Many of the wives have learned that even though lack of time together is a sore point in their marriage, little benefit is gained from arguing about it because it's not something they have any control over. One wife said it's easier to put it in its place when you consider "[p]eople all over the world have much more demanding and dangerous careers. So, if this is the role I will play for the rest of my life as a coach's wife, then I don't have it so bad. Whenever I hear wives complain about the amount of time their husbands spend at the office, I am quick to remind them that a soldier's wife has it much worse."

If an upside to the lack of time coaching couples are able to spend together exists, it appears to be their ability to make the most of what time they do have. Many of our respondents told us they cherished these times, and in fact, several said they believed their husbands' jobs have actually brought them closer because they appreciate each other more since he's not around very much. Age and length of time in coaching don't necessarily make things any easier. One wife said: "The longer we are married, the harder we work to have those moments together." Those wives who have demanding careers themselves have to work especially hard to carve out time to spend together.

One thing that's important in coping with the coaches' prolonged and frequent absences from home is to have a strong personal relationship with each other to begin with because that makes it much easier to cope with the limited amount of time together. For some wives, the old idea that absence makes the heart grow fonder seems to be true, and other mentioned that reuniting after time apart is wonderful (although that's not always the case, as we will discuss later).

For any couple, the presence of children affects the amount of time they can spend together. But for coaching couples, it's an added strain. Kate, the mother of two young children, said she and her husband have really tried in the past to spend time together, but lately, that hasn't worked out very well, and it's a topic of conversation between them at the moment. She said that before they had children, Thursday night would be the one night they would go out for dinner, but now with the kids' activities, they don't always manage to do that, and if they do, it's no longer couple time but family time.

Our respondents told us that the husbands' attitudes make a big difference. One wife said her husband "… really honors our time together and doesn't have a lot of hobbies that would take away from us." Another said: "Because of the demands of his job, he is more willing to spend as much of his free time with me as he can." The wives' attitudes are also extremely important in coping with so little time with their spouses, and several women told us they try not to think about it very much because when they do figure out the amount of time they actually get to spend with one another, it can be depressing. Others came up with what they see as advantages to the lack of time together. One said not having to make him dinner every night was a definite plus, and another mentioned she looked at football season as her time to do as she wants in the evenings. An online respondent put a positive construction on the limited amount of couple time in her marriage, saying: "Although we do not have as much time together as most couples or as much as we would like, I believe that we appreciate our time more than most, and it really keeps things in perspective." Finally, a veteran wife told us about a year in which her husband was out of the coaching business. She said they went to a lot of things together that they had never been able to do before, and she actually realized that when they retire, they'll be able to enjoy each other even though they had spent 40 some years not being together very much. She told her husband that maybe time apart is the secret to a long marriage.

Communication Issues

It's important to remember that the partners in any marriage must continually define and redefine their relationship through communication. Marriage isn't static, and as we have discussed earlier, it changes in response to many factors. How well couples deal with change in their relationship depends on how well they communicate with each other. Unfortunately, for coaches and their wives, lack of time together inevitably results in difficulties in communication. It appears to us that given their time constraints, coaching couples use communication that's direct, goal focused, and practical because they have little opportunity for any other type of communication. Many wives told us that they're only able to communicate with their husbands late at night for much of the year. The potential for breakdown in communication is especially great at the times during the year when the coaches are subject to the greatest stress. One wife said: "During the season, we get about 10 minutes before bed—if I wait up for him—[and that's] not enough." Several wives also mentioned that their husbands' exhaustion when he's home only adds to this problem, especially as one wife said: "My husband is too tired and worn down to really listen to me. This is especially the case during two-a-days or the season, when his mind is miles away."

In addition, we were told that communication difficulties often mean that the exchange of needed information regarding events and activities can result in misunderstandings when a husband forgets to tell his wife or thinks he's already told her where he'll be or where she needs to be. Many times, especially during the season, the husbands are so distracted that their wives find they have to repeat themselves often, and even then, they aren't sure whether the husbands have actually heard them. One wife said: "I never know if he is coming or going." Ultimately, the long stretches of inadequate time for communication and the strain of long hours and little sleep may result in arguments and fights that most likely would be avoided if they had enough time for discussion.

Although establishing effective communication in a coaching marriage can be perilous, many of our respondents seem to have overcome the difficulties and have passed on their strategies. For example, one wife said: "No matter what has happened that day, we make time for each other just to talk and reconnect—even at midnight." She went on to say: "We always get away for a week together before the season starts for some 'us' time to reconnect." Other wives agree that working on communication every day is important, as is a willingness on the part of both partners to improve the relationship through communication. The importance of listening to each other was stressed many times as well as the need to be direct and open. Many mentioned that they're fortunate they've the ability as a couple to talk to each other even when things are tough.

We don't mean to suggest that successful communication eliminates all arguments or disagreements. In their national study of communication, conflict, and commitment, Stanley et al. (2002) noted that couples who are able to handle conflict constructively create an environment "… that allows for deeper levels of self-disclosure and acceptance of vulnerabilities, which are central aspects of intimacy." One of our older wives pointed out that she and her husband communicate much better now that they've been married for a while and have learned the importance of a lot of give and take. In fact, they've finally learned how to fight. Another said: "We have the ability to put anger or fighting behind us quickly so that we don't ruin what time we do have together." They've learned that destructive communication doesn't create marital satisfaction.

Some women mentioned that their husbands' personalities help to make communication easier. One said that her husband was easygoing and didn't criticize, while another said: "Sometimes, I wish we talked more, but he's not a big talker in general. I think that's why we work: I talk and he listens (most of the time)." A couple of wives stressed the importance of taking a stand sometimes. One said: "I keep him grounded. I listen to him when he needs to vent and put him in his place when he is not looking at both sides when it comes to work." Another noted: "I am not afraid to tell my husband when it becomes too much and he needs to pull back."

Finally, Sarah-Grace, a veteran wife, told this story about the importance of speaking up when she needed to, even though it was a lesson she didn't learn until later:

> [Now] I would tell myself that it is okay not to be strong, it is okay not to feel that you can do it, and it is okay to feel that you need somebody to put their arms around you and say it is going to be okay. … I think that if I had to live my life over again, I would say that it is okay to express displeasure—it is okay to say that is a stinking decision that you made and I'm angry about it. But I didn't. So, I do tell my daughter—and I tell my boys too—it is better to get it on the table and say I feel this way about it.

Lack of Attention, Intimacy, and Affection

Another aspect of the marriage affected by lack of time is the limited attention the wives often receive from their husbands. Several mentioned that especially during the season, they feel as if they're put on the back burner and they're essentially alone for the entire season. Even when the coaches are at home, they're often so exhausted they just want to crash and zone out. A number of wives said that not being the most important thing in their husband's life and always coming in second is very hard. One wife said she understands that the "… marriage doesn't always come first (not that it's not his priority), but obviously, game schedules and recruiting preclude normal activities." Others noted that they know their husbands love them and understand that they make them a priority as much as they can. As one wife put it: "He is very devoted to making our marriage a lasting one, and I believe he does place me above his profession. So far, I have never felt neglected or unloved. …"

Although we didn't specifically ask about their sex lives, a number of respondents mentioned that because of lack of time together and the physical toll coaching takes on their husbands, their sex lives suffer, especially during football season and recruiting. However, others painted a different picture—from the wife who said "The sex is great when I can get it—when he's not too tired or has to get up early" to those who said how great their sex lives were without qualification. And then we heard from the wife who said of her husband: "He can still pull out some romantic home runs." (This last comment caused the authors to wonder if her husband may be in the wrong sport.)

Lack of Social Life and Couple Friendships

In general, married couples enjoy spending time with other couples, but this isn't something that's easy for coaches and their wives to do. Their ability to form and maintain couple friendships is often negatively affected by the hours the husbands spend at work, the time they spend on the road, and their frequent moves. Many of our respondents said they have few if any couple friends because their husbands are never home. One woman said: "We don't have any couple friends we can do things with." Another said: "We have no social life. He falls asleep at 8 p.m. most nights." Even when they do have friends, maintaining the friendships can be difficult because basically the only time they can do things together is during May, June, and July because they're busy with football from August through April. Some wives mentioned that the friendships they have are usually with couples on the athletic and football staff because they don't have the normal weekend time to be with other friends either.

One of the biggest problems in attempting to create friendships is that it's very difficult to get non-coaching couple to understand the limitations the coaches' job places on them and that he isn't choosing football over his family or his social life—he's choosing to meet the requirements of his job. Rachel, the wife of a Division II head coach, told this story:

> We have next door neighbors that we have been best friends with for the past seven years, but they still don't understand the program. The husband called me during spring ball and asked if my husband could come over and help him with something. He still, after all these years, didn't realize that my husband wouldn't be home until 9 or 10 o'clock.

Our respondents report that they've lost couple friendships over the years because of the hours their husbands work. They'd like to go to parties, participate in neighborhood gatherings, or go out to eat with other couples from time to time. Although many of the wives have long since resigned themselves to having to attend social functions alone, it's obvious that this is something they really don't enjoy. Neither do they enjoy having to continually explain to family and friends why it is they're always alone at various events.

Heidi, the 45-year-old wife of a Division I BCS coordinator, is one of the very few respondents who said they have friends as a couple who aren't connected with football. Heidi believes these friendships work for them because football isn't the focus when they get together. She said it's like taking a step away, which is a nice change.

Areas of Conflict

Extensive research by John Gottman and others suggests that how couples resolve conflict is more important than what it is they're arguing about. These writers believe that marital conflict is an important and inevitable part of happy and unhappy marriages (Gottman 1994; Gottman and Krokoff, 1989). Coaching marriages don't exist without conflict but, as is apparent from Figure 10-1, the partners argue surprisingly little, according to the wives. The online survey participants were asked to rank how frequently the issues listed in the table were a concern in their marriage.

Marital Concern	Frequency of Concern				
	Never	*Occasionally*	*Fairly Often*	*Often*	*Very Often*
Money	57 (19.7%)	158 (54.7%)	23 (8.0%)	24 (8.3%)	16 (5.5%)
Couple Time	72 (24.9%)	130 (45.0%)	37 (12.8%)	26 (9.0%)	10 (3.5%)
Family Time	73 (25.3%)	128 (44.3%)	39 (13.5%)	23 (8.0%)	10 (3.5%)
Parenting	81 (28.0%)	145 (50.2%)	22 (7.6%)	10 (3.5%)	8 (2.8%)
Allocation of Household Tasks	77 (27.9%)	134 (49.3%)	30 (12%)	21 (8%)	8 (2.9%)

Figure 10-1. The frequency of "typical" marital concerns

It appears from this table that around half of the wives said that all these topics were occasionally an issue, but only a very small percentage said that they were often or very often problematic. Several wives did talk about financial issues in their responses to other questions. Most of their comments had to do with the difficulty of managing on a coach's salary, particularly when their husbands are assistant coaches. One woman said: "The events that we get to attend related to his career are always fun and, on a coach's salary, sometimes the only events we can attend." Other wives mentioned their husbands' attitudes toward money as being an issue. For example, one woman said that money causes conflict between them because her husband is "so tight." Other comments had to do with the husbands being overly concerned with money or conversely with having no concept of finances and no desire to learn. Finally, several wives found it hard to deal with seeing their husbands not being compensated for their effort and hard work. As one wife said: "The lack of finances does not match the amount of effort and work that coaches do."

An additional question asked the wives to identify any other issues that cause conflict between them and their husbands. One wife wrote:

> We have a lot in common, and we see eye to eye on most things, which is important since he isn't always around when I'm making decisions. We support each other as best we can. We are in it for the long haul, so we work out the challenging situations that our lifestyle presents us with.

The issue of time together has been discussed in depth earlier in this chapter, and parenting and the allocation of household tasks are discussed in other chapters.

Re-Entry

One area of conflict in the marriage that we didn't specifically ask about on the online questionnaire but which the respondents often brought up is the problems that arise when the coaches "re-enter" the family after the season and recruiting, when they've been absent for significant periods of time. In some cases, it takes awhile for everyone in the family to adjust to their presence. Work by Robinson et al. (2001) explains that in these situations, the wife and children may well complain about the father's absence, but when he moves back into the daily life of the family, they also complain about his attempts at integration. Several of the wives we interviewed had much to say on this topic. Justice, the wife of a Division I BCS coach, said:

> But after the first couple of days, you're like, "Okay, you're under my feet. Go do something." I know other wives that are the same way. It's like you have a certain way that your household runs and certain expectations of the children and how things are done and how you coordinate with other wives or parents. When they come home, they screw all that up.

Another wife had this to say:

> When he is gone for long periods of time, everything runs according to my decisions and/or priorities. The kids and I have a groove and a shared understanding of how life and our house rules flow. When my

husband comes back from recruiting or is working less and around more, suddenly I have to check with him before making a decision or consider his needs when they were never an issue before. Invariably, I usually make the decision or plan differently than he would, and we have to go through all sorts or drama to resolve a situation which would have been a nonsituation if he wasn't there.

Some of the wives said that while they welcome assistance in the home when their husbands are working fewer hours in the summer, this can nevertheless create problems too. Kate, the young mother of two small children, said she gets into a routine during the season and gets used to not having his help and then when he's available, it throws her off.

Other problems related to re-entry include the difficulty of having someone tell the wives what to do and jumping in without always knowing everything that has preceded a situation. A number of wives mentioned that they're not sure their husbands really understand and appreciate everything they've done when they weren't around. Problems also exist, some wives noted, when the coaches are home after long absences because they like to be "the good guy" with the children, which often disrupts established rules and routines. Several wives identified what they called a "you and the kids versus him" feeling in the beginning as everyone tries to adapt to his being home again.

A final area of conflict that we identified from the respondents has to do with their extended families. Many of the couples live long distances from one or both sets of parents, and they have the difficulty of trying to decide when they do have a vacation whose family they'll spend the most time visiting. Out-of-town extended family members who come for home games are also sometimes a problem when they want to spend time with the coach but don't understand that the couple needs time together and family time when he finally does get home. Other extended family issues include those also encountered in non-coaching marriages, such as caring for elderly parents or mother-in-law problems.

Coaching Marriages Aren't "One Size Fits All"

As we noted in Chapter 1, the marital experiences of coaches' wives vary on several dimensions. We identified five factors that appear to have the greatest impact: age; life stage; presence and ages of children; husband's division and rank; and whether a wife knew what she was getting into when she married a coach.

Age

It's obvious that the wives' perceptions of their marriages are different according to their ages. For example, many of the younger wives find themselves in traditional marital roles that they never anticipated occupying and which can be sources of frustration.

Kate, who is 39, who has been married for 13 years, and whose husband was a head coach at the time she was interviewed, said she was intrigued by the nature of football coaching, as it creates traditional gender roles and expectations in the coaches' marriages and families. She said that many of her struggles have had to do with the almost 1950s structure of the coaching marriage, which she believes by its very nature relegates the wife to a lesser position in the relationship than that of the husband. She went on to say that to her knowledge, football coaching is the only occupation that has no *spouses,* only *wives.* Although we don't have the data to support this position, we suggest that conflict almost certainly exists for the younger coaches as well as their wives, as they find themselves torn between current expectations of young husbands and fathers and their inability to fulfill them because of the demands of their jobs. Another age-related issue was identified by this older wife, who said:

> It is fine when you are young and the other coaches and their wives are young too. You can do things together, and there is a sort of camaraderie. But when you get older, you have nothing in common with the younger coaches and their wives, and there is no time to develop other friendships because he is gone so much.

Life Stage

In addition to the ages of husbands and wives, research into marital satisfaction suggests that happiness in marriage isn't constant over the course of the marriage but varies according to the life stage of the partners and is directly related to the amount and type of stress accompanying each stage with which the partners have to contend (Glenn, 1991). In most cases, early marriage is a time of excitement and happiness in the relationship. Early parenthood brings great joy too but also stress from lack of sleep, anxiety about adequate parenting skills, and financial worries if the wife's income disappears. Middle- aged parents of teenagers often experience anxiety and stress, and this life stage may also coincide with increasing responsibility for aging or ailing parents and may therefore be detrimental to life satisfaction.

However, one of our respondents believes she and her husband are managing their middle years well. She said: "We enjoy our children and grandchildren beyond measure. We do truly try to work together concerning problem areas, such as being in the sandwich generation." The experiences of wives in long-term marriages in which the children are grown and gone are quite different from the experiences of women with young children still at home. Beth, who's married to a Division I BCS assistant coach, noted how the ages of the children alter the responsibilities of the wives as well as the family logistics. She said that as the mother of teenagers, her obligations to her children are very different from those of a coach's wife with small children.

Older women, having navigated the earlier life stages, may find that their responsibilities are fewer, their attitudes more relaxed, and their satisfaction greater than when they were younger. As one wife said: "After 35 years of marriage, we don't argue much anymore. Had I taken this survey 10 or 20 years ago, the answers would be much different." Earlier research has found that people who have been married for long periods of time are least likely of all age groups to identify specific areas of conflict (Stanley, Markman, and Whitton, 2002). This was confirmed by a veteran wife, who said she and her husband had many more areas of conflict in their earlier years than they do now, but she can no longer remember what they were. She goes on to say that a lot of the problems were caused by immaturity. It's logical to assume that all the life stages, with their attendant responsibilities and stresses as well as their joys and satisfactions, affect the attitudes of individuals toward their marriages as well as toward their partners.

Presence and Ages of Children

The presence and ages of children in the home is a third major factor likely to cause variation in marital satisfaction. How many children are present as well as how old they are determine to a large extent the responsibilities, schedules, and obligations of many of our respondents. In their study of physicians' wives and their marriages, Sotile and Sotile (2004) found that the age of a couple's children affects marital satisfaction for the wives and, in particular, as the children grow older, the wives' levels of marital adjustment increase.

The inability of their father to be as active in the children's lives as everyone in the family would like was frequently mentioned by the coaches' wives as a major difficulty for all concerned. The hours the coaches work during the season and recruiting and the days they spend out of town directly impact the amount of time for which wives with children at home find themselves for all intents and purposes "single parents." Tina, now in her 50s and married to a head coach, remembers how much she wished her husband could have been home more to help with the children when they were young.

The Team's Division and the Husband's Rank

As we discussed in the preceding chapters, the division in which his team is located as well as the husband's rank have a direct impact on the amount of stress and pressure he experiences at work as well as the number of hours he works each week. These factors determine the amount of time he's able to devote to his marriage, which in turn affects the marital experiences of his wife.

Beth, age 46, told us that her husband has coached in all divisions at one time or another. At the Division II level, she said, "… there wasn't a lot of pressure, and we were peons, so to speak, in the coaching profession." The biggest pressure, she noted, was financial because her husband didn't make much money. As her husband moved up the ladder and coached at the Division I FCS level, Beth said there still wasn't a lot of pressure, but once they hit Division I BCS, the pressure was "just crazy" and the expectations were so much greater. A younger wife said: "I realize my husband and I have only been married a short time, but he is a wonderful husband, and I completely encourage his involvement with the football program. That being said, if he were a Division I coach, I might feel differently about the lifestyle." However, the wives' experiences in the lower divisions, especially Division III, aren't always easy. An online respondent said:

> I think you need to remember the DIII wives in a special study. I have "coached" at all levels of coaching, and trust me, *nobody* works harder for less money than DIII coaches and their wives. The hours away are the same as DI, *but* the pay is not. What other level has coaches mixing Gatorade® before a game because the trainers are busy taping? I have much more respect for DIII wives and coaches than those at any other level.

Did the Wives Know What They Were Getting Into When They Married?

The final factor we believe contributes to the wives' happiness and satisfaction in their marriages is whether they knew what they were getting into when they married because this prior knowledge has a large impact on the wives' expectations of the marriage. If they're aware of the demands of their husbands' career on their relationship, their expectations will be realistic and the potential for disappointment, resentment, and unhappiness diminished.

As long ago as 1973, Ralph Sabock, in his book *The Coach,* said:

> Most of the unhappiness that occurs with coaches' wives arises because they never really understood what is involved in coaching and what kind of demands this profession makes on the coach and the family. It takes a special kind of wife to cope with this. ..."

Is that still the case almost 40 years later? Several of our wives' comments seem to indicate that not much has changed. An online respondent said she found being married to a coach especially hard in the early years because she knew nothing. Other participants mentioned how in the beginning, it was difficult for them to become accustomed to many aspects of life with a football coach, but with time, they learned to deal with it. Sarah-Grace, a veteran wife, recalled her experiences during her husband's first football season, when he would leave the house at 6:30 a.m. and be lucky to be home by 10 p.m. She said it took her about three weeks to make peace with the situation, and she finally thought: "If this is what it's going to be, I might as well realize that it is what it is and find a way to fill my day without depending on him." Similarly, an online respondent said:

> I sure wish that someone had told me what life would be like before I became a coach's wife. It wouldn't have changed whether I married him or not, but it would have prepared me to get more involved in my own interests and expect less help with the house and kids during the season. It seems so obvious now, but I wasn't prepared for it.

On the other hand, several others mentioned that knowing what the life of a football coach was like beforehand was really important in their ability to accept and adapt to the absences, the lack of time together, and the other disadvantages that can make their lives difficult. A number of our respondents mentioned that their fathers had been football coaches, and they knew from growing up what their lives were going to be like, but they did it anyway. The husband of one of the wives in our study had a football coach for a father, and this wife said that her mother-in-law was a mine of information and gave her a valuable piece of advice before she got married: "Your life with a football coach won't be easy, and there will be days when you could lay naked on the driveway and he will drive right over you." Another respondent told us she believes she enjoys being a coach's wife as much as she does because she was a coach's kid. She knew what to expect as far as time away and the disruption of family time are concerned.

A few women did tell us that if they had known what they were getting into, they probably wouldn't have married their husbands. The following remark is typical of this group: "I married my husband before going through an entire season. If I had known all the hours involved with this occupation, I may not have married him." Another said that if she had to do it over again, she's not sure she would because she's not sure she's cut out to be the wife of a football coach—she's not sure that it's worth it.

It's important to note that in addition to the influences we have just discussed, the marriages of football coaches and their wives, like marriages in general, are also affected in other ways. For example, knowledge of another person is always limited, and husbands and wives may not always reveal the more problematic aspects of their lives or personalities until after the wedding. In addition, people change over time. Both partners will be different in 10, 20, or 30 years and may experience difficulties because of this that they couldn't have anticipated at the outset. Finally, people's needs and interests change over time. None of these changes can be predicted. We don't know who or what will change nor how extensively; we simply know that almost every marriage experiences change.

Personal Qualities That Make the Marriage Work

In addition to asking our respondents about the positive and negative aspects of being married to a football coach, we asked the wives to tell us which of their personal qualities made it possible for them to succeed as coaches' wives. We also asked them to list the five words or phrases they believe best described the personal qualities of their husband that they thought were most helpful in maintaining their marriages. Overwhelmingly, the words and phrases they chose to describe their husbands were positive. Only a few used negative terms.

However, we have no way to know for sure if the words and phrases chosen by the wives to describe their husbands are accurate reflections of their feelings because two things may be at work here. First, many of our respondents completed the questionnaires after the football season had ended and some even after recruiting was over. As one wife pointed out: "My answers might have been quite different had I completed this questionnaire during football season." Second, loyalty in many forms is an integral part of football; loyalty to the school, loyalty to the team, loyalty to the head coach, and loyalty to one's husband are all behaviors that the wives of football coaches are expected to display. Perhaps this loyalty has become such a part of the way in which these wives think that speaking about their husbands only in positive terms has carried over into the responses to this particular question.

What Are the Qualities of the Wives That Enable Them to Have Successful Marriages?

The qualities mentioned most often by the online respondents as well as the wives we interviewed were independence, self-confidence, and self-sufficiency, which we'll discuss in depth in Chapter 11. Large numbers also mentioned their organizational and management skills, which we already addressed in Chapter 6. The remaining frequently mentioned qualities were patience and understanding. Many respondents believe these qualities contribute to the quality of their marriages, even though they're sometimes difficult to maintain. One wife told us: "Years of playing the good, patient, and understanding wife just wore me out. I hated his job and our life. My faith in God got me through that horrible time."

What Are the Husbands' Qualities?

The husbands' top 10 qualities identified by our respondents are:
- Hardworking
- Loving
- Caring
- Loyal
- Dedicated
- Honest
- Passionate
- Intelligent
- Strong
- Family oriented

It's not surprising that being a hard worker is the number one quality identified by the wives, but what did surprise us was that in second and third place are loving and caring, respectively. These are expressive (having to do with feelings and emotions) qualities not traditionally associated with men in general and especially not in a profession in which coaches are expected to be competitive, driven, forceful, and, above all, masculine. Almost 200 times on the online survey, the wives used such words as caring, compassionate, considerate, loving, sensitive, and understanding to describe their husbands. Wilcox and Nock (2006) suggested that men's marital emotion work is very important in determining marital quality, especially when other sources of marital satisfaction have declined. The fact that these coaches meet the emotional needs of their wives may go a long way toward compensating for their physical absence and other issues that the wives report. We suggest this is a major contributing factor to the wives' happiness and willingness to remain in their marriages.

One wife commented on the importance of the support she gets from her husband. She said:

> He supports me in whatever I want to do. (I think he feels he owes me because of all the craziness his career puts on me—and he does owe me.) He and his nutso job keep me on my toes, ready for action. His job has made me enjoy the good times when we have them because the good times (i.e., winning seasons) don't last forever.

Many wives said their husbands are men of integrity, and more than 170 times, such words as honest, loyal, sincere, and dependable were used. As far as job-related qualities are concerned, in addition to their being hardworking, the wives also said they're driven, intense, motivated, organized, and passionate about what they do. One woman said this about her husband: "It doesn't matter if my husband is a college football coach, investment banker, or even a lawyer. I know that he would spend just as much time away from home. It's who he is. He gives 100 percent of himself in everything he does."

The Synergy of Husbands' and Wives' Qualities

The question, then, is how do the qualities of the wives and husbands complement each other and allow these marriages to work as well as they do? Could the husbands do their jobs without the support of their independent, competent, and endlessly patient wives? It seems doubtful—at least if they want to have any kind of home life at all. Do the coaches' softer sides make up for their time away from home, their absence from family and social situations, and their exhaustion and fatigue when they're home? Almost certainly, they do. It's much easier for people in any relationship to accept, tolerate, and adapt to its disadvantages when they care for the other person. Knowing they're loved by their husbands, realizing that the coaches would rather spend time with them if they could, and being aware of their importance in the coaches' lives seem to make it possible for coaches' wives to deal with the more negative aspects of their marriages. In addition to personal qualities that work well together, the spouses' sharing of common goals and visions seem to be part of what makes these marriages work. We talked about this in detail in Chapter 9.

Summary

At the beginning of this chapter, we asked why coaches' wives stay in relationships that seem to have more costs than benefits for them. The least satisfying characteristics (costs) of a coaching marriage our respondents identified center around circumstances and situations brought about by the long hours that coaches must work. Despite their acknowledgment of the "worst" aspects of the marriages, the majority of the wives in our study appear to be devoted to their husbands. They recognize the personal qualities of themselves and their husbands that contribute to the success of their marriages, and many expressed how much they love their husbands and how much they also admire them.

11

When in Doubt—Punt!
(and Other Coping Strategies)

From what we've written so far, it's clear to see that wives of football coaches frequently experience problems or stress in several major areas, including money, parenting, allocation of household and family responsibilities, life in the public eye, moving, the fear of losing, and the lack of time their husbands are able to spend with them and their children. We've identified several strategies that the wives in our study use for coping with these issues, including being flexible, planning, establishing and maintaining support systems, learning to be independent, accepting and learning to live with the way their lives are, and taking care of themselves. The lines between these strategies aren't always clear, and several of them overlap, which is part of the reason they work so well. Together, they form a web of coping strategies.

The Importance of Flexibility

The coaches' wives recognize the importance of flexibility (in this case, flexibility means the ability to respond and adapt to change) as far as any expectations for routine and normalcy in their lives are concerned. A veteran wife said: "You just kind of roll with it, I guess. Things change and you have to change along with them." Another told us: "You have to live in the moment of where you are." These wives know that plans can change without notice and that nothing, including holiday traditions or family celebrations of birthdays and anniversaries, is immune. As one of our respondents noted: "In this profession, you can't put too much emphasis on one day or somebody is going to be disappointed." Another said: "You kind of have to be flexible … and you have to love what they do because if you don't … if you don't like football and what he is doing, I don't know how it's ever going to work. It's just a different life."

Some of our respondents told us they were lucky because they were flexible by nature or were blessed with the ability to be able to change plans "at the drop of a hat." Others are more like veteran coach's wife Dianna Coker, who was quoted as saying:

> … [I]n the beginning I didn't like it [football] because it took too much time away from me and my family life. But then I thought wait a minute, this something that he loves to do and I cannot ask him not to do it, so I've got to be creative enough to fit into the process. (Kaufman, 2006)

A number of wives in our study mentioned that for them to cope with the hours and demands of their husbands' careers, it was important to have occupations with flexible hours or employers who understand the nature of their lives, although they noted that these weren't always easy to find. Ann has been lucky in that respect:

> I was very fortunate to have a job where I worked Monday through Thursday from 8:30 to 1:30 and I was off on Fridays. I was able to travel with the team and was able to always be at their events. Now that we've moved, I'm going to be able to do all the billing and stuff through the computer. … The people I've worked with have always been football fans. They always kind of understood that the football coach has such a different lifestyle.

And Heidi, an accountant, said:

> I don't think I could work full time and be able to do everything that I am able to do with the kids and the running. … I can come and go, and that is where the flexibility of my job makes it ideal. If I had an 8 to 5 job where I could not leave, I couldn't have the job. … That is one of the factors when I would go to look for a job: How much flexibility would I have?

Leslie told us she was always grateful that the schools where she has taught were good about letting her resign in December or January—whenever her husband moved on to new positions. Our respondents also noted several other areas in which they needed to be flexible. For example, Julie said it was especially important to be flexible in spending habits, especially in the early years. She said: "You just cut back. You just don't have a new car every two or three or four or five years. It lasts until it drops on the sidewalk." According to Tina, moving forces wives to be more adaptable and flexible than they might otherwise be. Learning to be flexible is an ongoing process, according to Ann, who said: "I can't say we've had 25 years of wonderful times because it's been pretty rough on occasion. But he's gotten older, and I've learned and he's learned, and we're going to have to keep working at it." Several wives pointed out that even for those who are flexible by nature or have learned to be flexible, this isn't enough by itself. They need to have a plan whenever possible.

Strategic Planning

Coaches' wives know the importance of strategic planning (a designed plan to accomplish a specific purpose) even while they're aware that the most carefully crafted plans may be sidetracked and derailed at the last minute. They have game plans, they're goal driven, and many times, they see themselves on the offensive or defensive line as they protect and support their husbands. They think carefully about when, how, and why to do things—from planning ways for their children to have "Dad contact" during the football season to moving, family celebrations, attending games, and much more. The coaches' wives know that family weddings and other celebrations have to be arranged to accommodate the coach's schedule or he probably won't be able to attend. Some of the strategies we've learned about include one huge family celebration in the summer for all birthdays and anniversaries and scheduling the children's weddings for the few times in the year the coach is available. One wife, whose three children were married in the same year, said:

> Our oldest got married during spring break in Jamaica. Our middle daughter did July in Missouri, and our son got married at Disney World right after Signing Day [February]. All three of them knew that was their only chance.

This planning can even extend to the birth of children. As mentioned earlier, several wives planned caesarian sections so their husbands could be at the birth. One of our online respondents talked about the planning strategy that works in her marriage. She said: "We give each other freedom to do what is important to us. I support my husband in what he does, but I have not chosen to give up my life just to be at his side at all times." Another online respondent said the strategy that works best for them is for her to take the lead in paying the bills, cleaning the house, cooking meals, and organizing any family functions so that when her husband comes home from work, all he is expected to do is listen to and read with their sons and put them to bed.

Support Systems

The wives in our study are adept at creating and maintaining support systems (people or resources that provide reliable assistance and strength when needed) wherever they happen to be. One of our online wives said this is easy for her because she has an outgoing personality that allows her to create her own support group whenever they move. Included in these systems are family members, faith and churches, other coaches' wives, and friends.

Family Members

As we mentioned earlier, one of the most difficult aspects of the coaching life for many of our wives, especially those with young children, is being away from their families.

The coaches and their families often miss out on family reunions, weddings, and even funerals. The wives hate that their children aren't able to see their grandparents and other relatives on a regular basis. In some cases, the grandparents are older or in ill health and can't travel long distances to see the grandchildren.

However, despite the distance separating them, many still rely on their family members for support. For example, Marissa said: "My mom is my best friend. My family will make an effort—they will come down to at least one game a year. During the season, we actually see our family a lot." Claire talks to her parents every day, and Jamie is lucky that her family isn't too far away. She said:

> We're both from the next state over, so they're close. And they try to get to most of the games. … They're very supportive, and now, during two-a-days my mom is coming next week to help me out. They know how many hours my husband puts in, and they are very supportive with that. I have two sisters, and they come to a lot of games too. We try to make a family weekend out of it. I can vent to my sisters. I don't necessarily vent to my mom because then she'll worry too much. But to my sisters, I usually do. By the end of two-a-days, I'm ready to.

In addition to the moral support Jamie receives, having a father not too far away can also be a practical asset. She went on to say:

> We just got a dishwasher today, and they wouldn't put it in and said it's up to my husband to put it in, so I'm like, "Huh?" I called my dad and said, "Can you come up some weekend and put our dishwasher in?" because I just know he [my husband] doesn't have time to do it.

At the time of her interview, Heidi was living in the same town as her mother and brother. She said: "My mother is very active and helps me a lot, which has been great living that close. I have a brother who lives here in town, and he helps me a lot actually. … I see my mother at least on a weekly basis." Beth's mother-in-law was an important resource for her. She said: "My husband's dad was a coach, and his mom, who has been dead for five years, was a coach's wife, and she was really instrumental in bringing me up in the profession." Tina, whose own parents are deceased, has also been blessed with support from her in-laws:

> My in-laws are like my parents. I'm very close to them, and, yes, they are very involved. … I'm very close to my mother-in-law—closer than a few of her own daughters. I'll confide in my mother-in-law. She's a great one to vent to because she really sympathizes with us.

Surprisingly, given the hectic schedule of most of their husbands, some wives mentioned they relied on them for support. Michaela said: "My husband I talk a lot, which is really important to me. He's so supportive, and he always knows the right thing to say. … When I'm anxious … he's really good at helping me calm down."

In addition, a number of the older wives mentioned that they rely on their adult children for support when they need someone to talk to.

Friends

Friends are also an important source of support for many wives. Most wives actually have two types of friends: those who are also coaches' wives and those who have nothing to do with football. Both kinds of friends are important. Beth said:

> But you learn to find that family—those people that you can count on. For me, it made me mature a lot. I became better at judging people— became better at forming relationships where you knew I will take care of your kids and do anything and they would do the same. I have some really, really deep relationships I probably would have not had in my life if I had not been a coach's wife. … Some of these friendships are with other coaches' wives, but some are not. I found too that it wasn't healthy to be so consumed by the profession. You need to have friends outside of coaching.

Several wives agree with Beth that it's really useful to have friends outside of football. Tina said: "I like to always have at least one friend that's not involved with football. … Of course, most of my good friends are involved in football, and it's good to have them too because they really know what you're going through. …" Pam said: "I have a really good friend that lives about a half hour away from here now and I talk to her quite a bit. She's the one that I can just lay it all out there for. Everybody needs a friend like that, I think." Julie told us that most of her friends have been outside of the profession, but she didn't know if that was something she deliberately did or if it just ended up that way. Heidi also likes having friends not connected to football. She said: "So, when we are with those friends, it is not all about football, and it is like taking a step away and talking or doing or just meeting and things that aren't football related. It is a nice change." She went on to say:

> I have a great support group as far as my friends, and I talk a lot. I have a couple of really, really close friends that I let off steam with, and we just cry and say whatever is upsetting us, and it seems to help just to verbalize it. … I think I tend to kind of talk things out with one or two of my really close friends that know me and know our situation and who I trust, and by the time I kind of work through it, it doesn't seem as bad as what it really was.

Claire has a very good girlfriend in another state who she talks to all the time, and Beth finds a lot of camaraderie through her work. For young moms who are more confined to the house, having friends is especially important. Several wives mentioned that they tend to develop friendships with women their own age and/or women with children in the same age group as their own. Marissa, the mother of four small boys, told us about her friends:

In the moms' group I belong to, we have a moms' night out once a month. I also have lots of playdates with friends, where we meet at each other's houses and we let the kids play, and we sit and relax and have a cup of coffee. My main thing is to have adult time during the day and not just kid time.

As we discussed in Chapter 4, the friendship and support of other coaches' wives is invaluable, even for those wives who also have strong non-football friendships and family support.

Church and Faith

For many of our wives, their churches and their faith are valuable sources of support. In her article "Honored to Serve," Margaret Moore (2008) wrote that she found that making faith her top priority has sustained her when things were bad in her husband's career. She said that even in a year when his contract was up for renewal and the team had to win or else, her faith allowed her to have more peace than she had ever had before. These sentiments were echoed by many of our wives—online and in interviews. One wife said that her faith is her most important resource because "God never changes." Another mentioned: "You just know that God has a plan for everything." A third noted: "I really do have faith that the Lord will take us wherever we need to be." Leslie sees her faith as an important means of dealing with anxiety. She said: "God has a plan, and to have faith in what he is doing is more important than worrying about what you can or can't do because ultimately, his hands are going to be on it and you are going to be doing what he wants you to do anyway, so you really can't worry about it."

Sarah-Grace sees the constancy of God as a way of coping with what she calls "the fickle existence" of coaching with its highs and lows. She said she taught her children that however unstable their lives may be, they can never move away from God and that he goes with them everywhere. Ann, whose husband had experienced some health issues, talked about the importance of faith for them. She said:

> My faith is important to me—all through his sickness. … I mean, when he got sick and everything, we really looked to God. And it's really changed our lives. … And I believe it's helping with his coaching career. You know, to have faith in God and to let him handle things, and I think that's helped a lot.

A number of other wives mentioned the strong faith of their husbands as being a source of support for the entire family. Marissa said: "I am so happy that I do have a husband who has strong beliefs and that we can talk about it and discuss it." Several wives told us that one of the first things they do when they move is to find a church. Rachel mentioned that her church offers a mom's weekend retreat, which has been very helpful to her, and Beth's church membership and involvement in the congregation has been a big help in making friends in a new place.

The Importance of Independence

Although we briefly mentioned independence (the ability to function with little or no outside help; self-sufficiency) in Chapter 11 as it contributes to the success of coaching marriages, it seems more important to include a detailed discussion here as a coping strategy. From the start of this project, it was obvious to us that the coaches' wives are fiercely independent and proud of it. They're willing and able to do many things on their own and are confident in their abilities. Mostly, they see little option. As one wife put it: "If I were a dependent woman who required a lot of attention and time, there is absolutely no way our marriage could survive."

Many wives indicated to us that they were not by nature independent people but have had to learn to be so to cope with the vagaries of their lives. For example, Catherine, the young wife of a Division I BCS assistant coach, said: "I think if you're not independent in this business, you learn to be or it's not going to work—that and not being high maintenance. So, you learn to be independent. You learn that that's okay." It may not be easy in the beginning, but eventually, most of our respondents said becoming independent is possible. For example, one wife said: "I have learned to be strong and fairly independent in order to enjoy our life together and make it possible for my husband to do his job without added distractions at home. I am proud of the way I have grown in this business; it wasn't easy in the beginning."

Another wife said that being married to a football coach "[f]orced me to grow up and become more independent than I would have otherwise. I needed to develop my own goals, dreams, and aspirations." That's also the case for this wife:

> I think it takes an independent, strong woman to be a coach's wife. I'm still striving for that strength. I'm not the type of wife that lives and breathes his job, and my husband and I believe that this is part of what makes our marriage work. I have become independent, and I think he respects that.

Some of the wives were proud of the fact that they were "low maintenance" and saw this as an important factor in their ability to survive and flourish. They believe that their self-sufficiency is a quality that helps their marriages succeed. Catherine, the wife of a Division I BCS assistant coach, told us:

> I think the things that other women see as disadvantages I probably see as advantages. I am very self-sufficient. … I don't think I could be married to someone who came home at five every day and was always under my feet and needing constant attention. I think it would drive me insane. … I'm not one of those women who went from Mom or Dad's house straight to college and always had someone. I lived on my own more than once—no roommate. It doesn't bother me to be alone.

And Claire said:

I'm not needy. I don't bother him for anything at work. He knows that I'm just going to fix whatever it is and do whatever is necessary to take care of it.

Lesley, the wife of a Division I FCS coach at the time of her interview noted: "You really need to be your own person and be satisfied with that and not depend on your husband to always be there because he might not be. You have to be willing to be happy being yourself." Other wives told us that they've seen wives who aren't independent and it's not good. Justice said: "Sometimes, you see one of the coaches marry someone and you go, 'I don't know if she's going to make it.' Because it's such a different profession that you're like, 'I don't think she's self-sufficient enough to make it.'" An online response describes these same concerns with a happy ending:

I mean, there's been one [wife] that I would have thought, "Wow, does she know what she is getting into?" She was one of those very needy kinds of people who can't change a lightbulb without him, but she morphed into a coach's wife OK.

Jamie, the young mother of two small children, said: "I would say, for the most part, you have to be an independent person because otherwise nothing would get done. You'd sit home all day by yourself, and you know you just kind of go out and do things that you have to do." Having their own interests is essential to their ability to be independent, according to several wives. Problems could surface, according to Pam, if her life revolved around when her husband was going to be home and how much time he's spending away. Tina said the same thing: "You have to have interests—your own interests—or else you'll go crazy. If you're the type that's going to sit waiting for your husband to get home, you're in trouble. ... You definitely can't be the type that's going to be mad when he's not home." One wife said: "A wife needs to be independent. She needs her own interests and can lose her identity if she is just the coach's wife."

Diana Tucker (2001) noted that independence in coaches' wives isn't always consistent. For example, she said that the wife must lead the family and be independent when the husband isn't around but must then follow him wherever he wants to go. She sees football coaches' wives as being "constantly asked to change from being independent to being dependent and then back again."

However, the question that remains is which came first? Perhaps those who were independent by nature appealed to some coaches as future wives because they knew that dependent or needy women wouldn't survive and, therefore, they didn't "make the cut." For those women, their independence made it possible for them to thrive in a coaching marriage from the beginning. However, others told us that being married to a coach forced them to become independent. We have evidence to support both positions. Rachel, a Division II head coach's wife, said her independence "… is ingrained from growing up. I don't need to be entertained. I can go and find my own entertainment." This is also true for Marissa, who said:

I do everything. I know how to change a tire. I could probably change my own oil if I wanted to. I can fix just about anything in the house. I grew up where you do it yourself—anything in our house from laundry to dishes to fixing things. I put our fence up in our backyard. I stained and painted everything on the house outside.

Kate believes being older when she married was useful. She said:

I was already 27, so I was used to being very independent. I thought of it like, "Well, this guy's going to be busy a lot, so that means I'm going to need to be very independent." Well, I am now, so that's fine. No big deal. But actually, that first year, I was miserable. I thought, "Well, independence is really lonely."

Although they acknowledge that being independent is a valuable asset for coaches' wives, some of them say when they look back on things, they think it might have been better not to have been so self-sufficient. One wife told us:

I had a miscarriage but didn't feel as though I could call my husband at work—it was so ridiculous, and I think back on it, and I think, "My gosh, how silly"—so I called two of the other assistant wives to help me.

Although some wives are proud that they are or have learned to be independent, they're not always happy about it. Kate said:

I don't like being alone as much as I thought I was okay with it. I think I'm more confident and strong, and I can handle it. I think it takes a tough woman and being able to kind of advocate for yourself and be smart enough and aware enough to not get bullied once someone figures out you're the decision maker.

Jamie said:

Even though I'm okay to do things by myself, there are a lot of times you don't want to do things by yourself, but you just have to. I would say for the most part, you have to be an independent person because otherwise, nothing would get done.

Acceptance and Learning to Deal With Life the Way It Is

It's quite clear from our respondents that acceptance (the ability to deal with reality) is essential to the survival of some of these wives and to the maintenance of the sanity of others. Making peace with the life and schedule of the coaches is a key factor, as is an understanding of the priority the team will often take over the marriage and family. One wife said: "It is not going to get any better; it's really about accepting and understanding." Another said: "You need to realize that it is never going to be 50/50." The wives learn early on that living in the public eye, moving, and single parenting are facts of life and nonnegotiable, and their acceptance of this helps them to cope and adjust. One wife notes that wives "… need to accept where you are going and enjoy it." A veteran wife said emphatically: "It is what it is. It is what you make of it. It's not just a job but a way of life." Another older wife said: "But it could all change tomorrow. … That is one thing you learn about football—life is only what it is at the moment."

The earlier in the marriage that wives accept the reality of their circumstances, the better it is. Rachel said:

> It's not going to get any better. Being the one that truly is running the household, it is always going to be that way and to accept that early on rather than being resentful and thinking, "Well, he should be home, and he should be here to do this, and he should be here when we eat supper." I think that is what it takes, and I won't say that I am totally fine with it all because there are times when I'm like, "Can you just come home and eat with us as a family one night? Could you?" It really is about accepting and understanding the schedule and adapting to it.

Heidi echoed those sentiments:

> I'm just so used to the hours. I knew about that from the get-go. I never had high expectations. I never have and I probably never will. … I just knew from the get-go that is how it was going to be—that there were going to be a lot of hours away. … In this profession, you have to look at it this way. You can't look at it any other way.

Marissa believes that prior to the marriage is the time to come to terms with the realities of life as a coach's wife. She said:

> You have to have that conversation before you say "I do" because if you don't, you might come across problems, and I think that is where some marriages do fail. … They don't have those conversations before.

An online respondent explained how she looks at things:

> Seriously, since the first year of our marriage, I have adopted the philosophy of trying to never have many expectations of my husband. Then, I am not waiting for him to get home, easily disappointed, etc.

And another online wife said:

> Understanding that coaching is not a 9 to 5 job and that game day is just the end of the week and the beginning of the next week. Also, being aware that the off-season is not any easier than the season work wise, and it seems half the time that the time coaches devote actually increases in the off-season.

In her interview, Ann told us:

> I don't think I could be married to him right now if it was an 8 to 5 job because you just get used to the lifestyle. It's hard at the beginning, but you know there are a lot of times when he's gone and then he's home in the summer, and you wonder, "When are you going back to work?" You get used to him not being around.

Jamie said:

> As a football wife, I think you have to live for your husband's job and just accept that because there is nothing you can really do about it. They have to put in the long hours.

Some wives don't stop at simply accepting the limits and disadvantages of their husbands' careers but put a positive spin on things. This is especially true of some of the younger wives we interviewed. For example, Marissa said:

> I feel like I'm the only one who enjoys going to a lot of the events that you do with the university. For me, it's time we have together. … This is our chance to go and spend some time together and enjoy some quality time.

And Michaela noted:

> I just try really hard to be positive about everything that happens because I think there are so many worse things that could happen in the world, and we are really, really blessed to be here and be with each other.

Catherine had a similar outlook. She said:

> There are numerous other occupations in our country that are just as demanding. They really are—whether you're working on Wall Street or you're an attorney. I don't know if the longevity or the guarantee of the job is the same because this can be very quick. A quick climb up and a quick climb down.

After several difficult years, Kate said:

> In the early years, I wanted to know, "Why can't you do that? Why aren't you here for that? "I really struggled with that. I thought I would have more of a 50-50 partner in our home life—that somehow that stuff would get taken care of, and it didn't. I would say not to take it all so seriously—to just enjoy the ride. It's kind of neat. It's kind of fun and to really focus on the good and not get so hung up on the hard parts.

Taking Care of Themselves

While many of our respondents were quick to recognize the importance of taking time for themselves, in reality, this was something that few of them were actually able to accomplish, especially those with children at home and especially during the football season and recruiting. They pointed out that after doing all the things involved in running the family and household, working at their occupations, and doing those tasks their husbands would normally do if he were home to do them, there was little time and energy left over at the end of the day to indulge in anything much for their own enjoyment. Several wives did mention that they've finally learned the importance of making time for themselves. Jamie, the mother of two small children, stressed this. She said:

> I have learned that I have to make time for myself. I'll just get a babysitter. Like today, I sent the kids to daycare all day, so then I could get things done around the house or I could go shopping and do things like that. This summer, I sent them one day a week, so then I have that day to do things. Then, I don't feel so backed up.

Tina, a veteran wife, told us that the best advice she would give to younger wives would be: "Take better care of yourself. Make time for yourself even with kids. Learn to say no. You know, you have to stop and smell the roses." Some of our respondents have come up with some strategies to make sure they do have some downtime. For example, a couple of wives told us they have a particular spot in their house where they go when the need to recharge their batteries or escape from the family for a bit. Claire has an office downstairs in the house that she called "my spot." Rachel has one too. She said: "When I get home from work, I can just sit in my favorite chair in the living room where it is quiet and I can just sit and read the paper or read the mail—just to take a few minutes to unwind." Others, like Marissa, make sure they have a little time to themselves. She said: "First thing in the morning, I've got about a half hour of just quiet, calm time, and that is usually my favorite time of day."

Other wives mentioned that they indulge in what one of them called "guilty pleasures," which include such activities as pedicures, reading, watching their favorite TV shows, and shopping. Heidi enjoys her nightly bath and said: "Just before I go to bed at night, I take a bath every night—a hot tub bath. … It has always been my time where I am by myself, it is quiet, and no one is asking me to do anything, and it is a ritual—every night. I have to take a bath, and that is my alone time."

Preserving their own identity is extremely important for many wives. Sarah-Grace said: "I told my husband that I'm going to quit telling people what you do. I'm going to just tell them that you work for the university … because I want to be interesting for who I am. I'm proud of you and I'm proud of what you do, but I'm a person in my own right." Julie also takes steps to remain anonymous to be able to just be who she is. She also keeps herself busy as a way of coping with her husband's absence: "I seem to find things to do. I can always cook. I can always bake. I can always go for a long walk. I meet friends here. I knit. I do a lot of reading. … I seem to keep busy. I enjoy my time alone."

Other ways in which our respondents take care of themselves include exercising, reading, and communicating with family and friends. A number of the wives discussed the importance of maintaining balance in their lives and keeping things in perspective. Kate, a young mother, said: "I think the biggest thing that can help him and our family is me finding my own balance and a daily life routine that works for me." Lesley told us:

> Usually, if something is not going well in my life, I try to listen and hear about somebody else's life that is not good, and I try to help them. That makes me feel better—to do something for somebody else. There is always something worse going on in someone's life than is going on in ours. I try to focus on other things.

And Sarah-Grace, a teacher, said:

> Because of what I do for a living and what I deal with on a daily basis where people are fighting for their lives, it was very easy to keep it in perspective—the significance of a job that might not work out as compared to the significance of a life that might not survive.

Summary

The strategies used by wives in our survey have enabled them to cope with the challenges of their lives as coaches' wives. Responses overwhelmingly point out that for the coaching marriage and the coaching wife to survive, she must be flexible and independent.

It's important for the wives to make plans for "husband time," "family time," and "Dad time" within the time constraints that coaches face as well as finding some "me time" for themselves. Support systems are essential regardless of who or what comprises the system, and the sooner these systems are established, the better. Faith plays an important role in the lives of coaches' wives. Many are convinced that God has a plan for their lives and feel that job opportunities, hirings, firings, and moves are all part of this plan.

Many wives mention that they must come to a place of acceptance with the coaching lifestyle—an "it is what it is" mentality—and that they choose to see the positives of this often chaotic life. This last sentiment will be prevalent in some of the parting words found in our next chapter.

SECTION IV

THE FINAL SCORE

The last chapter of this book reflects the final words of the wives. Toward the end of each interview, we asked the wives if they had anything they wanted the public to know about them, if they had something they'd like to say to the schools that employ their husbands, and what advice they might give to younger wives or to their "younger selves," if that were possible. The online respondents were asked in the final question if they'd like to say something that hadn't already been covered. Chapter 12 is based on their responses to all these questions.

12

Parting Words From the Wives

Given one last chance to discuss their lives as football coaches' wives, respondents took the opportunity to reiterate points that had been made throughout the book as well as add a few tidbits that hadn't already been addressed.

What the Coaches' Wives Want the Public to Know

Coaching Isn't a Part-Time Job

A number of the respondents were anxious to let people know that football coaching isn't a part-time job, as many people seem to believe, and that the hours their husband work are horrendous. Several wives mentioned that so many people have absolutely no idea that coaching is a year-long job. They told about being asked what their husbands did for the rest of the year after football season was over. Heidi said:

> I would say they [the public] have no idea the amount of time that goes into it. I say that over and over again. People will still say to me, "Well, football season is over. What does your husband do now?" They just don't get it. They don't realize that it is not just four hours on Saturday afternoon where you assemble two teams on a field and they go at it. They still just have no clue about how much is involved—with the recruiting, the academics, the off-season, going into the two-a-days—to actually get to the season. I don't think they have a clue.

Tina said she'd like people to know that coaching isn't just a Saturday job. She said:

> People have no idea. And a lot of people I've talked to over the years have asked me, "What does he do when the season is over? Does he get another job?" They are just appalled when you tell them the whole cycle about the job. You know, they had no idea college football was like that.

Ann had similar things to say:

> Sometimes, I think people think football coaches' only work 12 weeks out of the year. I mean, I really do—12 or 15 weeks. I don't think people realize it's an all-year-round thing. I mean, people who know football and all that stuff know that, but your average fan that thinks they know everything … they think, "OK, you worked that week and you played the game and after the season is over, you're done." … I don't think people realize first of all what a coach does. They're not only teaching someone how to play football—they are teaching them how to be a person and getting them through school. For a lot of them, he's their father. I mean, a lot of the guys don't have dads, so, you know, these coaches are their dads and raising them.

Football Coaches Have No Sick Days

The wives would also like the public to know that some of the benefits people in other occupations take for granted, such as personal days, public holidays, or sick leave, aren't benefits many coaches choose—or feel able—to use, even though they're entitled to them. Claire said: "You can't call in sick when you are a football coach, you can't call in sick, you can't take a sick day—they don't exist." One head coach's wife told a story about a young graduate assistant (GA) who called in sick:

> This GA had previously been a teacher in a public school system, where he must have justified taking sick days for a head cold. I guess he assumed that he should just do the same thing as a coach. I'm sure he was taken back when the head coach and assistant coaches responded to his call with roars of laughter and comments, such as "Are you kidding me?" He wasn't going to get much sympathy from the head coach, who had only missed two days of work in almost 30 years.

Not All Coaches Make Big Money (And Many Don't)

A number of wives brought up inequality in coaching salaries as something the public needs to be aware of. The wives point out that only a few coaches make the fabulous money that's so often mentioned in the media and that the majority of them, while mostly well compensated, aren't overpaid when the hours they work are taken into consideration. In some cases, the wives note that if the wife didn't work, the family would have a hard time surviving.

Football Coaching Is a Career

The public also needs to be aware that football coaching is a career. Just as people in other occupations do, the coaches have invested huge amounts of time and resources in their careers through hard work, networking, education, and training. The opportunity costs incurred by coaches in terms of time lost with family, health issues, and the many other things that have to be given up to coach are enormous. The wives want the public to be aware of the sacrifices made not only by the coaches but also by their families—sacrifices that families of men in other professions don't make. One online respondent said: "I really wish people in the stands knew the sacrifices that the coaches and their families make for the colleges and universities. Whenever I hear of a coach with a losing season, I always think of his wife and family." And another wife noted: "People have no idea that it isn't just a game. It is a career. They have no idea that the whole family sacrifices and it drives your life."

Fans Are Often Unfair

The final point the respondents told us needs to be brought to the public's attention is the frequent unfairness of the fans. Jamie said:

> You know, I think the public needs to know that my husband puts a lot of hours in. When you get on those message boards and they're so hard on the coaches, it's so frustrating because it's not like they're trying to do bad. … They're just doing their job, but their job is based on [the performance of] 18- and 19-year-old kids. What can you do?

Beth said she wants the public to know that coaching families are just like fans:

> We're just like you. We're trying to do our jobs, keep our homes, pay our taxes, raise our kids, and educate our kids. We believe the same way you do. I mean, we have feelings. I think the big thing the public needs to know is you can take a shot at my husband. He's a big boy, but when my kids are standing there, that's a different ballgame. … And so, when people say stuff about him, I don't think they get that we're a family. I think I would tell the public, "You've just got to understand that you need to keep this within the confines of the game. Yes, his job is very much in the public domain, but it is his job. It's not who we are."

It's important to our respondents that the public be made aware of their husbands' investment in and commitment to their careers and the sacrifices they and their families make for their programs. It's their hope that the more the public knows about their husbands' and their own lives, the less likely they'll be to engage in the types of negative fan behavior we've discussed in this book. Finally, the coaches' wives want people to know that they're just like everybody else.

Leslie said that she and her husband work really hard, they love their children, and they try hard to always do the right thing. Claire had similar things to say but added that she thinks it's important for the public to understand that coaches' ability to succeed in this demanding profession is in large part due to the support of their wives. She said that a man who would have to worry about the house, the lawn, the cars, and the children wouldn't be able to work in football coaching.

What the Wives Want Schools to Know

From what our respondents have told us, every school has its advantages and disadvantages. Some of the things they enjoyed at one school weren't available at others, and some of the problems at one location weren't encountered at another. Although most of the wives we interviewed had no suggestions for the schools that employed their husbands, a few ideas did emerge. For example, Rachel said she would like to see schools at the Division II level campaign for more scholarships. Tina would like schools to be more aware of the great discrepancies in coaching salaries—between and within divisions—and wouldn't be opposed to a standardization of salaries. She said:

> I think at lower-level Division I schools, like where we are, I don't think it's fair that coaches are paid so much less than other [Division I] coaches when they're doing just as much work and putting in just as many hours—if not more. You know, I think there needs to be more equalization of salaries of coaches. You know, you have somebody making six million and somebody barely making 100 grand. …

Summer money for student athletes is another of Tina's concerns:

> My heart breaks for these kids in the summer who come here to do their summer workouts. So many of these kids are from horrible backgrounds. … These kids have no money. They don't have food. And I know the NCAA is working on it, but I really have a passion for them passing some type of rule where these kids can get some type of allowance. They can't work. And it just breaks my heart. You know, we can only have them over so much. And … some of them are starving. I just think something has to be done about that, like the universities have a training table in the summer or something.

Rachel would like to see universities be more intentional in their focus on football, especially in those schools where it's not the most popular sport. She said:

> There are so many broad things that I think this university may do that some other universities don't. It truly comes down to the athletic administration, and that changes from university to university. It's all about the focus, and I wish they had a little more focus and intention with the football program at this university because the past three programs that we have been at have been way more focused on football.

It's can be a vicious circle when a lack of attention is paid to a particular sport because that usually results in a lower fan base, lower attendance, lower ticket sales, and, therefore, less money available to the program. Lack of adequate funding and support often means poorer facilities, difficulties in recruitment, and, eventually, fewer wins. Fewer wins, of course, means fewer fans—and so it continues.

Marissa would like it if all schools were able to provide seating away from fans where the coaches' wives could all sit together. As the mother of young children, she would also like it if schools had facilities for children to move around more freely than they can in the stands. She said:

> I know when you travel to other places and when you go to games, new places you haven't been, or even in your conference, there are always things about each particular place that you enjoy and you would love to put it all together. I love it when we are able to travel somewhere that we can sit in a box and I can just let the boys run around and we don't have to be squished in the seats by all the other fans. We have been to a stadium that has a playground, and I love that.

Leslie had similar things to say:

> I have to take the initiative with our ticket guy that when it is time to do tickets so he has us all together and we are away from as many fans as we can be. Here, they have a spot for parents, and that is pretty good, but most of the general admission and those kinds of people are away from us, so that's good. At one university where we were, there was nobody behind us—just the athletic department—so that was good. At another university, we were out in the middle of everybody, and that was terrible. As a head coach's wife, I want to make sure that doesn't happen here.

Although some schools have a person designated to assist incoming staff with their relocation, this isn't available everywhere. Some of our respondents mentioned that they'd like the administration to know how valuable that assistance is when it's available and that they'd like to see this kind of service be available in all programs. Claire brought up the subject of "perks" for the coaches' wives. She said she thinks schools need to be more aware of how important these perks are to the wives and why:

> They [the schools] are very conscious of not giving too many perks to the wives because it will seem an impropriety. We will be at a ballgame, and it will be like, we can't do this or we can't do a wives' trip because people will think we are just living it up and having a good time. It is really just a desire to be with your husband a little bit and see what he does and be with him.

On the whole, the wives didn't have many suggestions for athletic departments or the administration at their schools, and those that did understood that some of their ideas would be difficult to implement.

What the Wives Would Say to Younger Wives or Their Younger Selves

Almost all the wives we interviewed said the best thing they could tell younger wives or their younger selves would be to enjoy it, especially the wins. Kate said: "I would say to not take it all so seriously—to just enjoy the ride. It's kind of neat. It's kind of fun. And to really focus on the good and not get so hung up on the hard parts." Several respondents talked about how being married to a coach is never dull, especially with extreme highs and lows, and it's always exciting. Heidi said:

> I would probably say to just accept where you are going and enjoy it. Enjoy the wins because the losses can be so horrible. I look back to our first years here, and we took it for granted, and I think sometimes we take for granted how great your life is until all of a sudden, you are not winning. And you're thinking that was really great how we went to the Rose Bowl and everybody was so encouraged and so excited about us bringing a winning tradition here. Obviously, then people's expectations of us are much higher than they were and in many ways unrealistic, which is a whole other story, but it's something you deal with. The more you win, the more they expect. I think probably the biggest piece of advice I would say is to enjoy the wins, enjoy when you are winning, because when you lose, it comes back to you really quick how great it was when you have the wins.

Several wives mentioned that they'd stress to new wives the importance of making time to communicate with their husbands—no matter how hard that might be to do. Others were emphatic about the need for coaches' wives to have their own interests outside of football. A number of wives thought it was essential for new wives to know what they were getting into before they married coaches and that they need to learn the ropes early on in their marriages. One online respondent said:

> I know it's hard to be a wife of a coach, but the young wives coming in really do need help sometimes dealing with the schedules, the phone calls during "our time," etc. … I think the head coach's wife in particular should take some time with these gals and help them. Also, it would be nice to every once in a while have the head coach or the head coach's wife take charge of some sort of social for the group. They have done it at other places, and I find the more the wives think that the head coach really does want to make sure everyone is happy at home, the more support is given to not only that coach from home but to the program as a whole.

And another online respondent said:

> I sure wish that someone had told me what life would be like before I became a "coach's wife." … Seems so obvious now, but I wasn't prepared for it, and the insight sure would have shortened the "learning curve" for me.

Pam talked about how glad she was that she and her husband didn't have children early in their marriage, and that's what she would like new wives to know. She said:

> Well, I guess I was glad that we didn't rush in to starting out family. So, that would be definitely something because there are a lot of transitions that have to occur from getting married to a coach and then figuring out how the whole of the seasons work. I know that some of the wives think, "OK, well, if I have a baby, then I'll have somebody to keep me company while he's gone." But that's just adds all up to [a] different kind of stress, you know, to your life because you're doing it all yourself.

Other wives mentioned that they'd tell new wives about the importance of a positive attitude. One said:

> It is what you make of it. If you choose to think of the situation as positive, it will be that way, but once you turn toward the negative side of things … it can be hard to come out of that. My strategy is to see good in as much as possible. … Choose a positive attitude.

The importance of taking advantage of every source of support available, especially other coaches' wives, was something our respondents said young wives need to understand. Several wives also told us that they believe this book will be an important resource for the younger women. The comments of one online respondent seem to be a good note on which to end this book:

> I like to tell people how rewarding it is. It is all a matter of attitude. I wouldn't trade my life in a second. Yes, the hours are brutal, the schedule is intense, balancing family, work—football can be wild … but the rewards far outweigh it. Heaven help me, I love August. I can't wait for the new season, new coaches, new offenses, and new players. I can't imagine doing the same thing over and over year after year. That is the magic of college football coaching, and I feel very blessed.

Conclusion

The three of us have learned many things from this study. First and foremost, the wives confirmed what we already suspected: Being a coach's wife is a job in and of itself. Coaches' wives take on the responsibilities that come with this job in addition to their own careers and in addition to the normal responsibilities of wives and mothers.

We also learned just how unstable the coaching profession is—not just because coaches often don't know from one season to the next where they'll be working but because of the day-to-day precariousness of their lives—lives that depend on the actions and behavior of young men in their teens and early 20s. Even though the coaches may believe they're in control of the players for whom they're responsible, the negative actions of a handful of players can bring about repercussions for the players, team, and coaches. This fragility and instability affect the coaches' entire family, and it explains in part the importance of the "football family" as a source of support for the coaches' wives.

We were surprised by the number of coaches' wives who have managed to keep their own careers going despite their frequent moves. We understand that for many women, their careers are a means of coping with their husbands' frequent absences, but they're also important to the wives who want to put their education and training to use and who take great pride in what they do.

Because of our prior and continuing exposure to the lives of coaching families, we weren't surprised to find that for much of the year, the wives do most of the traditional female family work as well as most of the traditional male family work. This is an interesting situation because it's neither a traditional division of family work that has "women's work" and "men's work" nor is it the more modern version in which the spouses share it all. It's simply an adaptation to the ways in which coaches and their wives live their lives, which results in the tasks being done by the person who's available to do them. In these families, it appears to us that whether the husband and wife are okay with their arrangement is what matters and not which one of them is doing a particular job and how often.

We were disheartened to find that fan behavior today is still as difficult for the coaches' wives to deal with as it was 60 years ago and that some fans don't stop to consider the effects of what they say on the families of the coaches. In fact, because of technological advances, negative fan behavior appears to be even worse in some respects.

It's obvious to us that the husbands and wives in our study are committed to each other, to their marriages, and to their families. According to the information from the wives, those connected to football coaching have much to be optimistic about. Overwhelmingly, coaches and their wives see themselves as a team on a shared mission. Husbands are passionate about what they do and their success with the players—on and off the field. Wives love being a part of their husbands' job and contributors to their success, and they know it would be difficult for their husbands to make it in coaching without their dedication and support.

We're intrigued at the extent to which the coaches display so many expressive qualities in their marriages—qualities that most people would never associate with football coaches. We believe these qualities largely account for the success of the marriages in that they compensate in many ways for the drawbacks of being married to football coaches. We're also firmly convinced that coaching marriages survive and succeed because of the ways in which the spouses treat each other. As we noted earlier, husbands and wives can put up with many difficulties in their marriages if they love each other and feel loved in return.

Would we do anything differently if we were to do this study over again? Perhaps the only thing we would have liked to have done would have been to hear what women who had once been (but were no longer) married to football coaches had to say. We suspect that most of the issues that caused problems in their marriages would be the same difficulties we have talked about in this book, with the difference being the unwillingness or inability of the ex-wives to put up with them.

It hasn't been our goal to deter anyone from going into football coaching nor to deter anyone from marrying a coach. Our aim has been to make people aware of the best parts and the worst parts of football coaching and their impact on coaching marriages. In addition, we wanted to inform the general public about the effects of certain aspects of coaching on the lives of the coaches' wives and children, with which most people wouldn't be familiar. As Ann stated: "I would say, as far as what the public needs to know, they need to know just how devoted and how patient we have to be." She goes on to summarize what, for us, this book is all about: "… [I]t takes a very special person to be a coach's wife. We're all going to Heaven for what we've had to do."

Epilogue

We've long said in my family that only Sally could put up with the demands of Danny's job and only Sally could be married to Danny. I know now how true this is, but I also know many women have the same strength, independence, compassion, and drive that our family has always recognized in Sally. As a marriage and family therapist and a person who studies families, I know everything about the coaching marriage is wrong and should lead to marital dissatisfaction, but it doesn't. The coaches work hard, have very little time for their wives or family, and are under great amounts of stress. They're lucky to be married to the women that they are married to, and they know it. No one is a greater fan of coaches' wives than the coaches themselves. The opportunity to glimpse behind the curtain into the lives of these wives is an incredible privilege, and I'm thankful for it. I've learned a great deal as a researcher, therapist, mother, and football fan.

I'm proud of the quality of this book; it has been a long time coming. I'm fortunate to have grown up with two such amazing roles models: my mother and Sally. Much of this book is the result of their hard work, their sweat, and their insights. Thank you to both of them for allowing me to tag along. I'm especially pleased that not only are we all still speaking, but I think we're closer for it.

—Liddy

In 2006, Janet approached me with the idea of conducting a study of coaches' wives and possibly sharing the results in a book. As a head coach's wife, I'm very guarded and go out of my way not to let the general public "in" on my family members' personal lives, so my first reaction was "No way!" Once I rationalized that the book would be based on interviews and responses from many wives and wouldn't be about me or only a few individual wives, I became excited about the potential to pass knowledge from veteran coaches' wives to other coaches' wives, potential coaches' wives, coaches themselves, and the general public, and I agreed to assist in the study. Now that the book is nearing completion, I'm very proud to have been a part of a project that has given a voice to football coaches' wives.

My second thought about the study was that I already know everything one needs to know about being a coach's wife because I've been doing this "job" for more than 30 years. I continue to emphasize the objective of educating other wives (particularly younger and potential wives) and the general public, but it never occurred to me that

I was also going to increase my own knowledge about the lives of football coaches' wives. During the process of writing this book, I learned information about the responsibilities of coaches and their wives at the levels we had never coached at. I learned the various ways that different universities and coaching staffs handle similar responsibilities. While the themes that emerged from our study weren't surprising to me, I should thank our respondents for an "attitude adjustment." The many messages that emphasized keeping a positive attitude and leaning on one's faith as well as the wives' ability to be upbeat despite losing seasons, firings, negative fans, moving, etc., were very inspirational to me.

I thank Janet and Liddy for their many, many hours of work that went into the study and this book and for their patience as I adjusted to analyzing "touchy feely" data. I especially appreciate the wives who willingly shared their lives with our readers. And, finally, I thank my husband, Danny, for the experience of being a coach's wife—there has never been a dull moment.

—Sally

I agree with everything "the girls" have already said, and I'm grateful for all their contributions and hard work. This book has been a wonderful (and sometimes exhausting) part of my life for more than five years. Many times, I wondered if it would ever be done, and I sometimes thought I probably would have fired my coauthors if they'd been graduate students working on the project rather than relatives.

The interviews were amazing experiences for me. I treasure my time with those wives I talked to in person, their hospitality, and their generosity in sharing their lives with me. I learned so much from them. I was also amazed by the amount of information the respondents to the online survey provided. Analyzing it all presented quite a challenge, but I want them to know that everything they wrote was read and a large amount was used in the preparation of this book, even if it wasn't possible to quote all their contributions.

I know my colleagues and my students at the College of St. Benedict/St. John's University will be glad the project is complete. All too often, I've hidden behind my office door, emerging only when absolutely necessary and looking like some subterranean creature blinking in the daylight. They'll also be happy when I find other things to talk about.

Finally, I must reiterate what Liddy has said: This book would never have been written (at least not by us) if it weren't for Danny. Who knew when he played on his first football team where his love of the game would take him? Who knew when he had the good sense to marry Sally the important role she would play in his career? We had no idea that their lives together would be the inspiration for this book. Thank you both.

—Janet

Appendix A

College Football Coaches' Wives Questionnaire

1. Your age: _____

2. Your race: _____

3. Your husband's age: _____

4. Your husband's race: _____

5. How old were you when you and your husband married? _____

6. How old was your husband when the two of you married? _____

7. How long have you been married? _____ years

8. Do you and your husband have any children together? _____ Yes _____ No (If no, please go to Q10.)

9. Please list the age and sex of each of your children from this marriage.

   Age _____ _____ _____ _____ _____ _____ _____

   Sex _____ _____ _____ _____ _____ _____ _____

10. Have you been married previously? _____ Yes _____ No (If no, please go to Q16.)

11. If your answer to Q10 is yes, how many times have you been married prior to your current marriage? _____

12. If your answer to Q10 is yes, how did those marriages/that marriage end?

    _____

13. Are there any children from your prior marriage(s)? _____ Yes _____ No (If no, please go to Q16.)

14. If you answered yes to Q13, please list the age and sex of each of those children.

    Age _____ _____ _____ _____ _____ _____ _____

    Sex _____ _____ _____ _____ _____ _____ _____

15. If any of the children referred to in Q13 are younger than 18, with whom do these children live? _____

16. Do you have children from a previous (nonmarriage) relationship? _____ Yes _____ No (If no, please go to Q19.)

17. If you answered yes to Q16, please give the age and sex of each of those children.

    Age _____ _____ _____ _____ _____ _____ _____

    Sex _____ _____ _____ _____ _____ _____ _____

18. If any of the children referred to in Q17 are younger than 18, with whom do these children live?_____

19. Has your husband been married previously? _____ Yes _____ No *(If no, please go to Q25.)*

20. If your answer to Q19 is yes, how many times has your husband been married prior to this marriage to you? _____

21. If your answer to Q19 is yes, how did those marriages/that marriage end?

_____

22. Does your husband have children from a previous marriage? _____ Yes _____ No *(If no, please go to Q25.)*

23. If you answered yes to Q22, please give the age and sex of each of those children.

Age _____   _____   _____   _____   _____   _____   _____

Sex _____   _____   _____   _____   _____   _____   _____

24. If any of the children referred to in Q22 are younger than 18, with whom do these children live?_____

25. Does your husband have children from a previous (nonmarriage) relationship? _____ Yes _____ No *(If no, please go to Q28.)*

26. If your answer Q25 is yes, please give the age and sex of each of those children.

Age _____   _____   _____   _____   _____   _____   _____

Sex _____   _____   _____   _____   _____   _____   _____

27. If any of the children referred to in Q26 are younger than 18, with whom do these children live? _____

28. Are you currently employed outside the home? _____ Yes _____ No *(If no, please go to Q31.)*

29. If your answer to Q28 is yes, do you work: _____ Full time _____ Part time

30. What is your current occupation or job title? _____

31. If you are currently a homemaker, did you previously work outside the home? _____ Yes _____No *(If no, please go to Q35.)*

32. If your answer to Q31 is yes, what was your occupation?

_____

33. If your answer to Q31 is yes, did you work: _____ Full time _____ Part time

34. If your answer to Q31 is yes, what were your primary reasons for leaving your employment? _____

35. What is the highest level of education you have obtained? _____

36. In what discipline(s) did you obtain your degree(s)?
Degree   Discipline

_____   _____

_____   _____

_____   _____

37. What is the highest level of education obtained by your husband?

38. In what discipline(s) did your husband obtain his degree(s)?

Degree   Discipline

_____ _____

_____ _____

_____ _____

39. What is your husband's current job title? *(Please do not identify the school.)*

_____

40. In which NCAA division is your husband's football program located?

_____

41. In what conference does your husband's team play? _____

42. How long has your husband been in his current position? _____

43. Please list your husband's prior employment history in college football. *(Please do not identify the schools.)*

Year(s)	Position(s) Held	NCAA Division
_____	_____	_____
_____	_____	_____
_____	_____	_____
_____	_____	_____
_____	_____	_____
_____	_____	_____
_____	_____	_____
_____	_____	_____
_____	_____	_____
_____	_____	_____
_____	_____	_____
_____	_____	_____
_____	_____	_____

44. What is your approximate total annual family income?

____ $25,000 or less ____ $25,001 to $50,000 ____ $50,001 to $75,000

____ $75,001 to $100,000 ____ $100,001 to $125,000 ____ $125,001 to $150,000

____ $150,001 to $175,000 ____ $175,001 to $200,000 ____ $200,001 or more

45. What percentage of this income is currently provided by you? _____

46. Do you currently perform any volunteer services? _____ Yes _____ No *(If no, please go to Q48.)*

47. If your answer to Q46 is yes, please briefly describe the nature of volunteer work you do and the approximate hours involved. _____

_____

_____

_____

48. What is your religious affiliation? _____

49. What is your husband's religious affiliation? _____

50. On average, how often do you attend services at a place of worship?

_____ Never   _____ A few times a year   _____ Once a month

_____ Once a week   _____ More than once a week

51. On average, how often does your husband attend services at a place of worship?

_____ Never   _____ A few times a year   _____ Once a month

_____ Once a week   _____ More than once a week

52. How important is your faith/spirituality to you?

_____ Not at all important   _____ Not very important   _____ Fairly important

_____ Important   _____ Extremely important

53. How important do you believe his faith/spirituality is to your husband?

_____ Not at all important   _____ Not very important   _____ Fairly important

_____ Important   _____ Extremely important

54. Do you believe what you are doing (that is, your paid career or your career as a homemaker) is as important as what your husband does? _____ Yes _____No

55. Why or why not?

_____

_____

_____

56. Please list the *personal* qualities you provide to your marriage that make it possible for your husband to do what he does effectively.

_____

_____

_____

57. Please list any traditionally *female* family tasks that your husband performs on a regular basis.

_____

_____

_____

58. Please list any traditionally *female* family tasks that your husband performs on an occasional basis.

_____

_____

_____

59. Please list any traditionally *male* family tasks that you perform on a regular basis.

_____

_____

_____

60. Please list any traditionally *male* family tasks that you perform on an occasional basis.

_____

_____

_____

61. Please identify any area or areas of your life that you believe suffer or have suffered in the past as a result of the demands of your husband's career? *(If there is more than one, please order them so that the area of greatest concern is given first, the next most serious area is listed second, and so on.)*

_____

_____

_____

62. Can you identify any area or areas of your husband's life that you believe suffer or have suffered in the past as a result of the demands of his career? *(If there is more than one, please order them so that the area of greatest concern is given first, the next most serious area is listed second, and so on.)*

_____

_____

_____

63. Please list five words or phrases that you believe best describe your husband's personal qualities.

_____

_____

_____

64. Please list the characteristics of your marriage that you find the most personally satisfying. *(List as many as you like.)*

_____

_____

_____

65. Please list the characteristics of your marriage that you find the least personally satisfying. *(List as many as you like.)*

_____

_____

_____

66. All things considered, how satisfied are you with your marriage?

_____ Not at all satisfied   _____ Extremely dissatisfied   _____ Dissatisfied

_____ Neither satisfied nor dissatisfied   _____ Extremely satisfied

67. How often do you and your husband disagree on the following items?

	Very Often	Fairly Often	Often	Occasionally	Never
The allocation of household tasks	_____	_____	_____	_____	_____
Money	_____	_____	_____	_____	_____
Time spent together as a couple	_____	_____	_____	_____	_____
Time spent together as a family	_____	_____	_____	_____	_____
Parenting issues	_____	_____	_____	_____	_____

68. Please identify any other issues that cause conflict between you and your husband.

_____

_____

_____

69. How likely are you and your husband to use the following techniques when dealing with serious disagreements?

	Very Often	Fairly Often	Often	Occasionally	Never
I give in.	____	____	____	____	____
My husband gives in.	____	____	____	____	____
We compromise.	____	____	____	____	____
We drop it without resolution.	____	____	____	____	____
I leave the room.	____	____	____	____	____
My husband leaves the room.	____	____	____	____	____
I refuse to talk about it anymore.	____	____	____	____	____
My husband refuses to talk about it anymore.	____	____	____	____	____

70. To what extent do you agree or disagree with the following statements?

	Strongly Disagree	Disagree	Neither Agree nor Disagree	Agree	Strongly Agree
I am very disappointed in my marriage.	____	____	____	____	____
My marriage is no longer as important to me as it used to be.	____	____	____	____	____

71. How likely do you believe it is that you and your husband will divorce at some point in the future?

____ Very unlikely   ____ Unlikely   ____ Unsure   ____ Likely   ____ Very likely

72. To what extent do you agree or disagree with the following statements?

	Strongly Disagree	Disagree	Neither Agree nor Disagree	Agree	Strongly Agree
In a marriage, it is much better if the man earns the main living and the woman takes care of the home and family.	____	____	____	____	____
If the husband and wife both work full time, they should share household tasks equally.	____	____	____	____	____
If the husband wife both work full time, they should share the child-related responsibilities equally.				____	____	____

73. During the following times, how many hours per week does your husband usually devote to his work?

Football season   _____   Recruiting   _____

Spring training   _____   Summer   _____

74. Approximately how many nights per year do you estimate your husband is away from home? _____

75. When you married your husband, was he then (or did he plan to become) a college football coach? _____ Yes _____ No

76. Which aspects of your life as the wife of a college football coach give you the greatest rewards? *(List as many as you wish.)*

_____

_____

_____

_____

77. Which aspects of your life as the wife of a college football coach do you find the most distressing or difficult? *(List as many as you wish.)*

_____

_____

_____

_____

78. Which aspects of their lives as the children of a college football coach do you believe your children find most rewarding? *(List as many as you wish.)*

_____

_____

_____

_____

79. Which aspects of their lives as the children of a college football coach do you believe your children find most distressing or difficult? *(List as many as you wish.)*

_____

_____

_____

_____

80. Is there anything else you would like to say about your life as the wife of a college football coach?

_____

_____

_____

_____

Thank you for taking the time to complete this questionnaire.

Appendix B

Demographic Details of the College Football Coaches' Wives Online Survey

The data included in this handout are from the online responses only. The total number of usable responses is 285. Differences in Ns in the figures are explained by missing responses to various questions. All information (including data related to husbands) is from the perspective of the wife.

Sample Characteristics

Figure 1 illustrates the mean age and age range of participants and their husbands. A two-year difference exists between wives and husbands. The majority of the wives and husbands are Caucasian (86.4 percent), with slightly more African American husbands than wives. The vast majority of respondents (87.5 percent) are well educated, with a bachelor's degree or higher level of education. Similar education levels were reported for husbands.

Variable	Wife	Husband
Age (n = 280)	Mean = 39.24 Range = 24–73	Mean = 41.52 Range = 24–81
Ethnicity (n = 279)	African American = 7.1% Caucasian = 88.6% Asian = 1.4% Biracial = 1.1% Hispanic = 1.1%	African American = 12.1% Caucasian = 84.3% Asian = 1.1% Biracial = 1.4% Hispanic = 7%
Education Level (n = 280)	High School = 1.8% Some College = 6.4% Associate's Degree = 4.3% Bachelor's Degree = 41.8% Bachelor's Plus = 7.1% Master's Degree = 32.9% Master's Plus = 3.6% Ph.D. = 1.8% M.D. = .4%	High School = 0% Some College = .7% Associate's Degree = 0% Bachelor's Degree = 36.9% Bachelor's Plus = 1.8% Master's Degree = 58.1% Master's Plus = 1.4% Ph.D. = 1.1% M.D. = 0%

Figure 1. Participant age, race, and education level

Family

Marriage Statistics

- 99.5 percent of the sample is married, for a mean duration of 13.48 years.
- The range in number of years married is newly married to 52 years.
- The percentage of those (wives and husbands) who have previously married is 8.2 percent.

Children

- 77.3 percent of the sample have children.
- 1.1 percent were expecting at the time of the survey.
- The majority of participants have two children (36.7 percent), one child (27.4 percent), or three children (20 percent).

Employment

Wives' Employment

- 71.8 percent of the wives are employed outside the home.
- 73.2 percent work full time.
- 23.9 percent work part time.
- The five most frequent occupations within this sample are:
  - ✓ Educational/training   42.1 percent
  - ✓ Healthcare   12.2 percent
  - ✓ Business/management   13.7 percent
  - ✓ Sales   5.1 percent
  - ✓ Office support   5.1 percent
- Wives provide 29.8 percent of the total household income.
- 50 percent of wives are currently involves in volunteer activity.

Husbands' Employment

Participants were asked to list their husbands' coaching employment history, including job title, division, and number of years in each position. It's important to note that participants were provided only seven spaces in which to report this information. On average, for this sample, coaches stayed in each position for 4.63 years. Figure 2 lists the percentage of coaches and number of positions held to date. It's interesting to consider these data in light of the fact that the average age of these coaches is 41.5. Figure 3 shows the current coaching position of participants' husbands. In this table, fixed staff refers to such positions as strength coach or conditioning coach. Figure 4 illustrates the represented NCAA divisions within the sample. All divisions were well represented.

Number of Jobs	Percentage
1	100% (280)
2	96% (268)
3	84% (234)
4	68% (190)
5	50% (141)
6	35% (99)
7	19% (54)

Figure 2. Number of coaching positions

Job Title	Percentage
Fixed Staff	2.6% (7)
Graduate Assistant	.7% (2)
Positions Coach	26.3% (72)
Coordinator	24.8% (68)
Assistant Head Coach	8.8% (24)
Head Coach	36.1% (99)
Retired	.7% (2)

Figure 3. Current coaching position (title)

Division	Percentage
Division I BCS	36.2% (97)
Division I FCS	19% (51)
Division II	17.5% (47)
Division III	25.7% (69)

Figure 4. Current coaching position (division)

Husbands' Workweek

Figure 5 outlines the number of hours worked per week by season; the year was divided into four seasons: football, recruiting, spring training, and summer. Wives were asked to estimate the number of hours their husbands worked in a "typical" week during each season. The data reported have been condensed into those time increments, as illustrated in Figure 5.

Hours Worked in a "Typical" Week						
Season	Total Number	100+	75–99	50–74	25–49	24 or Less
Football (n = 264)	264	36.7% (92)	49.6% (131)	13.6% (36)	0	0
Recruiting (n = 251)	251	24.75% (62)	29.2% (75)	39.8% (100)	3.5% (9)	1.9% (5)
Spring Training (n = 254)	254	7.5% (19)	22% (56)	44% (112)	22.8% (58)	4.7% (2)
Summer (n = 232)	232	2.2% (5)	4.7% (11)	26.7% (62)	50.8% (118)	15.5% (36)

Figure 5. Coaching workweek by season

Income

Figure 6 lists the reported annual household income for wives and husbands combined. Given the known income discrepancy between divisions and coaching ranks, it's also important to consider income in relation to these variables. Figure 7 illustrates income level in relation to NCAA division. Figure 8 depicts the income level in relation to current position.

Income	Percentage
$25,000 or less	1.1% (3)
$25,001–$50,000	6.1% (17)
$50,001–$75,000	18.1% (50)
$75,001–$100,000	21.7% (60)
$100,001–$125,000	19.1% (53)
$125,001–$150,000	9.4% (26)
$150,001–$175,000	6.9% (19)
$175,001–$200,000	6.1% (17)
$200,001+	11.6% (32)

Figure 6. Total annual household income

Income	Division I BCS	Division I FCS	Division II	Division III
$25,000 or less	0% (0)	0% (0)	0% (0)	3% (2)
$25,001–$50,000	2.1% (2)	7.8% (4)	12.8% (6)	3% (2)
$50,001–$75,000	12.8% (12)	23.5% (12)	14.9% (7)	21.2% (14)
$75,001–$100,000	11.7% (11)	25.5% (13)	31.9% (15)	27.3% (18)
$100,001–$125,000	17.0% (16)	17.0% (16)	25.5% (12)	21.2% (14)
$125,001–$150,000	11.1% (11)	13.7% (6)	4.3% (2)	9.1% (6)
$150,001–$175,000	38.9% (7)	7.8% (4)	6.4% (3)	6.1% (4)
$175,001–$200,000	9.6% (9)	7.8% (4)	4.3% (2)	4.5% (3)
$200,001+	27.7% (26)	3.9% (2)	0% (0)	4.5% (3)

Figure 7. Total household income by NCAA division

Income	Fixed Staff	Graduate Assistant	Positions Coach	Coordinator	Assistant Head Coach	Head Coach	Retired
$25,000 or less	0%	0%	2.7%	1.5%	0%	0%	0%
$25,001– $50,000	14.3%	50.0%	8.2%	9.1%	4.2%	0%	0%
$50,001– $75,000	14.3%	50.0%	24.7%	22.7%	29.2%	5.1%	50.0%
$75,001– $100,000	42.9%	0%	19.2%	24.2%	20.8%	21.4%	0%
$100,001– $125,000	14.3%	0%	19.2%	15.2%	16.7%	22.4%	50.0%
$125,001– $150,000	14.3%	0%	9.6%	7.6%	4.2%	12.2%	0%
$150,001– $175,000	0%	0%	9.6%	3.0%	0%	10.2%	0%
$175,001– $200,000	0%	0%	4.1%	3.0%	8.3%	11.2%	0%
$200,000+	0%	0%	2.7%	13.6%	16.7%	17.3%	0%

Figure 8. Total household income by position title

References

Allen, J. (2002, February 3). "Married to football." *The New York Times*. Retrieved on November 26, 2012, from www.nytimes.com.

Allen, J. (2007, May 3). "A coach's wife, the true MVP." Retrieved on November 26, 2012, from NFL.com.

American Football Coaches Association. Retrieved on November 26, 2012, from www. afca.com.

Barnhart, T. (1999, July 4). "Inside colleges retreat is for coaches' wives." *Atlanta Journal-Constitution.* Retrieved on November 26, 2012, from www.ajc.com.

Bartlett, B. (2002, January 21). "Loving football." *The Courier-Journal.* Retrieved on November 26, 2012, from www.courier-journal.com.

Becker, G. S. (1991). *A treatise on the family.* Cambridge, MA: Harvard University Press

Berkowitz, S., & Upton, J. (2012, January 17). "Salaries rising for new college football coaches." *USA Today*. Retrieved on November 26, 2012, from www.usatoday.com.

Bianchi, S. M., Milkie, M. M., Sayer, L. C., & Robinson., J. P. (2000). "Is anyone doing the housework? Trends in the gender division of household labor." *Social Forces*, *79*(1): 191–228.

Bird, C. (1999). "Gender, household labor, and psychological distress: The impact of the amount and division of housework." *Journal of Health and Social Behavior*, *40*(1): 32–45.

Brown, G. (2005, February 14). "The academic progress rate." *NCAA News Online.* Retrieved on November 26, 2012, from www.ncaa.org.

Buchanan, O. (2006). "Fatherhood a priority for college coaches." Retrieved on November 26, 2012, from www.collegefootball.rivals.com/content.asp?CID=551870.

Cherlin, A. J. (2004). *Public and private families: An introduction* (4th ed.). Boston: McGraw-Hill.

Chizik, G., with Thomas, D. (2011). *All in: What it takes to be the best.* Carol Stream, IL: Tyndale Press

College Football Poll staff. (2010). "2010 head coaching changes and how they fared." Retrieved on November 26, 2012, from www.collegefootballpoll.com/coaching_changes_2010.html.

College Football Poll staff. (2011). "24 teams begin 2011 season under new stewardship." Retrieved on November 26, 2012, from www.collegefootballpoll.com/coaching_changes_2011.html.

Coontz, S. (2005). *Marriage, a history: How love conquered marriage.* New York: Viking.

Dooley, B. (1991). *Put me in, coach: Confessions of a football wife.* Atlanta: Longstreet Press.

Durando, S. (2011, June 12). "College football assistants' salaries soar." *St. Louis Post-Dispatch.* Retrieved on November 26, 2012, from www.stltoday.com.

Erickson, R. J. (1993). "Reconceptualizing family work: The effect of emotion work on perceptions of marital quality." *Journal of Marriage and the Family,* 55: 888–900.

Evans, T. (2006, November 28). "For a coach in demand, family trumps football." *The New York Times.* Retrieved on November 26, 2012, from www.nytimes.com.

Finkel, L. B., Kelley, M. L., & Ashby, J. (2003). "Geographic mobility, family and maternal variables as related to the psychosocial adjustment of military children." *Military Medicine,* 168(12): 1019–1024.

Folstad, K. (2002, February 2). "Why the wives get defensive." *West Palm Beach Post.* Retrieved on November 26, 2012, from www.palmbeachpost.com.

Football Scoop. (2012, January 8 and 9). Retrieved on November 26, 2012, from www.Footballscoop.com.

Fox, D. (2012, January 22). "Long-term deals are far from guarantees." Retrieved on December 14, 2012, from http://highschool.rivals.com/content.asp?CID=1321360.

Frey, J. (2002, December 16). "Team player: Whether husband Steve is at home or away, Jerri Spurrier is anything but a football widow." *The Washington Post.* Retrieved on November 26, 2012, from www.washingtonpost.com.

Galinsky, E. (1999). *Ask the children: What America's children really think about working parents.* New York: Morrow.

Glenn, N.D. (1990). "Quantitative research on marital quality in the 1980s: a critical review." *Journal of Marriage and Family,* 52(4): 818-831.

Gottman, J. (1994). *Why marriages succeed or fail.* New York: Simon & Schuster.

Gottman, J. M., & Krokoff, L. J. (1989). "Marital interaction and satisfaction: A longitudinal view." *Journal of Consulting and Clinical Psychology,* 57: 47–52.

Greenhaus, J. H., & Beutell, N. J. (1985). "Sources of conflict between work and family roles." *The Academy of Management Review, 10*(1): 76–88.

Hayes, M. (2004). "Expectations come with paycheck." *Sporting News, 228*(50): 34–35.

Hendershott, A. (1995). *Moving for work: The sociology of relocating in the 1990s.* Lanham, MD: University of America Press.

Higgins, R. (2010, September 23). "Relax, it's only a game (yeah, right): SEC coaches sometimes find it difficult to take it easy." *The Commercial Appeal.* Retrieved on November 26, 2012, from www.commercialappeal.com.

Hochschild, A. R. (1983). *The managed heard: Commercialization of human feeling.* Berkeley: University of California Press.

Hughes, P. C., & Dickson, F.C. (2005). "Communication, marital satisfaction, and religious orientation in interfaith marriages." *The Journal of Family Communication, 5*(1): 25–41.

Kaufman, M. (2006, September 29). "Support systems strongest at home." *Miami Herald.* Retrieved on November 26, 2012, from www.miamiherald.com.

Kuhnert, K. W., & Palmer, D. R. (1991). "Job security and the intrinsic and extrinsic characteristics of work." *Group and Organizational Management, 16:* 178–192.

Lowrey, S. (2009). "Megan Mullen's Journey." Retrieved on November 26, 2012, from http://hsalabama.scout.com/2/919150.html.

McCollum, A. T. (1990). *The trauma of moving: Psychological issues for women.* Beverly Hills, CA. Sage Publications.

McDonald, B. (2001). "The wives of Fresno State football coaches live through every down in every game right along with their husbands." Retrieved on November 26, 2012, from www.gobulldogs.com/sports/m-footbl/spec-rel/092801aab.html.

Mickelson, K. D., Claffey, S. T., & Williams, S. L. (2006). "The moderating role of gender and gender role attitudes on the link between spousal support and marital quality." *Sex Roles, 55:* 73–82.

Monson, G. (2004, April 10). "Finding purpose and priorities: Football is his job, but not his life." *Salt Lake Tribune.* Retrieved on November 26, 2012, from www.sltrib.com.

Moore, M. (2008). "Honored to serve." Retrieved on November 26, 2012, from www.afcwa.org/Newsletter/AFCWA_Fall2008.pdf.

NCAA. (2012). Bylaw 13.17.4 Football. *2012-13 NCAA Division I Manual.* Retrieved on December 14, 2012, from http://www.ncaapublications.com/productdownloads/ D113.pdf.

NCAA Academic Progress Rate. (2005). Retrieved on November 26, 2012, from www. ncaa.org/wps/wcm/connect/public/NCAA/Resources/Research/Academic+Progress+ Rate.

NCAA Division I Football Coaches Off-Campus Recruiting Guide. (2009). Retrieved on November 26, 2012, from http://fs.ncaa.org/Docs/AMA/recruiting_calendars/DI/ Football%20Guide.pdf.

Niehuis, S., & Bartell, D. (2006). "The marital disillusionment scale: Development and psychometric properties." *North American Journal of Psychology. 8*(1): 69–83.

Nock, S. L. (1995). "Commitment and dependency in marriage." *Journal of Marriage and the Family, 57:* 593–614.

O'Toole, S. (2006). *Wedded to the game: The real lives of NFL women.* Lincoln: University of Nebraska Press.

Ortiz, S. M. (2004). "Leaving the private world of wives of professional athletes." *Journal of Contemporary Ethnography, 33*(4): 466–487.

Pelak, C. F. (2002). "Women's collective identity formation in sports: A case study from women's ice hockey." *Gender & Society, 16*(1): 93–114.

Pietropinto, A. (1986). "The workaholic spouse." *Medical Aspects of Human Sexuality, 20:* 89–96.

Pointer, M. (2002, November 22). "Coaches' wives run home team during season." *The Indianapolis Star.* Retrieved on November 26, 2012, from www.indystar.com.

Price, S. L. (1998, July 6). "Greatest gift." *Sports Illustrated.* Retrieved on November 26, 2012, from http://sportsillustrated.cnn.com.

Reilly, R. (2003, November 3). "What about Bob?" *Sports Illustrated.* Retrieved on November 26, 2012, from http://sportsillustrated.cnn.com.

Riemer, J. W. (2000). "Job relocation, sources of stress, and sense of home." *Community, Work & Family, 3*(2): 205–217.

Rives, J. M., & West. J. M. (1993). "Wife's employment and worker relocation behavior." *Journal of Socio-Economics, 22*(1): 13-22.

Robinson, B. E., Carroll, J. J., & Flowers, C. (2001). "Marital estrangement, positive affect, and locus of control among spouses of workaholics and spouse of nonworkaholics: A national study. *The American Journal of Family Therapy, 29:* 397–410.

Rodriquez, R. (2005). "How's that feel? ... to be 'Mrs. Coach'?" *Sporting News, 229*(31): 23.

Rogers, S. J., & Amato, P. R. (2000). "Have changes in gender relations affected marital quality?" *Social Forces, 79*(2): 731–753.

Rotundo, E. A. (1985). "American fatherhood: A historical perspective." *American Behavioral Scientist, 29:* 7–23.

Russo, R. D. (2012, January 23). "Paterno could be last of ilk in college football." Associated Press.

Sabock, R. (1973). *The Coach.* Philadelphia: W. B. Saunders.

St. John, W. (2005, October 16). "His cheerleader, win or lose." *The New York Times.* Retrieved on November 26, 2012, from www.nytimes.com.

Smith, D. P. (2010, July 29). "It's also 'game time' for Megan Mullen." *Starkville Daily News.* Retrieved on November 26, 2012, from www.starkvilledailynews.com.

Sotile, W. M., & M. O. Sotile (2004). "Physicians' wives evaluate their marriages, their husbands and life in medicine: Results of the AMA-alliance medical marriage survey." *Bulletin of the Menninger Clinic, 68*(1): 39–59.

Stanley, S. M., Markman, H. J., & Whitton, S. W. (2002). "Communication, conflict and commitment: Insights on the foundations of relationship success from a national survey." *Family Process, 41*(4): 659–675.

Story, M. (2003, January 28). "Coaching carousel leaves wives and kids in limbo." *Lexington Herald-Leader.* Retrieved on November 26, 2012, from www.herald-leader.com.

Stuhldreher, M. (1948, October 23). "Football fans aren't human." *The Saturday Evening Post.* Retrieved on November 26, 2012, from www.saturdayeveningpost.com.

Suwanski, R. (2009, October 31). "KWC's Holsclaw juggles coaching, child care duties." *Lexington Herald-Leader.* Retrieved on November 26, 2012, from www.herald-leader.com.

Thamel, P. (2005, September 5). "Bowden and Paterno value their family ties." *The New York Times.* Retrieved on November 26, 2012, from www.nytimes.com.

Tucker, C. J., Marx, J., & Long, L. (1998). "Moving on: Residential mobility and children's school lives." *Sociology of Education, 71:* 111–129.

Tucker, D. L. (2001). "A gender drama in American football culture: The case of the coach's wife. *Football Studies, 4*(2): 58–76.

Tucker, D. L. (2006). "The making of the perfect sacrifice: A rhetorical analysis of football coaches' descriptions of their wives." In L. K. Fuller (Ed.), *Sport Rhetoric and Gender* (pp. 241–251). New York: Palgrave.

USA Today. (2010, December 9). "Salary analysis of 2010 Football Bowl Subdivision coaches." Retrieved on November 26, 2012, from www.usatoday.com.

USA Today. (2011, November 17). "College football coach salary database (2006–2011)." Retrieved on November 26, 2012, from www.usatoday.com.

Wieberg, S. (2008, December 2). "Coaches on shorter leashes: Rise in salaries brings more pressure to win. *USA Today.* Retrieved on November 26, 2012, from www.usatoday.com.

Wieberg, S., Upton, J., Perez, A. J., & Berkowitz, S. (2009, November 11). "College football coaches see salaries rise in down economy." *USA Today.* Retrieved on November 26, 2012, from www.usatoday.com.

Wight, V. R., Raley, S. B., & Bianchi, S. M. (2008). "Time for children, one's spouse and oneself among parents who work nonstandard hours." *Social Forces, 87*(1): 243–271.

Wilcox, W. B., & Nock, S. L. (2007). "'Her' marriage after the revolutions." *Sociological Forum, 22*(1): 104–111.

Wilcox, W. B., & Nock, S.L. (2006). "What's love got to do with it? Equality, equity, commitment and women's marital quality." *Social Forces, 84*(3): 1321–1345.

About the Authors

Janet Hope, Ph.D., recently retired as professor of sociology at the College of St. Benedict/St. John's University in Minnesota, where she had been a faculty member for almost 20 years. Before that, she was a faculty member in the Department of Sociology and Anthropology at Eastern Illinois University. She has studied, researched, and taught in the area of family sociology for almost 25 years. Janet received her M.A. and Ph.D. from the University of North Carolina at Chapel Hill and her B.A. from the University of Tennessee at Chattanooga. She is the mother of Dr. Liddy Hope and the mother-in-law of Sally Hope. Janet and her husband, Joe, are the parents of five children.

Liddy Hope, Ph.D., holds an M.S. in marriage and family therapy from Purdue University and a Ph.D. in family social sciences from the University of Minnesota. Her research interests center around issues of gender, parenting, and families. She's the mother of two daughters and currently works as a therapist in the Chicago area.

Sally Hope has been married to former Purdue University head football coach Danny Hope for more than 30 years. Sally has experienced the life of being married to a graduate assistant, position coach, assistant head coach, and a head coach at the high school, Division I FCS, and Division I BCS levels. Sally received her B.S. from Eastern Kentucky University and her M.A.T. from the University of Louisville in the area of pedagogy. Sally and Danny are the parents of a son, and she currently teaches in the Health and Kinesiology Department at Purdue University.